STOKVIS STUDIES IN
HISTORICAL CHRONOLOGY
AND THOUGHT
ISSN 0270-5338
Number Fifteen

I0160431

Politics

Quaker

Style

A History of the Quakers from 1624 to 1718

by

John H. Ferguson

Professor Emeritus, Pennsylvania State University

R . R E G I N A L D
The Borgo Press
San Bernardino, California ▫ MCMXCV

THE BORGO PRESS

Twentieth Anniversary, 1975-1995
Post Office Box 2845
San Bernardino, CA 92406
United States of America

*   *   *   *   *   *   *

Copyright © 1995 by John H. Ferguson

Library of Congress Cataloging-in-Publication Data

Ferguson, John Henry, 1907-
  Politics Quaker style : a history of the Quakers from 1624 to 1718 / by
John H. Ferguson.
    p. cm. (Stokvis studies in historical chronology and thought, ISSN
0270-5338 ; no. 15)
  Includes bibliographical references and index.
  ISBN 0-8095-0101-5 (cloth). — ISBN 0-8095-1101-0 (pbk.)
  1. Society of Friends—History—17th century. 2. Society of Friends—
History—18th century. I. Title. II. Series: Stokvis studies in historical
chronology & thought ; no. 15.
BX7676.2.F47 1995   95-1515
289.6'09'032—dc20   CIP

FIRST EDITION

TABLE OF CONTENTS

Foreword v

I. Quaker Beginnings 1

II. The Ideological Setting 22

III. Steps Toward Institutionalized Quakerism 51

IV. Beleaguered Monarchs and Protectors 72

V. Ideological Conflicts and Persecution Within England 110

VI. William Penn's Maturation and Colonial Governance 145

Notes 173

Bibliography 189

Index 198

ABOUT THE AUTHOR

Dr. John H. Ferguson retired in 1978 after a distinguished career as a professor of political science, dean, director at various universities and research centers, and government program evaluator. Born in Nebraska in 1907, he received a B.A. from Nebraska Central College and an M.A. and Ph.D. in political science from the University of Pennsylvania. In 1934 he joined the faculty of the political science department at Pennsylvania State University, where he later became department head and remains a professor emeritus.

He has also held many non-academic positions, including executive director of the Commonwealth Compensation Commission, secretary of administration and budget secretary under Pennsylvania governor George Leader, and executive board member of the American Friends Service Committee. He was director of a conscientious objector camp in Gatlinburg, Tennessee, during World War II.

Dr. Ferguson's books include *American Diplomacy and the Boer War*, *The American System of Governmen* (with Dean E. McHenry), *The American Federal Government* (with Dean E. McHenry), *Elements of American Government* (with Dean E. McHenry), *Municipally Owned Waterworks in Pennsylvania* (with Charles F. LeeDecker), *American Government Today* (with Dean E. McHenry and E. B. Fincher), and *The Minor Courts of Pennsylvania* (with David L. Cowell),. For many years his college texts on American government were considered definitive; and two of them went into fourteen editions. He received a Distinguished Service Award from the American Society of Publishers in 1956.

A member of the Society of Friends, Dr. Ferguson extensively researched the history of the Quaker founding fathers in England and America. This book represents the fruition of that lifelong interest.

FOREWORD

Although early Quakers disclaimed political intent, they neverthe-less set out to conform human societies with the teachings of Jesus. England was the first to feel the brunt of their messianic objectives, as indicated below and throughout this treatise.

Quakers, properly known as "Friends," made their appearance in England well over three centuries ago and their Society still exists. Their numbers today approximate 200,000, most of whom are concen-trated in the British Empire, North America and quite recently Kenya, a republic on the equator in North Africa. Early Quakers were not a new sect but a spinoff from Catholic, Protestant and other independent religious bodies, many of whom considered themselves "Primitive Christians," as did sixteenth century Germanic Anabaptists. Typi-cally, they opposed highly structured religious bodies which usually were affiliated with political entities known as "states" and governed by feudal lords.

George Fox, the founder of Quakerism, had a modest upbringing in England's Midland counties but little, if any, formal schooling. Religiously, he was a Protestant of Anglican persuasion with Presby-terian overtones but left home at a tender age to serve an apprentice-ship, the details of which are scarce. Deeply religious, serious and emotionally distraught, he left his master, began a pilgrimage during which he cobbled shoes, studied the Bible, conversed endlessly with both skeptics and kindred spirits over theological issues and near the end of his travels had an ecstatic mystical experience which clarified his thinking and launched his ministry.

While Fox was pilgrimaging, he paid little attention to the brutal civil war and such historic antecedents as the Puritan Revolution, Protestant Reformation and the seemingly endless warfare which en-compassed not only England but also Western Europe. Rather, he was preoccupied with mystical religion as represented by Jesus, his disciples and subsequent "Primitive Christians." Given that preference, he wrangled incessantly with both Protestants and Catholics, especially their preachers and priests.

Religion was but one of several factors which set the stage for England's Civil War and its aftermath inasmuch as the King professed Episcopalianism while Presbyterians controlled Parliament. At issue fundamentally, however, was the ancient doctrine of the divine right of kings. Traditionally, that right implied that a monarch could do no wrong but there were limits in the past or at least accommodations.

The King and Parliament clashed repeatedly over that doctrine. An early disagreement centered on The Petition of Right which the King opposed vigorously but Parliament approved in the famous "Grand Remonstrance." Other major disputes hinged upon the King's desperate need for revenues and qualified manpower. The outcome was civil war, the King's defeat and his execution, and the "Kingless Decade" dominated by Oliver Cromwell. Neither of the two restored Stuart kings, Charles II and James II, repudiated divine right although they chafed over Parliament's preference for the King-in-Parliament formula, explained below.

Although King Charles was euphoric over the Stuart Restoration, his political "honeymoon" was cut short in less than a year by the Fifth Monarchist Uprising, which was quickly and unmercifully crushed. That event had historic consequences not only for the King but also Quakers, their sympathizers, and British politics generally, including the North American colonies.

Fox began his ministry in 1647 in the vicinity of Nottingham. While there he suffered his first of eight debilitating imprisonments for reasons which in retrospect seem trivial. His second incarceration was at nearby Derby. Meanwhile, his reputation had spread and institutionalization took form, fostered in part by soldiers recently discharged from the devastating Civil War. A trip northward from Derby exceeded Fox's expectations and laid the foundation for the Religious Society of Friends, headquartered at Swarthmoor Hall. Meanwhile, Oliver Cromwell strove mightily to find a viable alternative for the deposed Stuart dynasty, despite considerable odds. Although he could be brutal, and often was, he nevertheless mitigated Quaker persecution somewhat and showed a personal interest in Fox.

Most Quakers lamented the demise of Cromwell lest restored Stuarts wreak vengeance upon those who favored the Commonwealth. All went well for several months until the Fifth Monarchists staged a coup d'état for which the unpopular Quakers were rounded up as suspects. Although totally innocent, and despite their historic pacifist declaration of 1661, their popularity plummeted and severe persecution followed until relieved somewhat by James II and more so by the Glorious Revolution. Chapter 5 provides statistics and other data, including selected examples.

Persecution in the British Isles prompted migration to the North American colonies. Fox and his party traveled among them to Barbados, then headed for Virginia, fostering Quakerism as they went. The tour lasted about two years, starting from mid-1671 to mid-1673. Arriving in Virginia, the party followed coastal areas northward but stopped short of the most hostile colonies, such as Massachusetts and Connecticut.

Of all the early Quakers, none was more famous than Fox, Margaret Fell Fox, William Penn and Robert Barclay, although there were countless others who played significant roles. Of those persons, Barclay was the most distinguished scholar and author of the famous Apology without which Quakerism might have been devoid of the scholarly content essential for long-term survival. Both Penn and Barclay were deeply involved with the development of New Jersey and Pennsylvania, although Barclay did so while remaining in England.

The chapters which follow focus not only upon Quakerism but also its historical antecedents dating back to the first century A.D., when absolutism was the rule. Roman Catholicism was equally autocratic and so was Protestantism until challenged by sectarianism, which over time helped moderate tyranny.

Quakers came into existence toward the end of England's Civil War and came to rely heavily upon such sectarians as English Baptists, Congregationalists, Independents, Muggletonians and numerous others detailed in chapter 1. Meanwhile, the persecution of dissidents was both widespread and cruel until relieved somewhat by the Glorious Revolution of 1688.

Early Quakers were by no means homologous, hence reliable generalizations about their behavior are of dubious value. Countless attempts have nevertheless been made, including the following recent one by Professor W. K. Jordon:

> Cromwell's policy toward Quakerism, which under
> highly effective leadership began to spread with amazing

rapidity about 1855, was the consequence of more complex considerations. No other sect in the Civil War period was so universally or as vigorously hated and feared as the Quakers. Their contempt for public authority, their apparent irreverence, their disavowal of the literal truth of Holy Writ, their strange habit and stranger conduct, and extreme intolerance toward other Christian sects made them appear dangerous to civil and religious stability and aroused the concerted wrath of an age disposed to deal violently with eccentric and anti-social exhibition. The restraints under which the Quakers labored in the revolutionary era were the consequence of an outraged public sentiment which the government strove steadily to placate and modify.[1]

That appraisal, though harsh, had reference to an absolutist era during which embattled Quakers and their protagonists were moving slowly but surely toward religious and political moderation.

John H. Ferguson

I

QUAKER BEGINNINGS

George Fox, the founder of Quakerism, was born in 1624, while England's first and only civil war was brewing. He and his associates were religionists in a hurry to persuade their generation that human perfection was the only sure route to the Kingdom of God on earth. Like Jesus of Nazareth, they considered themselves not *of* this world but *in* it for the purpose of making all things holy,[1] including the political entities, territorial rulers and governments detailed in the following chapter. This book attempts to place the Quakers' mission in political perspective.

Looking back on the Foxian era, it seems odd to discover that the terms "politics" and "political" were not then in common usage, or mentioned by Fox in his voluminous writings. Both words are derivations of *poli*, which had reference to the Greek city-states renowned for their common history, social, economic and political interests. Delayed usage of those words was due primarily to the long continuance of absolutist governance by caesars, popes, kings, czars and similar potentates. Genuine politics require a substantial degree of voluntarism, liberalism and toleration which were lacking in Western Europe until the seventeenth and eighteenth centuries.

Early Quakers did not formulate a coherent political theory or system, as did Aristotle (384-322 B.C.), and such scholarly contemporaries of Fox as Thomas Hobbes, John Locke and James Harrington. Rather, their basic assumption was that God created the heavens and earth, but for reasons which are not explicitly stated in the Book of Genesis, another power, known as Satan, became chief of the apostate angels, archenemy of God and the prince of worldly sinners. Whether Fox ever addressed that formula existentially is doubtful. Moreover, whether an omnipotent God would bifurcate his sovereign prerogatives has confounded theologians and philosophers ever since.

Fox's biblical approach differed radically from that of Aristotle who declared in *Politics* that "Man is by nature a political animal." If that proposition is true, all interactions among people bearing upon public affairs within and between organized societies raise serious questions which were controversial during Fox's life. When and where, for example, did interaction among people begin? Did it happen within a short period of time, as suggested by the Genesis account of creation, or was it an evolutionary development at numerous places where chemistry was favorable? The statement also suggests there were legitimate governments whenever communities entered into binding compacts and by doing so established "natural law," about which the contemporary scholars mentioned above were debating and writing. Fox himself contributed little to that profound discussion of social origins.

Even so, both Fox and his followers professed to be apolitical, or withdrawn from traditional coercive governance. Robert Barclay (Tottenham) confirmed that observation with these words:

> There is no feature of Fox's character more striking than his absolute separation from all the political aims and objects of the men of his time. It is the more important to notice this, since a view has been taken by several writers of ability, that a covert intention existed in the Society to interfere with matters of State. While the Early Baptists and Independents started in the movement, in which Fox bore his part, with the same purely religious views, and a large number of their Churches steadily adhered to them, there cannot be a doubt that the irreligious influence was gradually lessened by their meddling with politics. This feature he succeeded in impressing on his followers; and the almost entire absence of political allusions in the great mass of the religious literature of the Society, and even in the more private correspondence of Fox and the early preachers, proves beyond a doubt the entirely religious character of the movement. There was, however, no morbid shrinking from political life on the part of Fox's followers, nor did Fox teach the incompatibility of the duties of a Christian, and of a magistrate. They were, however, fully occupied

with the salvation of men's souls, an object which absorbed their energies.[2]

One great exception, Barclay went on to say, was state support for religion, particularly the compulsory payment of tithes for that purpose which they openly and vigorously resisted.

How does one reconcile Aristotle's premise with that of early Quakers? One plausible answer is that he lived at a time when heathenism was unconstrained by institutionalized religion. The Quakers, on the other hand, were constrained by monotheism, as taught by the Hebrews, and what they perceived to be "Primitive Christianity." Moreover, they adhered closely to biblical teachings and shunned "worldly" behavior, including secular politics and power. That is not to say, however, that Aristotle was incorrect; indeed, all human behavior, whether planned or otherwise, has a bearing upon one or more body politics proportionate to ambition, ability and zealotry.

Given those possibilities, one seeks in vain for Fox's opinions and judgments about the critical secular issues of those troubled times. He said nothing substantive, for example, about the Civil War, its causes, conduct and consequences; whether monarchy based upon divine right was preferable to other alternatives; the devastating Thirty Years War then coming to an end; Hugo Grotius's famous treatise on international law published about the time Fox began his ministry; whether mercantilism was preferable to other economic systems; needed parliamentary reforms, such as those advocated by the Levellers; and future relationships between England, Scotland and Ireland. It could be, however, that comments on such issues were overlooked or unrecorded.

The Quakers' brand of politics was shaped considerably by the "Puritan Revolution," which had been gestating since the Middle Ages. It was those Puritans who struck the first blow to the Roman Catholic Church and strove later to "purify" the newly established Protestant churches rather than separate from them. Puritanism remained a potent force far beyond the mid-1600s, when Quakers made their appearance, and is remembered today for its intense enthusiasm; self-righteous dogmatism; advocacy of millenarianism, predestination, theocracy and moral perfection; strict compliance with literally-construed scriptures and what became known as the Protestant work ethic. Used in a popular sense, the term "Puritanism" came to apply loosely to all Protestants and Quakers whose outward appearance and behavior resembled those of strict Anabaptists and Calvinists.

George Fox and John Bunyan were up front in that Puritan drama as displayed in their day, with fictitious Christian Pilgrim in the wings. Both men were contemporaries and now lie in nearby cemeteries. Bunyan, the son of a tinker, was a lay-Baptist preacher who, like Fox, suffered cruel imprisonments on several occasions. Bunyan became famous for his writings; Fox for his polemics. They disagreed on some theological issues, particularly Fox's conception of the Inner Light. Of Bunyan's numerous writings, *Pilgrim's Progress* was the most popular. It was printed, read and translated more than any book other than the Bible for well over two centuries. But from a literary point of view, his first book, *Grace Abounding to the Chief of Sinners,* is the most illustrious.[3]

Quaker "peculiarities" were well known at that time and often led to shunning and imprisonment. Among such customs were refusals on the part of males to doff hats inasmuch as only God was worthy of "hat honor," regardless of social rank or legal requirements. Other customs included "knee-bending refusals" to upper class people, among whom were lords, ladies and public officials; usage of "thee" and "thou" rather than "you" because of the latter's plural inference. Other oddities included plain dress, unpretentious living, rustic meeting houses, silent worship except for deeply-felt oral preaching or prayers, nonhierarchical church organization and governance. In retrospect, the affronts mentioned to upper-class persons appear to have been rude and contrary to the Golden Rule. Early Quakers were nevertheless often uncompromising, hoping thereby to "level" standards of personal conduct in a class-ridden society.

Fox's Youth and Apprenticeship

Fox was born in the Midlands of England about a year before King Charles I ascended the throne in 1625. The exact date of birth is uncertain, but the month of July is indicated on his tombstone. His birthplace was a village of perhaps two dozen dwellings then known as "Drayton-in-the-Clay" because of its fenny or boggy soil. Drainage and cultivation have since enhanced and beautified the still-small village now known as Fenny Drayton. Fox died on January 13, 1691. His remains lie in the modest burial grounds of Bunhill Friends

Meeting, located in London, a short distance from St. Paul's Cathedral.

Fox's father, Christopher, did silk weaving at his home, which has since disappeared. Locally, he was well regarded for his integrity, devotion to duty, and righteous behavior. The mother, Mary, appears to have been better educated than most women in the community. Of her family, the Lagos, George Fox said they "were the stock of martyrs," perhaps the Protestant "Mancetter Martyrs" of Catholic Queen Mary's reign. The term "Mancetter" referred to a village located on the Old Watling Street of Roman times. Fenny Drayton was but a few miles away in the adjacent county of Leistershire. Two of the persons martyred were Robert Glover and Mrs. Joyce Lewis; both were burned at the stake, he at Coventry in 1555, she at Litchfield two years later. Memorial tablets were placed much later in the Anglican Church at Mancetter.[4]

Fox was one of several children, about whom Elfrida Vipont writes:

> There were other children in the family [besides George], but nobody knows how many. The relevant pages of the baptismal records of Fenny Drayton were torn out by the sexton's wife some time in the eighteenth century, to make covers for her preserves. Only the youngest child's name, Sarah, survived, though Thomas Hodgkin records that the then vicar of Fenny Drayton had discovered mention of another sister, Mary. Other names have been traced through references in the writings of George Fox—a brother John, later of Polesworth, and two more sisters, Dorothy and Katherine.[5]

The Fox home and work place appear to have been austere, but whether the family was tender and loving is speculative. George, when composing his *Journal*, acknowledged and complimented his father and mother, as indicated below, but said nothing which would characterize his five siblings. In retrospect it seems odd that more about that sizable family and household has not come to light.

Fox had this to say about his youthful years:

> In my very young years I had a gravity and stayedness of mind and spirit not usual in children, inasmuch

5

that, when I had seen old men carry themselves lightly
and wantonly toward each other, I have had a dislike
thereof risen in my heart, and have said within myself,
"If ever I come to be a man, surely I would not do so
nor be wanton."

When I came to eleven years of age, I knew pure-
ness and righteousness; for while I was a child I was
taught how to walk to be kept pure. The Lord taught me
to be faithful to God and outwardly to man, and to keep
to "yea" and "nay" in all things.[6]

Those words, spoken by a boy brought up in a puritanical household
and community, reflected not only solemnity but also priggishness.
Genius though he came to be, fun-loving was not one of his youthful
traits.

Fox's remarks quoted above suggest that he aspired to perfection,
an objective he continued to emphasize for himself and others
throughout his ministry. Could it be that his "gravity and steadiness of
mind and spirit not usual in children" presaged the traumas which
plagued him as a young man?

Eulogizing Fox on the occasion of his death, William Penn made
these comments:

But from a child he appeared of another frame of mind
than the rest of his brethren; being more religious inward, still solid and observing beyond his years, as the
answers he would give and the questions he would put
upon occasions manifested to the astonishment of those
who heard him especially in divine things.[7]

In a similar vein, the Rector of Fenny Drayton, Nathaniel Stephens,
said of the youthful Fox that "never such a plant was bred in England."[8]

Fox's *Journal* seldom mentions his parents, but the few references made are kind and generous. He said of his father, "he was by
profession a weaver, an honest man, and there was a seed of God in
him. The neighbors called him 'Righteous Christopher.'"[9] Of his
mother, he said she "was an upright woman" and on the occasion of
her death, at age 70, he said "I did in verity love her as ever one

could love a mother, for she was a good, honest, virtuous and right-natured woman."[10]

At home and nearby Protestant Episcopal state-related church young Fox became familiar with the Bible, the Authorized Version of which appeared in 1611, approximately thirteen years before his birth. He was also exposed to the *Book of Common Prayer,* which set forth officially approved doctrines and liturgies, and to gripping tales of martyrs past and present. And despite hard benches and long sermons, regular attendance was surely a source of intellectual stimulation and enlightenment. The dogmatic theology, ritualism, sacramentalism, and class consciousness then exhibited prominently at church services may have predisposed the sensitive youth to the mental anguish, eccentricities, and rebelliousness which characterized his adult life.

The Drayton area had been, from 1582, well known for its radical Puritanism and Presbyterianism. Speaking of those influences, Pickvance added:

> The tradition of religious dissent in the Fenny Drayton district . . . is closely bound with the fortunes—economic, social and political—of the Purefey family. The Purefeys were in Thomas Hodgkin's phrase, the "territorial aristocracy" of Fenny Drayton for more than 100 years, from 1400 to 1706.[11]

Tombstones and living descendants were constant reminders of Purefey power and grandeur and may have affected young Fox negatively. The tomb of George Purefey, who died in 1661, has since dominated the nave of the Drayton church.

Young Fox's schooling appears to have been limited to parental instruction and whatever pastoral or tutorial assistance the nearby parish church provided. Noting his serious demeanor, his relatives suggested that he become a clergyman but "others persuaded him to the contrary." Instead, he was apprenticed to a shoemaker at the age of twelve for reasons unexplained in the *Journal.*[12] Limited schooling accounted for not only his poor handwriting and spelling but also lack of comprehensive reading, which may have been a more serious handicap. Moreover, apprenticing the lad at such a tender age may have had a bearing upon his melancholic behavior toward the end of his apprenticeship, throughout the pilgrimage, and well into his ministry.

The decision made is understandable given the father's tradesman status. Furthermore, there were children to support, a paucity of nearby inexpensive schools, and such deeply rooted puritanical community values as austerity, self-reliance, frugality, industry and disdain for erudition. Those values were crudely reflected when an emotionally distraught George Fox interrupted his pilgrimage to return home. Seeking help while there, a clergyman advised him to "take tobacco and sing hymns" and relatives suggested that he marry or join the "auxiliary band of soldiery."[13]

Fox's *Journal* account of the apprenticeship is, for all practical purposes, the sole source of information about that crucial stage of his life. That his master was basically a "shoemaker by trade" appears to be a certainty. Doubts remain, however, about such fundamentals as the master's name and the place where the apprenticeship was served. A footnote by Braithwaite suggests this clue: "Probably George Gee of Mancetter, a neighboring village."[14]

Gerard Croesce, Fox's earliest general biographer, does not mention the master's name but implies, albeit ambiguously, that Nottingham, the base of many of Fox's future endeavors, was the site.[15] William Sewel, the Quaker historian who shared some materials with Croesce, mentioned the apprenticeship but neither confirmed nor denied the latter's account.[16] A brief biography of Fox appearing in the *Dictionary of National Biography* relied upon Croesce's statement that Nottingham was the site.[17] A more recent account by Elfrida Vipont stated that Fox "was apprenticed to a shoemaker in Mancetter" but neither the source nor the master's name is mentioned.[18]

Those uncertainties are confusing not only to casual readers but especially to biographical analysts. Fox was still quite young and his apprenticeship lasted about seven years. Where, how, and with whom he spent those formative years were not inconsequential matters. If nearby Mancetter were the site, proximity to his family, home church and neighborhood might have been advantageous. More-distant Nottingham, on the other hand, might have fostered greater independence, self reliance, perspective and familiarity with the many "dissenting and separatist people" known to have settled there.

Fox's *Journal* account of the apprenticeship said nothing about learning to cobble shoes but stressed his part in conducting business dealings. His words were:

. . . whereupon I was put to a man, a shoemaker by trade, and dealt in wool, and used grazing, and sold cattle; and a great deal went through my hands. While I was with him, he was blessed; but after I left him he broke, and came to nothing. I never wronged man or woman in all that time, for the Lord's power was with me and over me, to preserve me. While I was in that service, I used in my dealings the word 'verily,' and it was common saying among people that know me, 'If George says "Verily" there is no altering him.' When boys and rude people would laugh at me, I let them alone and went my way, but people had generally a love to me for my innocency and honesty.[19]

Few other details have been verified. The tasks he performed can readily be imagined but the *Journal* does not mention the master's name, where the apprenticeship was served, and whether anyone else lived in the household. It is certain that he read the Bible assiduously, but whether he attended church services regularly is speculative. Moreover, the *Journal* does not indicate whether he had intimate female companions or how closely he kept in touch with his family. His usual moody and serious demeanor may have been aggravated by melancholia, an ailment then common in England.

Otherwise, Fox's maturation appears to have been normal, although it seems odd that the *Journal* says little about his family. Comments about his mother were generous, but no other contemporary woman, including his four sisters, was mentioned before his ministry began at about age 23 when he first met Elizabeth Hooton. It could be that psychosexual factors accounted for his lack of interest in women and perhaps also his temperamental behavior. He remained a bachelor until about age forty-five when he married Margaret Fell, widow of the late Judge Thomas Fell, who was about ten years older than Fox. Whatever may have accounted for the circumstances mentioned, his ministry showed no deliberate inclination to demean or discriminate against women because of their sex. On the contrary, as we shall see, his views on such matter were, for the most part, charitable and liberal for those bigoted times.

Near the end of his apprenticeship, a poignant episode redirected his life. He tells of that event in these words:

When I came toward nineteen years of age, I being upon business at a fair, one of my cousins, whose name was Bradford, being a professor [anyone who professed a religious faith] and having another professor with him, came to me and asked me to drink part of a jug of beer with them, and I, being thirsty, went in with them, for I loved any that had a sense of good, or that did seek after the Lord. And when we had drunk a glass apiece, they began to drink healths and called for more drink, agreeing together that he that would not drink should pay all. I was grieved that any that made profession of religion should offer to do so. They grieved me very much, having never had such a thing put to me before by any sort of people; whereupon I rose to be gone, and putting my hand into my pocket I took out a groat and laid it down upon the table before them and said, 'If it be so, I'll leave you.' So I went away; and when I had done what business I had to do, I returned home, but did not go to bed that night, nor could I sleep, and cried to the Lord, who said unto me, 'Thou seest how young people go together into vanity and old people into the earth; and thou must forsake all, both young and old, and keep out of all, and be as a stranger to all.'

Then, at the command of God, I left my relations and brake off all familiarity or fellowship with young and old. . . .[20]

The beer drinking episode provides one of the few available portraits of Fox at that stage of life. Having called upon the Lord for help and received what he thought was a command to withdraw from fellowship with people, that is apparently what he did. He may have terminated his apprenticeship at that time but the *Journal* does not specifically say so. Nor does it say how long he remained reclusive.

What happened is important because it reflects Fox's puritanical upbringing, temperament, values, and straightforwardness in dealing with people whose conduct he found offensive. It also suggests that he may have been unduly self-righteous, insensitive, and tactless. His *Journal* and other writings indicate that similar emotional displays were not uncommon.

Looking back on Fox's childhood and apprenticeship it is surprising to find no direct evidence that he was interested in secular politics. It would be helpful to know what his youthful perceptions were on such facts of life as king, parliament, courts of law, local governments, church-state relationships, crime and punishment, taxes, war, elections, voting and other civic obligations. We now know that children as young as six to ten have identifiable perceptions of such common phenomena, but researchers were not around in Fox's day with the necessary skills for probing youthful attitudes and behavior.

Pilgrimage

Shortly after the drinking episode Fox set forth, in September, 1643, at the age of nineteen, on an extended pilgrimage, but how it was financed is unclear. Croesce states that the funds needed were obtained by stopping en route to practice his shoemaking trade, and that probably is the case.[21] Whatever the source, Fox financed not only the pilgrimage but also had money enough to help the needy. Of the latter he said:

> And when the time called Christmas came, while others were feasting and porting themselves, I would have gone and looked out for poor widows from house to house, and have given them some money. And when I was invited to marriages, as I sometimes was, I would go to none at all, but the next day, or soon after, I would go and visit them, and if they were poor, I gave them some money; for I had wherewith both to keep myself from being chargeable to others, and to administer something to the necessities of others.[22]

Journal references to happenings after leaving the master's household included no appreciative or complimentary remarks, nor is his former master ever mentioned again. His comment that "After I left him [his master] he broke, and came to nothing" appears callous and self-serving, to say the least. Bernstein says that "Fox abandoned the apprenticeship" but provided no confirmation.[23]

It could be that Fox's anguished state of mind after the beer-drinking event prompted an abrupt and ugly departure from his master's household. Available dates for the start and ending of the apprenticeship are too imprecise for accuracy, but it could be that Fox did leave before serving seven full years, as usually required by law. The *Journal* provides no evidence that fulfillment of his contractual obligations was ever officially certified. Nor is anything said to indicate that he ever considered becoming a journeyman (one who has completed an apprenticeship but does skilled work for someone else).

After leaving the master's premises Fox may have returned to Fenny Drayton en route southeastward as far as London, where he took lodging and visited an uncle named Pickering, of General Baptist persuasion, but other details are lacking. He spent about nine months on that part of his pilgrimage then returned home to allay parental anxieties over his welfare. While at home, advice was plentiful, not only from relatives and lay neighbors but also Rector Nathaniel Stephens and other nearby inquisitive priests.[24]

Throughout the pilgrimage, Fox roamed leisurely conversing, reading the Bible, meditating, fasting and otherwise searching for "truth" and "perfection." He traveled lightly wearing what probably were self-made leather outer garments and resting either in guest rooms (commonly known as chambers, garrets and attics), open fields, hedgerows and hollow trees. While pilgrimaging for about four years—from departing his master's household until he first preached publicly—he discussed repeatedly, and often aggressively, the most inflammable biblical and doctrinal issues of those troubled times. In retrospect, his trekking has the appearance of a roaming seminar, interspersed with traveling, contemplation, Bible reading, mental distress and occasional shoemaking.

Fox's quest peaked toward the end of his pilgrimage with a mystical experience best explained in his own memorable words:

> And when all my hopes. . . in all men were gone, so that I had nothing outwardly to help me, nor could tell what to do, then, Oh then, I heard a voice which said, "There is one, even Christ Jesus, that can speak to thy condition," and when I heard it my heart did leap for joy. Then the Lord did let me see why there was none upon earth that could speak to my condition, namely, that I might give him all the glory; for all are concluded under sin, and shut up in unbelief, who enlightens, and gives grace, and faith, the power. Thus, when God doth

work who shall let [prevent] it? And I knew this experientially.

That "leap for joy" marks the beginning of what became Quakerism.[25]

Fox does not mention the place where that experience happened, but it probably was in the vicinity of Mansfield to which his pilgrimage had brought him. His melancholic moods continued but diminished somewhat, despite two short-term imprisonments, as public recognition and opportunities for ministration increased. Meanwhile, his reputation spread, or as he said:

> . . . a report went abroad of me that I was a young man that had a discerning spirit; whereupon many came from far and near, professors, priests, and people. And the Lord's power spake unto them of the things of God, and they heard with attention and silence, and went away, and spread the fame thereof.[26]

Sewel said that Fox's first public preaching

> consisted of some few, but powerful and piercing words, to those whose hearts were already in some measure prepared to be capable of receiving this doctrine. . . It set the professors of those times in a rage, that some of their adherents hearken to this preaching; for they would not endure to hear perfection spoken of, and a holy and sinless life, as a state that could be obtained here.[27]

Fox's growing popularity was fostered in part by the miraculous cures for psychic and physical ailments young Fox reputedly was capable of performing. More fundamental reasons included endemic civil and religious strife and such personal characteristics as zealousness, stamina, readiness to suffer, forensic skills, truthfulness and his spectacular command of the Bible. He lived in an intolerant age and his confrontational tactics may have fallen short of Jesus' Sermon on the Mount, but none could doubt the depth of his conviction and commitment to what he perceived God's will to be. In retrospect, it is amazing how such a young man without formal schooling could sift and settle upon the numerous inflammatory theological issues then

13

current for which he was willing to stake his freedom and life. Time and experience reinforced and modified his early views, but fundamentally they changed little.

As Fox began his ministry in the vicinity of Nottingham he sought out kindred spirits, some of whom were General Baptists. One such person was Elizabeth Hooton, a married woman with children, who had been a Baptist preacher. She first met Fox in 1646-1647 and cast her lot with him and a few other followers. Given Fox's hallucinatory tendencies at that early date, she may have contributed to his emotional stabilization. She may also have helped form "The Children of Light," the first title given to a small assembly of Fox's earliest followers.

Speaking of those developments, Gerard Croesce wrote that she

> . . . was born and living in Nottingham, a Woman pretty far advanced in years, was the first of her Sex among the Quakers who attempted to imitate Men and Preach. . . . After her Example, many of her Sex had the confidence to undertake the same Office.
>
> This woman afterwards went with George Fox into New England, where she wholly devoted herself to this Work; and after having suffered many Affronts from that People, went to Jamaica, and there finished her life.[28]

She was in New England on two occasions. While in England she was imprisoned on several occasions, the first time at Derby Gaol well known to Fox.

Early Ministry

By mid-1647 the time had come when Fox could no longer be merely a wandering seeker; he had now to decide what to preach and how to proceed. External sources which shape a young man's ideology can seldom be pinpointed, but available evidence provides clues, as indicated by this quotation from the *Journal:*

> Now after I received that opening from the Lord that to be bred at Oxford or Cambridge was not sufficient to fit a man to be a minister of Christ, I regarded the priests less, and looked more after the dissenting people.

14

> Among them I saw there was some tenderness, and
> many of them came afterwards to be convinced, for they
> had some openings. But as I had forsaken all the priests,
> so I left the separatist preachers also, and those called
> the most experienced people; for I saw there was none
> among them all that could speak to my condition.[29]

That quotation is the first *Journal* reference indicating his esteem
for dissenting people. He doesn't specify, however, which of the
many types of "dissenters" he had in mind, but contemporary General
Baptists were high on his list. Their spiritual progenitors included,
among others, continental Mennonites, Brethren Hutterites, and
Schwenkfelders. When and why he formed such preferences is
speculative, but it accords with his puritanical small-village upbringing, minimal schooling, apprenticeship experience and life-style.
Available evidence suggests the people he preferred were then quite
numerous in and around Nottingham. Indeed, there is a strong prob-
ability that he ended his pilgrimage and began ministering in that vicinity because of the presence of such "tender" people.

Fox's preference for dissenting people raises the question of what
happened to his youthful commitment to Episcopalianism. There
probably was no formal withdrawal from the Fenny Drayton church,
but it is clear that disenchantment with that faith increased as he grew
older. We noted above that the *Journal* said nothing about his church-
going habits during the apprenticeship. While pilgrimaging, he spoke
many times with priests, but made no mention of regular attendance at
any particular church. He did say, toward the end of that sojourn, that
he forsook "all the priests" and even the "separatist preachers."[30]
Sewel suggests that as between Episcopalians and Presbyterians, Fox
concluded there was little difference;[31] and as persecution intensified,
he denounced both of those churches.

Richard T. Vann reported that during the mid-1600s there were
"no less than 199 sects" in England, 29 of them in London,[32] but
whether all were "sects" from a technical point of view is questionable. Such large numbers were due to the long struggle for power,
secular as well as ecclesiastic, during the illiberal Protestant Reformation and the aftermath of the Civil War. That blend of Catholicism,
Lutheranism and Calvinism, allied with the nobility which controlled
numerous secular states, left an intolerant legacy that had little appeal
to Independents and minor religious groups, including Quakers.

What happened in England is illustrative. Catholicism was out-lawed by King Henry VIII and displaced by Episcopalianism, a slightly modified version of Catholicism without a Pope. Episcopalianism remained dominant, except for the brief reign of Catholic Queen Mary, until displaced by Calvinist Presbyterianism more than a century later, in 1643. Episcopalianism returned to power with the restoration of King Charles II, 1660. Meanwhile, neither Lutheranism nor Menno Simon's brand of Anabaptism had taken root in England. To suggest where Quakers fitted into that complicated picture, Episcopalianism was dominant for all of Fox's life, except for his four-year pilgrimage and the first thirteen years of his ministry, during which Presbyterianism was legally ascendant.

The numerous sects plagued not only national and local governments but at times gave the appearance of anarchy. Fox became acquainted with many of them during his four-year pilgrimage and early ministry. Indeed, it was he, more than anyone else, who played the role of catalyst for the numerous ideological groups detailed below.

The general term *Dissenters* refers to those who disagreed with the beliefs and practices of the Church of England, whether controlled by Episcopalians or Presbyterians. *Separatists* chose to withdraw from the Church of England rather than conform to its requirements. *Independents* preferred freedom of religious belief and congregational governance. Robert Browne, an English clergyman whose followers were known as "Brownists," founded the first body of Independents as early as 1581. That self-governing concept was anathema to the Church of England. Quakers were in fact Independents.

Seekers were not, strictly speaking, a sect, but dissatisfied people searching for "Truth," either as free individuals or as participants in a simply structured fellowship of kindred spirits. They antedated the Civil War and became quite numerous; some were hostile to the earliest Quakers but later became enthusiasts and many affiliated with them.

English Baptists were at that time the spiritual descendants of continental Anabaptists. John Smyth usually is credited with founding the first Baptist Church in England. The liberal wing of that body, known as "General Baptists," was far more numerous and sympathetic to Fox and his followers than Calvinistic "Particular Baptists." The former was more likely to have Mennonite background than the latter.

Familists, known as the "Family of Love," were initially led by Hendrik Niclaes, who was born in 1502 at Münster located in Westphalia. Later, his followers settled in Holland from which some moved to England where they became quite influential. They stressed, with much emotionalism, that religion consisted primarily of love. Some members kept their Episcopalian or Catholic affiliations, but no form of worship was mandated. Some became Quakers.

Muggletonians were named for Ludowicke Muggleton, an English tailor and visionary who, with his cousin John Reeves, denied the Trinity and proclaimed a new spiritual and political dispensation resembling the Kingdom of God. Although they were aggressive, their numbers were never large. Some became Quakers.

Socinians were followers of Faustus and Laelius Socinus, Italian Protestant theologians and forerunners of what became known as Unitarianism. They accepted Christ as the Messiah but denied His divinity and also the doctrine of Holy Trinity. Of special interest to Quakers was their stress upon the innate goodness and rationality of man.

Ranters, though not a sect, became a political force during the Commonwealth and Restoration periods. Their beliefs combined elements of Christianity, pantheism and antimonianism. More particularly, they believed Christ's blood had purchased and unleashed them from sin and by doing so made them free spirits unconstrained by moral law, especially as set forth in the Old Testament. God, they said, is present in all nature, including human beings, and as free spirits they were entitled to behave as led or prompted individually and collectively. The Ranters were quite numerous; their disputations were often noisy and unbridled; some became Quakers.

Fifth Monarchy Men were millenarians who prophesied the imminent return of Christ to earth and the resurrection of all faithful dead, as foretold in the Old Testament Book of Daniel and the Apocalypse portrayed by St. John the Divine in the New Testament Book of Revelations. According to Daniel's account, the four previous monarchies had been Assyrian, Persian, Greek and Roman. Fifth Monarchists, many of whom were Catholics, deplored existing established churches and advocated their forceful overthrow. Assassination attempts were made unsuccessfully on the lives of Lord Protector Oliver Cromwell and King Charles II. Drastic reprisals and punishments had severe consequences for the Quakers as well as the Monarchists.[33]

Fox unwittingly politicized himself within a year or so after beginning his ministry. From then on, the *Journal* is replete with instances where his preaching prompted beatings, threats, fines, trials, incarcerations and other forms of harassments, but he usually took them in stride. Inspired by the *Book of Revelation,*[34] Fox likened such conflicts to a Lamb's War fought by saints with spiritual weapons for truth and righteousness. Indeed, he and many of his followers were firmly convinced the apocalypse would soon come whereupon Christ would return, destroy evil rulers and resurrect the righteous who would live eternally.[35]

Fox's first imprisonment recorded in the *Journal*[36] occurred at Nottingham shortly after his ministry began in 1647. On that occasion he went to what probably was a Presbyterian Church and during the sermon the "Lord's power" became so strong he "could not hold, but was made to cry out" his disagreement with the priest, whereupon he was arrested, charged, tried and imprisoned "for a pretty long time." Whether Fox, who was then in his mid-twenties and without formal legal training, knew what statutory provisions governed such matters is uncertain. They dated back to Queens Mary and Elizabeth and forbade maliciously disturbing a preacher by word or deed during a sermon.[37]

The prison was, according to Fox, "a pitiful stinking place," but fortunately the "head sheriff" and his wife were cordial. Indeed, they went so far as to allow a "great meeting" in their house, during which they were "convinced" and later preached repentance in the market place.

Following his release, Fox attended a church service at Mansfield-Woodhouse and spoke after the priest had done, but despite that precaution a mob gathered afterward and beat him severely. Although bruised, he said "after a while the Lord went through me and healed me, . . . glory be to the Lord for ever."[38]

What an eye-opening experience those episodes were for the "tender" and reclusively inclined young Fox! Lessons learned were aplenty, but certainly not a deterrent for the messianic preacher who was to be imprisoned often thereafter, spanning and sapping his energies for more than a quarter of a century. His experience at Nottingham marked the start of more than three centuries of Quaker concern for what became known as humane and enlightened justice, including prison reform. Meanwhile, his popularity spread, calls for merciful

18

assistance increased, audiences became larger, but controversies remained endless.

Fox's politicization was reinforced about a year later while at Derby, which was located a short distance from Nottingham. The charge on that occasion was for blasphemous remarks spoken during a dispute with army officers, priests and preachers over the doctrine of sanctification. While still in prison, but near the end of his term, Fox was proffered a captaincy in the militia which he rejected for reasons explained below.

The trial at Derby was notable, not only for the seriousness of the charge, but also happenings of special interest to the Religious Society of Friends. As the trial proceeded, one of the Justices, Jervase Bennet, noticed Fox was trembling and dubbed him "Quaker," a term detested by Fox and many of his followers but gradually accepted with the passage of time. Imprisonment lasted a year or so and prompted two policy declarations having far-reaching significance for both religion and politics: capital punishment and pacifism.[39]

The following comments on capital punishment may have been the first written by Fox on that subject. Apparently, while imprisoned at Derby two men were executed for stealing cattle, whereupon Fox wrote to the judges as follows:

> I am moved to write unto you to take heed of putting men to death for stealing cattle or money, etc.: for the thieves in the old time were to make restitution; and if they had not the wherewith, they were to be sold for their theft. Mind the laws of God in the Scriptures and the Spirit that gave them forth and let them be your rule in executing judgment; and show mercy, that you receive mercy from God, the judge of all. And take heed of gifts and rewards, and of pride, for God doth forbid to give liberty to sin, God hath forbidden it; but that you should judge according to his laws, and show mercy, for he delighteth in true judgment and in mercy. I beseech you to mind those things, and prize your time now you have it, and fear God and serve him, for he is a consuming fire.[40]

Two aspects of that letter merit special emphasis. He spoke of "laws of God that gave them forth in the Scriptures" with emphasis upon the "Spirit that gave them forth," not the hard-line approach then widely preferred. He also stressed mercy at a time when forbearance and compassion were rarities, especially in criminal proceedings.

While still at Derby Prison, Fox confronted the issue of capital punishment again with a more fortunate outcome. A young woman was the prisoner and "carried to execution," whereupon Fox wrote to the judges, who spared her life, following which she was, according to Fox, "convinced of God's everlasting Truth." Fox also wrote to the judges saying "what a sore thing it was that prisoners should be so long in gaol, and how they learned badness one of another in talking of their bad deeds, and therefore speedy justice should be done."[41]

While still imprisoned at Derby, Fox was importuned to join the army as a captain to fight Scottish Royal Forces at Worcester, a county town lying southwesterly from where Fox was confined. His response, as stated in the *Journal* was in two parts; the first was as follows:

> But I told them I lived in the virtue of that life and power that took away the occasions of all wars, and I knew from whence all wars did rise, from the lust of James's doctrine (James, iv. 1).[42] Still they courted me to accept their offer and thought that I did not compliment them. But I told them I was come into the covenant of peace which was before wars and strife were. And they said they offered it in love and kindness to me because of my virtue, and such like . . . and I told them if that were their love and kindness I trampled it under my feet. Then their rage got up and they said, "Take him away gaoler, and cast him into the dungeon amongst thirty felons" in a lousy, stinking place in the ground without any bed. Here they kept me a close prisoner almost a half year, unless it were at times; and sometimes they would let me walk in the garden, for they had a belief of me that I would not go away.[43]

Fox's refusal deprived him of sharing in Cromwell's victory and the complete rout of Charles I and the Scots on September 3, 1651.[44]

Shortly thereafter, recruiters stopped by to enroll manpower for the upcoming battle. Fox's account of what happened is as follows:

20

So Worcester fight came on, and Justice Bennet sent the constables to press me for a soldier, seeing I would not accept a command. I told them I was brought off from outward wars. They came down again to give me press-money but I would take none. Then I was brought up to Sergeant Hole's, kept there awhile, and then taken down again. After a while at night the constables fetched me up again and brought me before the Commissioners, and they said I should go for a soldier, but I told them that I was dead to it. They said I was alive. I told them, "Where envy and hatred are there is confusion." They offered me money twice, but I would not take it. Then they were wroth, and I was committed close prisoner without bail or mainprize. Thereupon I writ to them again, directing my letter to Colonel Barton, who was a preacher, and the rest that were concerned in my commitment.

Now when they had gotten me into Derby dungeon, it was the belief and saying of people that I should never come out; but I had faith in God, and believed I should be delivered in his time; for the Lord had said to me before, that I was not to be removed from that place yet, being set there for a service which he had for me to do.[45]

The two *Journal* extracts quoted above were based upon biblical passages which Fox knew very well. His premise was that Adam's fall in the Garden of Eden was the cause of war and Friends should conform with Jesus's teachings regardless of consequences to themselves. Stated otherwise, his approach was nonresistance and total commitment to what he perceived to be God's will. It is well known, however, that he was not always consistent.

II

THE IDEOLOGICAL SETTING

At birth George Fox was not only a member of a family, but he had obligations as well. Legally, at birth he had dual status: one based upon nationality, the other domicile. The former applied to all subjects wherever they might live within the British Empire. Both place of birth and residence were legally significant.[1] Thus, Fox at birth was British by nationality and English by domicile. His sovereign was James I, who died the following year and was succeeded by Charles I. Baptism shortly after birth enrolled him in a state-related Protestant Episcopal Church. Thus, he unwittingly became enmeshed with three basic social institutions—family, political entity, and church—from cradle to grave.

Fox appears to have taken his subordination for granted. Revocation of an English person's subject-status was then rare, although executions and banishment were common. Fox did mention, from time to time, the rights and privileges of subjection. He also professed respect on numerous occasions for his King and Queen and lesser magistrates and nation. Except for two brief trips to Holland (one of which included Germany), one to the West Indies and America, one to Ireland and another to Scotland, he spent his entire life in his homeland.

Writing today about mid-seventeenth century English politics one quickly runs into semantic thickets. One finds some help by turning to the writings of such famous English philosophers as Thomas Hobbes (1599-1678), James Harrington (1611-1677), and John Locke (1632-1704), all of whom were contemporaries of George Fox. Also helpful were the writings of Hugo Grotius (1583-1645), the Dutch lawyer and jurist who published the celebrated *De Juri Belli Ac Pace* (translated "Concerning the Law and War and Peace") in 1625,[2] the year after Fox was born.

Political Systems and Concepts

The political nomenclature in England at that time is confusing, chiefly because of rising nationalism during and after the Anglo-Saxon period which began in 450 A.D. The "British Isles" included England (i.e., the southern geographic sector), Wales (added in 1636), Scotland (added in 1707) and nearby Ireland (added in 1800), whereupon the title was changed to the "United Kingdom of Great Britain." The "British Empire" embraced all territorial possessions wherever they might be. Unification was then, as now, a "fighting" word and seldom came quickly even for such small political entities as villages, parishes, town, boroughs, and counties. If and when that happened, growing consciousness of identity and commonality among inhabitants usually had taken place.

The term "nation" may have been appropriate for England and Scotland before their union, in the sense that each had distinct lineage, language, customs and history. That term was undoubtedly appropriate for Great Britain and later the United Kingdom of Great Britain, despite lingering doubts over how "united" the collective political entities were. George Fox used the term "nation" frequently but never defined it. The continuing struggle for unity accounts in substantial measure for both the Civil War and the persecution of dissidents such as the Quakers.

Western Europe also had numerous political entities, many of them small feudal preserves of dominant aristocratic families. One finds, for example, duchies, bishoprics and archbishoprics ruled by dukes, princes, counts, etc.; all of whom had previously been Catholics subject to the Pope's ecclesiastic jurisdiction and canon law. Succession to the highest offices usually was by "divine right." The Protestant Reformation (1517-1607) left unsettled territorial, dynastic, and religious issues which prompted counter-reformations, led by powerful Catholic families such as the Hapsburgs, to unite for defense and retaliatory action.

Rebellion in Bohemia triggered the Thirty Years War (1618-1648) which had far-reaching consequences. Reformationists included petty German political entities, France, Sweden, Denmark and England; counter-reformationists included Austria, Germany, Italy, the Netherlands and Spain, all of whom were allied through the Holy Roman Empire whose spiritual vicar was the Pope. Costly fighting and carnage were comparable to those of modern world wars, with civilians suffering as grievously as combatants. Despite the horrible costs in both money and bloodshed, the war set in motion the rudiments of today's international law, conciliation and such institutions as the United Nations and World Court.

Grotius's famous treatise appeared shortly before the war ended.[3] It was favorably received, particularly by the small states which had grown wearier than others of international lawlessness. It drew heavily upon both ancient and recent legal codes, judicial rulings and commentaries. His focus throughout was upon how societies settle both private and public disputes honorably, justly and peaceably. Both Old and New Testaments were taken into account and all questions touched upon both religion and politics. The issues included types of enforcement, the lawfulness of war and who is responsible, what punishments are just, what things belong to men in common, how great is the force of an oath, and who may be rightly killed in war.

Some early Quakers were deeply impressed by Grotius's masterpiece. Penn, for example, wrote and published *An Essay Towards the Present and Future Peace of Europe* in 1693, about which Tolles and Alderfer observed:

> Penn was not the first European to dream of a world united for peace; Dante, Erasmus, Henry IV of France, Hugo Grotius, a handful of other farsighted men, had caught a glimmer of that bright vision and had drawn up schemes to give it reality. Penn's Essay is notable among those early peace plans for its combination of idealism and realism, for the noble and disinterested nature of its end and the practical character of its proposed means.[4]

Penn's plan was written while yet another European war was taking place, known at first as the War of the League of Augsburg and later as the Grand Alliance. The latter coalition was formed in 1689 and consisted of England, France, Sweden, Spain, Savoy, Holland and several minor German states; the intention was to constrain French expansion.

Fundamental to this discussion is the doctrine of divine right, the origin of which is unknown. Its acceptance obviously required belief in a god, or gods, whether pagan or otherwise; a reasonably stable body politic; and a non-egalitarian social structure. England had employed the doctrine for centuries; even before it could properly be

24

called a "state," as when settled by Celts, Romans, Scandinavians and Germanic tribes. The first five books of the Hebrew Old Testament, which probably were written by Moses about 1000 B.C., did much to spread the doctrine of divine right. Speaking of that supposition, John Neville Figgis stated it rested upon four hypotheses:

1. Monarch is divinely ordained
2. Hereditary right is indefeasible
3. Kings are accountable to God alone
4. Non-resistance and passive obedience are enjoined by God.[5]

Controversy over the divine-right issue subsided somewhat during the Kingless Decade (1649-1659), but Charles II continued arguing for it as late as 1681 when he addressed the topic at Oxford University. His remarks, briefly stated, were:

> We will still believe and maintain that our Kings derive not their title from the people but from God; that to Him only they are accountable; that it belongs not to subjects, either to create or censure, but to honour and obey their sovereign, who comes to be so by a fundamental heredi-tary right of succession, which no religion, no law, no fault or forfeiture can alter or abolish . . .[6]

Not once in that important statement did Charles concede that sover-eignty rested in King-in-Parliament. The divine right concept was badly fractured, however, when his brother, James II, was forcibly deposed. Moreover, this concept has since been drastically modified (as in England, Norway and Japan) or rejected (as in France, Russia, and the United States of America). The orderly succession of rulers is so vital to political entities that divine right may have served primitive societies better than other possibilities, but for major powers of the seventeenth century the practice was an imperfect one, to say the least.

The word "state" gained acceptance in Western Europe gradually during medieval times. Aristotle spoke of "city state" or *polis*, mean-ing an autonomous city or similar polity, in his classic *Politics*. The Latin word "state" stems from "status," a cognate of which is "estate," meaning a social or political class of high order, such as nobility, clergy and commons. The French word is *état*. Niccoli Ma-chiavelli (1483-1517) is credited with having validated the word gen-erically in his famous book *The Prince*. It was published in England, under the title *England,* by Thomas Stareky in 1538.[7] Petty hereditary "states," most of them feudal and some of them papal in character, existed from time to time in Italy and Central Europe. Later, the words "nation" and "state" came to be used synonymously and quite recently the term "nation-state" became acceptable.

The favorable reception given to Grotius' treatise, particularly by small entities, led to a redefinition of the word "state." A modern version reads: A state is a permanent association of independent people politically organized on a definite territory and habitually obeying the same sovereign.[8] For such a state to exist legally, then, the following are essentials: (1) population, (2) definite territorial boundaries, (3) political organization or government, (4) independence, (5) sovereignty, and (6) unity sufficient to provide consensus, or at least acceptance, which will permit sustained collective action. Behind each of the six elements lies a vast reservoir of experience, controversy, international law and jurisprudence.

While all the elements mentioned are essential, sovereignty, defined as supreme temporal authority and power, is the key one. Where sovereignty rests and by whom it will be exercised are among the most vital questions known to mankind. It has at various times resided in an emperor, monarch or similar potentate, church, pope, cabal, political party, people, parliament, class, or the state itself conceived as an ideal person. The theoretical and legal location of sovereignty may, and often does, differ from its actual situs; or its exercise may be ineffectual because of widespread factionalism, dissent, corruption, revolt, or civil war. While monarchical sovereignty was the rule in mid-seventeenth century England, the assumptions upon which it rested were then undergoing radical change.

The word "sovereignty," as defined above, raises more questions than it answers. Its elements often are not readily discernible. What, after all, is supreme temporal power and authority? The word "temporal" brings meaning down to earth but makes nothing else obvious. External evidences provide clues, but still leave essence undisclosed. Of the many answers provided by scholars, this one has considerable acceptance: The essence of sovereignty consists of a bundle of conventional and hypothetical concepts acceptable over time to a particular body politic. However defined, sovereignty is fundamental to effective lawfulness in viable political entities.

Politically speaking, there are three principal schools of thought on the issues involved: monist, pluralist, and anarchist. Monists insist that sovereignty is an indivisible whole. Pluralists prefer divisibility, but seldom concur on what the consequences would be of having a multiplicity of sovereign territorial and/or functional authorities, particularly in highly industrialized and urbanized areas. Anarchists contend that both monism and pluralism are self-serving concepts preferred by those presently holding supreme authority and power. Rather, sovereignty should rest in each individual; the public interest would be better served by voluntary personal actions or cooperative endeavors. Lawful coercion by a body politic is considered evil by many advocates of this point of view.

The term "popular sovereignty," in vogue since the late 1700s in some democracies, usually is based upon monist concepts, with sovereignty resting in "the people." As a practical matter, monist concepts underlie nearly all firmly established political entities, but debate is endless over the wisdom, justice, and morality of such arrangements. The Quakers were among the debaters.

The term "Puritan Revolution" has reference to the conflicts which precipitated the Civil War (1642-1649), but its origin dated back to the Middle Ages. Among the Pre-Reformationists was John Wycliffe (c. 1320-1384) and his "poor preaching priests" collectively known as "Lollards." It was they who struck the first of many blows to the Roman Catholic Church and strove later to "purify" the newly established Protestant churches rather than separate from them. In England, and despite King Henry VIII's drastic disestablishment of the Catholic Church, Puritan leaders continued to insist that he and his successors had been too liberal and willing to compromise with unscriptural and corrupt practices retained from the former Roman Church.

Puritanism remained a potent force far beyond the 1600s. Indeed, it is remembered today for its intense enthusiasm; self-righteous dogmatism; millenarianism, predestination, theocracy, and moral perfectionism; strict compliance with literally-construed scriptures; frugality, and other traits which became popularly known as the "Protestant work ethic." Used in a popular sense, the term "Puritanism" applies loosely to all religionists whose outward behavior resembles those popularized by John Calvin.

England had for nearly a millennium an "Established Church," meaning one recognized by law and supported by civil authorities. That privileged position came about gradually; its evolution makes interesting reading.

Roman soldiers secured a foothold on the British Isles in 43 A.D. and, as Christianity spread, Catholicism took root. Friction soon developed between Catholics and Celtic Druids who worshipped the forces of nature as gods. The arrival of pagan Germanic Jutes, Angles and Saxons, at about 450 A.D., intensified rivalries which culminated in the acceptance of Christian faith by Æthelbert, King of Kent (560-616), and a triumph for the Catholic Church in 664. Canterbury, then England's temporal capital, became the ecclesiastical center as well, and has remained so ever since. Church governance from Canterbury was in the name of the Pope through an appointed archbishop and subordinate bishops. During the years that followed, robed clergymen, cathedrals, monasteries, convents, monks and nuns became commonplace. Moreover, the Church was assigned seats in Parliament and given other coveted prerogatives. Its landholdings and other assets were both extensive and enormously valuable.

That traditional church-state relationship was altered drastically by widespread acceptance of Calvinism early in the Protestant Reformation. King Henry VIII led the way, in 1531, by disestablishing England's Roman Catholic Church and replacing it with an Episcopal Church of England. That historic event was prompted by mixed motives, but a major one was the Pope's denial of the King's request to divorce Katherine of Aragon. The King's action was formalized by the Act of Supremacy in 1559, which designated the monarch as "the only head of the Church" and sovereign over both church and state. Modifications were made in 1559 to clarify constitutional questions which had arisen and provide that the monarch's ecclesiastical powers were to be exercised through the Ecclesiastical Court of High Commission. That Court became increasingly controversial; it was abolished in 1641, restored in 1661, and abolished again in 1689.

The Act of Supremacy also imposed draconian constraints upon the Roman Church and Catholics generally. That, and subsequent legislation, were intended to terminate all papal authority within the King's domain; abolish Catholic institutions, many of which had existed for centuries; and render ineffectual what remained of the priesthood, customary modes of worship, and sources of revenue. Such drastic treatment was not only humiliating and costly but left a legacy of bitterness that threatened political stability and left marks visible even today. Meanwhile, countless non-Catholics with long memories of papal tyranny showed little sympathy.

Prosecutions for recusancy, the refusal of Roman Catholics to attend the Church of England, were legion and continued for well over a century. Enforcement by unprofessional officials, often with the help of spies and "common informers," was capricious at best, but frequently harsh, cruel, and corrupt. Evasive tactics on the part of recusants were nevertheless often ingenious and successful.[9] Similar constraints were imposed upon Separatists and Independents, the latter of whom included Quakers when they arrived on the scene. The persecution of Catholics in Ireland, when under British rule, was even more severe.

In addition to the official constraints mentioned, others applied to Catholic laymen and clergy for offenses committed and punishable by canon law, ecclesiastic courts, and old pre-Reformation rules of the Roman Church. Moreover, compliant monarchs, by using their inherent prerogatives and favors, could and often did, reward, punish, and harass Catholic offenders, sometimes unmercifully.[10]

Lewis H. Berens summarized as follows the religio-political alignment as it stood during the interim between the disestablishment of the Roman Church and the restoration of the Stuarts in 1660:

> On the one hand, the English Roman Catholics became a distinct and persecuted religious body, whose members were generally regarded, despite repeated evidence to the contrary, as necessarily enemies of England. On the other, despairing of further changes in the direction they desired, a large number of the extreme Protestants separated themselves from the National Church—though by doing so they rendered themselves liable to be accused not only of heresy, but of high treason, and to suffer death—and formed themselves into different bodies of Separatists and Independents, differing on many points among themselves, but united by a common animosity of all outside ecclesiastical control. Within the Church the Catholic sentiment crystallized into the Episcopalian, the Protestant sentiment into the Presbyterian section of the Church of England.[11]

Most of the official restrictions on Roman Catholics detailed above have since been terminated. They are, however, still excluded from the Throne, a few civil offices and others connected with the Church of England.

Throughout the epochal period here under review, monarchical succession was violently interrupted as never before since the Norman Conquest of 1066. Transitional periods from Henry VIII to William III and Mary were as follows:

- Henry VIII (1491-1547)—Catholic at first, then Episcopal
- Edward VI (1547-1553)—Episcopal
- Mary Tudor (1553-1558)—Catholic; often referred to as Bloody Mary
- Elizabeth (1558-1603)—Episcopal
- James I (1603-1625)—first of Stuart Dynasty; mother, Queen Mary
- Charles I (1625-1649)—Episcopal; married to a Catholic
- Commonwealth-Parliament (1649-1653); sectarian rivalries
- Protectorate (1653-1659)—headed by Oliver and Richard Cromwell; Puritan; first national republic but actually an oligarchy
- Charles II (1660-1685)—Episcopal, with Catholic leanings
- James II (1685-1688)—avowed Catholic; deposed from throne
- William III and Mary (1688-1702)—Episcopal; the Glorious Revolution
- Anne (1702-1714)—the last of the Stuarts
- George I (1717-1727)—the first of the Hanovers

While the concept of having an established church and preference for Episcopacy remained controversial in England, their continuance was never again in great jeopardy after the coronation of William and Mary.

Catholic persecution, as sketched above, reminds one that Jews were banished from England in 1290 by King Edward I. Their non-Christian religion, superior abilities, professional reputations and wealth set them apart from other residents. Those living in populous places were required to live in segregated wards known as "Jewries," and wear special dress or other distinctive insignia. Legally, their status was inferior and invited all sorts of indignities, including violence.

Recognizing the Jews' undoubted abilities and value to the kingdom, special royal protection was provided. But as hatred and conflict intensified King Edward ordered all Jews expelled on a designated date under pain of death. They were, however, permitted to take with them all possessions, including money, and free passage was provided for the very poor. An estimated 16,611 left; a few found ways of remaining. Most expellees settled in Western Europe, many of them in the Netherlands.

The ban was lifted in 1655, three hundred and sixty-five years after expulsion, by Lord Protector Oliver Cromwell and his Privy Council.[12] Puritan respect for Judaic values may have prompted that historic decision. Efforts made for exclusion after the Stuart restoration came to naught. Although readmitted to residence, discriminating statutory constraints remained in force until late in the nineteenth century.

England was not the only country where Jews were expelled and otherwise persecuted. Rather, Jews were tormented from the start of the Crusades in the eleventh century until the eighteenth century. They were expelled from France in 1392; from Spain in 1492, about which time 100,000 Jews were killed; and Portugal in 1497. In retrospect, it appears that when a country suffered economically or from war, the Jews were likely to be scapegoats. Political emancipation began with the American and French Revolutions; rising capitalism also improved their condition throughout the Western World. The Nazi holocaust of the 1930s and 1940s is a reminder that Judaic values are still not everywhere respected.

Anabaptism and Primitive Christianity

The Anabaptists were among the many other pre-Reformation critics of the Roman Church. They are of special interest to us because, of all the "dissenting people" Fox encountered on his pilgrimage, none fascinated him more, even though their doctrines and practices had been modified with the passage of time.

The term "Anabaptist" is a Latin derivative of the Greek word meaning re-baptism. Its usage in the pre-Reformation period sprang from heated controversy over child versus adult baptism. More was at stake than differing scriptural interpretations; indeed, the issues went to the very core of church authority and governance.

Infant baptism presupposed an unbreakable continuum between child, family and the visible Catholic Church; baptism of adult believers, on the other hand, presupposed freedom to choose between faiths, churches, or none of them. Catholic doctrine insisted upon the former; critics contended for adult baptism and also the rebaptism of infants already baptized when they attained adulthood. Of that controversy, Franklin Hamlin Littel says "The important point to emphasize is that the real issue was not the act of baptism, but rather the bitter and irreducible struggle between two mutually exclusive concepts of the church."[13]

Littell found the term "Anabaptist" difficult to define. Indeed, he said, the term became a "slippery word, an epithet flung contemptuously in much the same way the word 'Bolshevik' recently has been hurled at those of unpopular views."[14] Generally, he said, it embraced radical Protestants; more precisely, it referred to Swiss Brethren, South German Brethren Hutterites, and Dutch Mennonites. He lumped under the term "Left Wing" all the "varicolored individuals and groupings associated with the movement at the first and later hanging on its periphery." Among the "Left Wingers" were the Anti-Trinitarians, Spiritualizers, and revolutionary prophets.[15] For working purposes, Littell provided this definition: The Anabaptists proper were those of the radical reformation who gathered and disciplined the "true church" upon the apostolic pattern as they saw it.[16]

Historians still dispute whether Anabaptists arose in and around Zurich, within the context of the Swiss Reformation, or in Saxony, a region and former duchy in Northwestern Germany. American Reformation scholars appear to accept the premise that it was the Zurich area.[17]

The Anabaptists were at first widely scattered congregations led by strong-minded persons who were determined to revive "primitive Christianity" and restore the apostolic church. It was Menno Simon's (c. 1496-1561) leadership which welded the besieged congregations into a permanent association of Anabaptist churches.

Born of Dutch Catholic parents living near the North Sea in Friesland Province, he became a priest but never a monk. Although an admirer of Luther, he continued to be independently minded, resigned his priestly office, remained a pastor and dedicated the rest of his life to fulfilling his vision of the True Apostolic Church. His latter

32

years were spent in Holland. The churches in that area, some of which had 500-600 members, were the first to be called "Mennonites." Simon's writings consisted of twenty-four books and pamphlets.[18]

Writing of Anabaptist origins, Robert Barclay (Tottenham) had this to say:

> . . . the rise of the anabaptists took place long prior to the formation of the Church of England (in 1534), and there are also reasons for believing that on the Continent of Europe small hidden Christian societies, who have held many of the opinions of the "Anabaptists" have existed from the time of the Apostles. In the sense of the direct transmission of Divine Truth, and the true nature of spiritual religion, it seems probable that these churches have a lineage or succession more ancient than the Roman Church.[19]

Of the "apostolic pattern," also known as "primitivism," Rufus M. Jones wrote:

> There has been a persistent feeling, a perennial recurring faith throughout all centuries of the Christian Church, that the culminating period of religion was in the Galilean circle and in the apostolic age. Men have steadily looked back to that period as the "golden age," when the Divine and the human were completely united in one Life, and were brought into joyous fellowship in many lives. The supreme aspiration of the spiritual men and women who have travailed for the regeneration of humanity, has been a return, a restoration, of that golden time. The cry, "Back to Christ," or "Back to apostolic Christianity," is not at all a new cry. Every profound movement toward a more spiritual and unfettered Christianity than that embodied in the dominant historical Church of the period has been initiated by a rediscovery of Christ, or by a fresh interpretation of the Gospel, and in nearly every instance the leaders of reform have asserted their particular movement to be a "revival of primitive Christianity."[20]

With primitive religion as their ideal, the Anabaptists and "Left Wingers" glorified the Early Church as portrayed in the New Testament. They also deplored the worldly accommodations made with the passage of time, especially the cozy alignment of church and state in 324 A.D. by Constantine, who was then Emperor of Rome based at Constantinople. Also distasteful to the Anabaptists were growing centralization of Papal power, the Pope's insistence upon infallibility, burdensome church tithes, and heavy-handed suppression of alleged heresy. Numerous remedies were proposed, chief of which were separation of church and state with non-hierarchical churches whose members were freely committed to the literal teachings of Jesus.

Speaking of the genuineness of Anabaptists, a recent writer said: "The price was well known to all: contempt for the many, persecution, and perhaps martyrdom . . . Strange as it might seem to modern man, the Anabaptists accepted martyrdom 'with shining eyes.' . . . By the middle of the sixteenth century more than five thousand of their group had suffered cruel death and all kinds of torture."[21]

Persecution and martyrdom took their toll among early primitives, who had formed sectarian divisions and cults. One such division became known as the Catholic Church, which, with the passage of time, aligned itself with the Byzantine Empire, as mentioned above. That development has been ably recounted in these words:

> Speaking of church and state in the Byzantine Empire (Eastern Orthodox) Christianity was not merely the cult of a new god (or gods—the Christians were not quite clear on this point). It was an *organized* cult, as none of the pagan cults had been. It was also an *intolerant* cult, not only intolerant of those who worshipped other gods without the state's permission (this paganism had often been), but intolerant, by inheritance from Deuteronomy, of anyone who worshipped any other god at all, and then, by theological extension, of anyone who practiced Christianity "incorrectly." These two characteristics were complimentary: The intolerance had done much to build up the organization; the organization made the intolerance effective.[22]

More recently, Elaine Pagels added the following comments pertaining to "primitive," "true" and "real" Christianity:

What I did *not* find in the process of this research was what I started out to find—a "golden age" or purer and simpler early Christianity. What I discovered instead is that the "real Christianity"—so far as historical investigation can disclose it—was not monolithic, or the province of one party or another, but included a variety of voices, and an extraordinary range of viewpoints, even among the saints (witness Augustine and Chrysostom!), as well as among those denounced as heretics, from Valentinus to Julian, and even as we have seen, within the New Testament writings themselves. From a strictly historical point of view, then, there is no single "real Christianity."[23]

Enthusiasts for "Primitive Christianity" may have been overly romantic. Life at that time was demanding and harsh. Moreover, ignorance was widespread, archaeological evidence was scanty, historical records of what happened in the tiny area known as Judea are questionable, and opposition was both relentless and cruel, not only by Judeans (Jews) within Palestine and Transjordan, but also by the many thousands of them scattered throughout the Greco-Roman Empire. Other oppressors included champions of Caesarism, paganism, cultism and agnosticism. Given those circumstances, some historians continue to doubt whether the New Testament account of Jesus' life is true or mythical. The writings of early Quakers, however, reflect no such doubts.

Henry J. Cadbury, a recent distinguished Quaker scholar of the New Testament, came to these conclusions:

> I find the quest for the historical Jesus a challenge to curiosity and also to integrity as a historian. . . I recognize that every historical statement is a hypothesis. As such I give it as my judgment that Jesus was a historical character. That he never lived at all seems to me simply a less probable hypothesis, as it is in the case of King Arthur or William Tell. The probability of his existence does not make possible all that the gospels record, nor does the improbability of some features in the gospel throw doubt on his existence.

The eschatological elements of the gospels . . .
probably go back to him. Indeed, the study of Judaism in
the first century seems to me one of the most fruitful
paths to understanding him. His differences from it are
fewer and less easy to indicate. His likenesses are reas-
suring of some veracity in the gospels.[24]

"Primitive Christianity" in general, and Anabaptists in particular,
were loathed by Catholic authorities and such leading Protestants as
Luther and Calvin. Calvin's vituperative remarks are representative:

Some Anabaptists in the present age mistake some inde-
scribable sort of frenzied excess for the regeneration of
the Spirit, holding that the children of God are restored
to a state of innocence, and, therefore, need give themselves no anxiety about curbing the lust of the flesh; that
they have the Spirit for their guide, and under his agency
never err. It would be incredible that the human mind
could proceed to such insanity, did they not openly and
exultingly give utterance to their dogma. It is indeed
monstrous, and yet it is just, that those who have re-
solved to turn the word of God into a lie, should thus be
punished for their blasphemous audacity. . . . Who is not
amazed at such monstrous doctrines? And yet this philosophy is popular with those who, blinded by insane
lusts, have thrown off common sense. What kind of
Christ, pray, do they fabricate? What kind of Spirit do
they belch forth?[25]

Illustrative of the "Spiritualizers" mentioned above was Kaspar
von Schwenkfeld (1490-1561), a Silesian nobleman. After attending
the University of Cologne and studying elsewhere he served briefly as
courtier for Duke Charles of Munsterberg and later as councilor for
the Duke of Liegnitz. Meanwhile, contacts with radical reformers and
admiration for Luther's defense against heresy before the Diet of
Worms in 1521, caused him to question his religion and return to private life for study and reflection. Thenceforth, he championed a dis-
tinctly spiritual brand of religion. Meanwhile, he was excommunicated by Luther, chiefly because of his Anabaptist leanings and belief

that the Eucharist was a spiritual symbol, not the "Real Presence" of Christ.

Merciless persecution followed for both Schwenkfeld and his disciples, who during his lifetime numbered from 4,000 to 5,000.[26] Later his followers fled to the Netherlands, England and North America, where a few small congregations remain in southeastern Pennsylvania. He wrote ninety books and tracts, most of which were destroyed, as were many Anabaptist publications, by both Protestants and Papists. He stopped short, however, of forming a new sect or aligning with any particular Reformation movement. Rather, he advocated a general *Stillstand* or "middle way."[27] That preference may have been due to his haunting fear of martyrdom. More than a century later his followers advocated withdrawal from state churches, for which they were severely persecuted.

Schwenkfeld is noted for stressing the "inward" as opposed to the "outward" aspects of Christianity. That emphasis led him to disagree fundamentally with Luther's doctrine of justification by faith and beliefs about such outward things as the scriptures, sacraments, church-order and prayer. What was needed, said Schwenkfeld, was not such outward things but deep and radical inward change. God does not, said he, merely forgive a man's sins and absolve him from guilt but gives the Holy Spirit who cleanses the heart, by the love of Christ, and makes him desire what is good and right. That stress upon the inward stemmed from what Schwenkfeld called the "Inward Light, Life, Word, Seed, etc." and Immediate Revelation.[28]

After reviewing the stormy times in which Kasper Schwenkfeld lived, Barclay (Tottenham) remarked:

> . . . his character was one of the most beautiful which that eventful period produced. He maintained the gentleness and purity of the Christian character as described in the Gospel, at a time when Luther fiercely attacked Christian men, and treated them as inspired by the Devil, because they differed from him in opinion, and expressed their views with learning and ability; when Zwingli did not raise his voice against the drowning of Anabaptists; and when, at a later period, Calvin also delivered men over to fearful punishment, for the sole crime of confuting his peculiar theological views.[29]

Jacob Boehme (1575-1624) was another "Spiritualizer." He was born of humble Lutheran parents in Silesia, at the small town of Alt Seidenberg near the City of Gorlitz. He had the usual village school education and herded cattle in the fields as did other children. A shoemaking apprenticeship, begun at the age of 14, was followed as he wandered over Germany cobbling shoes, whereupon he returned to Gorlitz, opened a shoemaking business, married a tradesman's daughter, and fathered four sons. Later he became a linen trader. Although modestly successful as a businessman, his genius lay in other directions. Small in stature, he was widely known as the "little cobbler."

Early in life, his acutely sensitive temperament, vivid imagination and extraordinary native ability became evident. From then on he observed and speculated about the meaning of life and natural phenomena; had frequent spiritually-meaningful visions; experienced periods of melancholia; and anguished over suffering, factional wrangling and war.

A simple, unsophisticated, gentle, sensitive mystic and theosophist, he went about his business without fanfare. He was an avid reader of books, especially the Bible, which suited his fancy and meditative inclinations. His philosophy grew slowly but surely enough to enrage his Lutheran pastor and other orthodox clergymen. In 1612, his first of thirty books, entitled *Aurora (Glow of Dawn),* made its appearance.

As fame overtook him, he continued to admire Martin Luther's brilliance and heroism, but more appealing was the inward religion exemplified by the Anabaptists and particularly the "Spiritualizers" such as Kaspar von Schwenkfeld. Harassment of himself and family, the Thirty Years War, and the psychic rewards of contemplation, writing, and spiritual maturation, accented those tendencies. His last melancholic "silence," which continued for seven years, was followed by a burst of energy that produced six of his most important treatises, including *The Way of Christ,* a collection which "epitomized the breadth and depth of . . . his thought in final form."[30]

Boehme's teachings spread overseas as well as on the Continent. They reached England as George Fox was on his pilgrimage and religious enthusiasm was nearing its peak. Margaret Lewis Bailey said the first printed mention of him in England was published in 1644.[31] From then on his works were widely read and a small sect sprang up, called the "Beheminists," which appealed to scholars and others interested in philosophy, science and religion. John Milton, the famous Puritan poet and author of *Paradise Lost* and *Paradise Regained*, was one of many English men and women impressed by Boehme's writings, especially his exegesis of mysticism and the Inner Light.

By the time George Fox came on the scene, the term "Baptist" had largely superseded "Anabaptists" on the Continent and in England. John Horst provides this introduction to what happened:

> By the year 1681, under the benign reign of William of Orange an attitude of general toleration prevailed in all parts of Holland.
>
> The modern Baptist Church is purely of Mennonite origin. The first congregations given the name "Baptists" were in fact Mennonites.
>
> The earliest Baptist congregation was organized in 1609 by John Smyth in Amsterdam, Holland. Smyth and his followers had been Puritans but had, with other Puritans, separated from the state Church of England and became "Independent" (Congregationalists). In consequent of persecution they had sought and found refuge in Amsterdam, where they came under Mennonite influence. A group of these people—the "Pilgrim Fathers"—somewhat later emigrated from England to America.[32]

Smyth had fled from England to Holland to escape persecution. He returned in 1611 and during the following year the first Baptist Church was established in London. Shortly thereafter differences arose among them; the major one was over the Calvinist doctrine of predestination. "General Baptists" insisted that atonement was general and not limited to the "elect." The "Particular Baptists" agreed with Calvin, saying atonement was particular and individual. The Generalists baptized by immersion; Particularists did not at first insist upon immersion but later (in 1644) they did. Fox and most other early Quakers preferred the Generalists, many of whom joined their ranks. Not until 1891 did the two bodies unite.

The Protestant Reformation

That historic event had its origin in Western Europe. The term had reference to the religio-political controversies arising from the power and behavior of the Roman Catholic Church which still considered itself "universal" in the sense that it had no limitations, territorial or otherwise.[33]

The term "Protestant," it should be noted here, was first applied when princes of the Roman Empire sympathetic to reform issued a formal *protestation* or protest, against recessing the Diet of Spires in 1529, after it failed to resolve sectarian differences and forbade further advocacy by Catholics of doctrinal deviations and ecclesiastical innovations. Since that time the term has been used variously; primarily with reference to major non-Catholic Christian societies and members.

The Roman Church had been challenged many times since its inception but during the Middle Ages its ascendancy became secure. Of that phenomenon the late John Neville Figgis said:

> In the Middle Ages the Church was not a State, it was the State; the State or rather the civil authority (for a separate society was not recognized) was merely the police department of the Church. The latter took over from the Roman Empire its theory of absolute and universal jurisdiction of the supreme authority, and developed into the doctrine of *plenitude potestatis* of the Pope, who was the supreme dispenser of law, the fountain of honour, including regal honour, and the sole legitimate earthly source of power, the legal if not the actual founder of religious orders, the guardian of international right, the avenger of Christian blood.[34]

Such absolute power had prompted numerous protests prior to the Reformation but they failed to coalesce sufficiently to lessen Catholic power. Illustrative of such efforts were those led by the Englishman John Wycliffe (c. 1320-1384), John Huss (1369?-1415), and the Anabaptists.

Wycliffe was a scholar, theologian, teacher, preacher, and Bible translator who attacked prevailing church doctrines and practices for which he was twice declared a heretic. He and his "poor priests," popularly known as Lollards, formed a link between English and Continental reformers, such as John Huss, Menno Simon, Ulrich Zwingli, Luther and Calvin on the Continent.

Wycliffe's criticisms focused on clericism generally, the doctrine of transubstantiation,[35] and the claim that the Church's good offices were an absolute prerequisite for receiving divine grace. For him, the scriptures were the supreme authority and should be accessible to all persons. His part in preparing the Wycliffe Bible, the first translation of the Latin Vulgate Bible, was looked upon by the Catholic Church with disfavor.

John Huss was a Bohemian religious reformer born of peasant parents. After studying theology at the University of Prague, he was ordained a Catholic priest. Although sympathetic to Wycliffe's view of transubstantiation, he stopped short of embracing that highly controversial doctrine but attacked clericism vigorously. In doing so he antagonized many priests and also the Pope, then involved in controversy over which one of two lines of popes was involved was legitimate and whether headquarters were to remain in Rome or centered in Avignon (France). A series of Hussite Wars followed, which set the stage for what became known as the Protestant Reformation.

Martin Luther (1483-1546), Huldreich or Ulrich Zwingli (1484-1531), and John Calvin (1509-1564) were the foremost spokesmen for reforming the Roman Catholic Church. Luther's operations centered in Wittenberg, province of Saxony, located in Northwest Germany. Both Zwingli and Calvin centered their activities in Switzerland.

Luther was born at Eisleben, Saxony, to a family of small, but free, landholders. He became a Catholic priest in 1507 and later a professor at the University of Wittenberg. After much spiritual agonizing over the ecclesiastical laxity of his church, he devoted himself to reconstructing doctrine and purifying practices. He was particularly incensed over the sale of indulgences for the remission of part or all purgatorial punishments due for sins committed. In 1517 he posted, as academicians were then wont to do, ninety-five theses on the Wittenberg Castle church door challenging others to debate the alleged abuses. By that act and subsequent developments, including formal excommunication by the Pope in 1521, Wittenberg became the cradle of the Reformation with Luther its chief mentor and spokesman.

Unwilling to recant, Luther took refuge from papal wrath at Wartburg, in the castle of Elector Frederick III of Saxony, where he concentrated on translating the Bible and writing doctrinal treatises. Disregarding personal safety, he returned ten years later to Wittenberg where he spent the remainder of his life writing, organizing and otherwise spreading his beliefs. Meanwhile, independent churches based on his teachings sprang up, which usually were called "Evangelicals" in Germany and "Reformed" elsewhere. The Lutheran Church emerged from those beginnings and by so doing marked the first institutional break in unity with the Roman Catholic Church.

Lutheran creedal documents were incorporated in the *Book of Concord* published in 1580. One of them was the Augsburg Confession, drawn up in 1530 by Philip Schwartz Melanchthon, a German scholar closely associated with Luther. That Confession became the primary statement of Lutheran faith.

Lutheranism was quite conservative compared with the views propounded by Wycliffe, Huss, Zwingli, Schwenkfeld, Boehme and the Anabaptists. Its creedal statements display high regard for the historic Catholic Church, including its mission, saints, sacraments, achievements and many of its doctrines. The intent was not to alienate, but to bring about reforms that would end the "tyranny of the Pope," including what were thought to be unwarranted claims to absolutism, universality and infallibility; and unjust applications of papal power, corruption and lax administration of the huge church establishment.

Following are selected extracts of Lutheran fundamentals as set forth in the Augsburg Confession:

> Scriptures are the Word of God and the only necessary guides to truth;
>
> Sin is inborn and hereditary and condemns to the eternal wrath of God all that are not born again through baptism and the Holy Spirit;
>
> The true body and blood of Christ are really present in the Supper of our Lord under the form of bread and wine there distributed;
>
> True perfection consists alone of the proper fear of God and real faith in God;
>
> Christians are obliged to be subjected to civil authority and obey its commands and laws "in all that can be done without sin. But when commands of civil authority can not be obeyed without sin men must obey God rather than men";
>
> Christ will return on the day of judgment to raise up all the dead, to give eternal life and everlasting joy to the

elect but condemn ungodly men and the devil to hell and everlasting punishment;

Salvation and justification are obtained by faith alone; consciences can not come to rest and peace through works, only through faith;

No one is required to believe in or receive the sacraments, no law is to be made consenting to it and no time or place should be appointed for it;

Inasmuch as the power of the church or of bishops bestows eternal gifts it does not interfere at all with government or temporal authority. The two authorities, the spiritual and the temporal, are not to be mingled or confused, for the spiritual power has its commission to preach the Gospel and administer the sacraments. Hence it should not invade the function of the other, should not set up and depose kings, should not annul temporal laws or undermine obedience to government, should not make or prescribe to the temporal laws or undermine obedience to government.

Luther's system of church governance was tailored to his version of scriptural design and intent, local customs and practicalities. As Lutheranism spread, governance became synodical in form, with boundaries drawn by clergy, possibly lay representatives and secular governments. Governance within each local church was similar with laity playing a considerable role. On matters of church policy, however, the bishops were dominant. Organically, church and state were unitary, as the Catholic Church had been for well over a millennium. Although bifurcation of the "two authorities"—spiritual and temporal—was a cardinal principle as mentioned above; state officials were often dominant and became increasingly so as nationalism grew and ultimately triumphed. Lutheran churches have remained state-related in many places, notably in Central Europe and Scandinavia.

Huldreth or Ulrich Zwingli was the forerunner of Calvinism and Protestant Reformed Churches. He was born in Switzerland, reared a Catholic and was deeply impressed with cantonal self-governance. While attending the University of Paris, he came under the influence of two famous humanists, Desiderius Erasmus and Pico della Mirandola, the former a native of Holland, the latter an Italian. Although both were Catholics, they abhorred the strict religious uniformity of the Middle Ages and welcomed the religious enthusiasm promised by the Reformation.

Zwingli was ordained in 1506, became a foremost advocate of humanism and published his controversial views in 1513 which have since been known as Zwingli's Sixty-Seven Articles, or Conclusions.[36] The displeased Catholic Bishop of Zurich tried silencing Zwingli, but civil magistrates intervened and took charge of the city's religious affairs. By 1525, the break with the Catholic Church was well underway and soon displaced by the Reform Church of Christ in both the city and canton of Zurich.

During the controversy, and with magisterial support, Zwingli launched a vigorous attack upon church liturgy and decor, but insisted that change elsewhere be gradual. Using his church as an example, he eliminated all but two sacraments, baptism and the Lord's Supper, and simplified all else. Moreover, he banished all music and painted images of saints, broke up the organ, knocked out stained glass windows, whitewashed the walls, installed benches for use by the congregation and celebrated the Supper with wooden cup and spoon.[37]

Meanwhile, bitterness peaked and polarized the nation, with urbanites supporting Zwingli and rurality committed to Catholicism. Civil War followed, during which Zwingli was killed while serving as chaplain for Protestant forces. So bitter were his enemies that after burial the body was exhumed and savagely desecrated. He had, nevertheless, laid the foundation for Calvin's comprehensive theological system. The Consensus Tigurinus of 1649 marks the transition from Zwinglian doctrine to Calvinist.

Zwingli and Luther were nearly the same age, but their backgrounds were quite different. They met only once, then as antagonists, shortly before Zwingli's death and parted coolly. Philip Schaff provides these comparisons:

> Zwingli's eyes were opened to the readers of the Greek Testament. . . and the humanistic learning of his friend Erasmus while Luther passed through the ascetic struggles of monastic life, till he found peace of conscience in the doctrine of justification by faith alone. Zwingli broke more rapidly and radically with the Roman Church than Luther. He boldly abolished all doctrines and usages not taught in the Scriptures; Luther piously retained what were not clearly forbidden. He aimed at a reformation of

government and discipline as well as theology; Luther confined himself to such changes as were directly connected with doctrine. He was a Swiss and a republican; Luther a German and monarchist. He was a statesman as well as a theologian; Luther kept aloof from all political complications, and preached the doctrine of passive obedience to established authority. . . . They could not but respect each other personally, though Luther approached the Swiss with the strongest prejudices, looking upon him as a fanatic and semi-infidel.[38]

Over time, the two men narrowed their differences on all but one doctrine—the Eucharist. Both rejected the Catholic Mass and the doctrine of transubstantiation, but Luther insisted that for believers having faith the body and blood of Christ coexisted with the substance of the bread and wine offered. For Zwingli, however, the sacrament was a *symbolical* acknowledgment of the absolute sovereignty of God.[39]

John Calvin was born and reared a French Roman Catholic. He attended several prestigious colleges in Orleans, Paris, and elsewhere, concentrating on theology, law, humanistic subjects, and the classics of ancient Greece and Rome. Those studies and other experiences made him increasingly critical of the Roman Church and ultimately, said he, a "sudden conversion, subdued my mind,"[40] which prompted him to join a growing number of Protestant reformers.

Forced by persecution to move from place to place, he settled in Geneva, Switzerland, which had long been a hotbed of religious controversy. Shortly before moving there he published, in 1636, *Institutes of the Christian Religion*. As revised from time to time, that treatise has been acclaimed the classic statement of Protestantism and one of the greatest of its kind. His many publications were written in imperious but modulated prose and encompassed a wide range of human activities.

The first Calvinists were Swiss Protestants, among whom were numerous "Huguenots," often suspected of being Jews because of their swarthy complexion. Among those Continental Protestants, none was more unmercifully persecuted than they, and many fled to England, Scotland and later the Americas.

Unlike Luther's priestly and scholarly approach, Calvin was more forceful, militant and "Puritan," as evident by his strict conformity to church dogmas and vigorous activism. His objective was no less than

45

the Kingdom of God on earth. Incidentally, he was the first Protestant leader to apply his doctrines to economic behavior and systems, while at the same time inveighing against exploitation and extolling the virtues of thrift, industry, sobriety, and responsibility. Those influences affected the world profoundly inasmuch as the Western world was then in a transition from a medieval-agrarian economy to what later became known as "capitalism." It was that thrust which prompted the phrase "Protestant work ethic."

Calvin's master plan provided for a theocratic state governed by Christians who would enact and enforce legislation pertaining to both secular and religious affairs. The intent was to institutionalize religion in such a way as to insure that the Will of God would be the canon governing both. More particularly, a major purpose was to effectuate the principles set forth in the *Institutes*.

Illustrative of what he had in mind was a code revision prepared by Calvinists at Geneva, a Swiss city which then had considerable autonomy. As revised, civil law became applicable to all aspects of communal life. At first, the municipal council displaced the bishop and undertook to appoint pastors and revise church rites. Later, a division of responsibility was made by which political councilors attended primarily to secular affairs, while religious and moral direction was entrusted to a body composed of all clergy and a Consistory of Elders appointed by the church congregation as approved by the municipal council.

That arrangement assured church ascendancy on a wide range of human behavior. The city council endorsed a code of conduct based on Calvin's teaching which minutely regulated thought and actions. Prosecutions were numerous for such sumptuary offenses as fornication, fighting, swearing, abstention from church services, laughing or sleeping in church, promiscuous bathing, gambling during church services and after nine o'clock at night, card playing in taverns, "indecent" dancing, and attending theatrical performances. Unrepentant wrongdoers were excommunicated, banned from fellowshipping with other church members, and forbidden to partake of the Lord's Supper. Those who ridiculed excommunication were bound over to secular authorities for punishment. For the church itself, discipline had become a primary function as well as teaching and preaching. A major objective was to ensure the purity of the Supper.

The model outlined was praised by many of Calvin's admirers in Central Europe and elsewhere but seldom emulated. Serious attempts were made to replicate it, notably in Scotland, England during the Civil War period, and the Massachusetts Bay Area, but those were short-lived. They did, however, help popularize and politicize Calvin's brand of Calvinism for countless people ever since.

Calvinists modeled their "Visible Church" after what they perceived to be the New Testament pattern. Governors included bishops who served as overseers and watchmen; presbyters, who served as elders; senators and church fathers; pastors; and teachers. Synods, or regional groups of churches, were set up to inquire about matters touching upon the life and doctrines of persons exercising ministerial power and disciplining those found ungodly. Laity as well as clergy participated in selecting and disciplining ministers through local and synodic councils. The key role of Presbyters gave rise to the appellation "Presbyterian."

As for the state, "the magistry, of what sort whatsoever it be, is ordained by God," and a friendly liaison between church and state is desirable. The magistrate should be honored and revered "as the minister of God." Personal obedience, just wars, oath swearing, and capital punishment were blessed by the Lord. Anabaptists were so despicable that severe persecution was warranted.

The stated position on church-state affairs differed little from that of Lutherans. In practice it retained a hand-in-glove relationship with the state, particularly on matters pertaining to morals and perceived self-interest, while at the same time striving to keep the state from interfering with ecclesiastical matters. The clergy, subordinate only to God and synodic authorities, had great power both within and outside the church.

While both Luther and Calvin opposed Catholicism, they differed theologically, notably over the doctrine of transubstantiation and predestination. Luther's view of the former was that the bread and wine offered at communion was the "Real Presence" of the body and blood of Christ. Calvin revered the sacrament but, like Zwingli, thought it a spiritual symbol, not the actual presence of Christ.

As for predestination, both men accepted the doctrine but differed over such details as how, when, and why God made such a fateful and discriminating decision. Basically, the doctrine rests upon two premises: (1) God, the Creator and Ruler of the universe, predetermined its design, lawful mode of operation, purpose and destiny; and (2) human beings are born sinful because of Adam and Eve's fall in the

Garden of Eden and every person is either elected by God for salvation or condemned eternally to damnation.

Calvin defined his version thus:

> By predestination we mean the eternal decree of God, by which he determined with himself whatever he wished to happen with regard to every man. All are not created on equal terms, but some are preordained to eternal life, others to eternal damnation; and accordingly, as each has been created for one or the other of these ends, we say that he has been predestined to life or death.[41]

Among those predestined for life were the seed of Abraham with whom God had made a special covenant. Calvin's words were:

> When God ever and anon gathered his Church from among the sons of Abraham rather than from profane nations, he had respect to his covenant which when violated by the great body, he restricted, that it might not fail. In short, that common adoption of the seed of Abraham was a kind of visible image of a greater benefit which God designed to bestow on some of the many. . . . We say, then, that Scripture clearly provides this much, that God by his eternal and immutable counsel determined once and for all those whom, one day to admit to salvation, and those whom, on the other hand, it was his pleasure to doom to destruction. We maintain that this counsel, as regards the elect, is founded on his free mercy, without any respect to human worth, while those whom he dooms to destruction are excluded from access to life by a just and blameless, but at some time incomprehensible judgment.[42]

Moreover, according to Calvin, caution is advised when speaking about predestination. "As a general rule," he said, "it is best that secret things of God are not to be scrutinized. . . . Whoever, therefore, throws obloquy on the doctrine of predestination, openly brings a charge against God, as having inconsiderately allowed something to escape from him which is injurious to the Church."[43]

While that gloomy doctrine pervaded Western civilization for several centuries and has still not totally disappeared, it was neither practical nor theoretically possible for Calvinist clergy to name the countless numbers who were foreordained for heaven or doomed to hell. One consequence was that Calvinist preachers emphasized increasingly the possibility of salvation by Grace with the hope of becoming a "saint," whether or not elected to "everlasting glory."[44]

One of the ablest non-European champions of Presbyterianism was Scotsman John Knox (1505?-1572), a zealous and strong-minded Catholic priest turned Protestant. Fearing the Catholic English Queen Mary Tudor, he fled to the Continent, stayed briefly in Switzerland, met Calvin and embraced many of his views on church doctrine and civil authority. While in exile, he wrote numerous letters to fellow-believers back home and published a pamphlet entitled *Admonitions* which urged the righteous to overthrow monarchs and persecute "idolatrous" Catholics. Upon Queen Mary's death, he returned from exile to see Presbyterianism confirmed in 1650 as Scotland's official religion. The reigning king at that time was James VI, who later became James I of England. Official status has continued since, but nowhere else.

Both Luther and Calvin met with unprecedented difficulties as they strove to institutionalize their "Evangelical" and "Reformed" churches in areas where Catholics had long been entrenched. Absolute dominance by the Roman Church over political entities had diminished, but the Pope remained powerful enough to resist forcibly growing and spreading Protestantism among numerous political entities. Meanwhile, growing nationalism and monist concepts of sovereignty prompted territorial rulers to make something more of their governments than—to use John Neville Figgis's words—merely police departments.

Luther and Calvin had other religio-political problems. Their transfer of sovereignty from Pope to scriptures and individual consciences, although severely constrained, did make a profound difference: It weakened Catholicism, fostered ideological dissent and even civil, regional, and what today would be called "international" warfare. Moreover, it subordinated church polities to secular. By the late 1600s the pope's Roman Catholic Goliath, described by Figgis, had become scattered Hobbesian monolistic leviathans. Of that impact, Figgis said:

All these functions [of the Pope during the Middle Ages] have passed elsewhere, and the theory of omnipotence, which the Pope held on the plea that any action might come under his jurisdiction, has now been assumed by the State on the theory that any action, religious or otherwise, so far as it becomes a matter of money, or contract, must be a matter for the courts.[45]

In England, controversy continued for nearly a century after the Reformation began and peaked during the Civil War. Presbyterians, then politically ascendant in England and Scotland, convened an Assembly of Elders at Westminster Hall in London to clarify and codify beliefs. What has since been known as the "Westminster Confession of Faith" was adopted in 1646; it was at that time the most fully developed creedal pronouncement of English-speaking Calvinism. It remains the most authoritative summary of Presbyterianism in England, Scotland, and with modifications, a few other places.[46] Coincidentally, George Fox was pilgrimaging during the Assembly's deliberations, but no mention is made of it in his *Journal*. Little did he then know how horribly that Confession would affect him and his followers.

III

STEPS TOWARD
INSTITUTIONALIZED QUAKERISM

Fox's release from Derby Prison in October, 1651, marked the end of his early ministry and the start of an extraordinary new one. He was still in his twenties, and though chastened by two encounters with England's legal and penal system, he headed northward where Puritanism was least entrenched and Seekers were numerous. The Civil War had ended ingloriously whereupon young warriors were released, some of whom cast their lots with Fox and his preachers, called "Publishers of Truth" in 1652 and "Valiants" two years later.

Preaching as he went, Fox soon encountered and "convinced" the first four Publishers—Richard Farnsworth, James Naylor, Thomas Goodaire and William Dewsbury. Moving onward, the party continued in the general direction of Carlisle, near the old Roman Wall separating England from Scotland. The terrain was new to Fox, but well known to his first Publishers. Sedgberg, near where Yorkshire and Westmoreland met, marked the party's first major triumph and the start of what became an institutionalized religious society.

When and where Fox began thinking about an organized effort is unclear. Nor is it certain when he first considered a rubric around which he might institutionalize, a term Fox would have detested as much, if not more, than "sect," "pulpit" and "tithes," which had been equally odious to earlier "Primitive Christians." Clearly, there was nothing in his background to qualify him as an institutional administrator, although helpful experience had been obtained during his apprenticeship, the management of his pilgrimage, church attendance and inquiries about ecclesial governance.

Unpopular, harassed and persecuted as early Quakers were, it is not surprising that they preferred as few institutional constraints as possible. Indeed, their behavior, amidst fiercely competing secular and theological dogmas, bordered on anarchy. Biblicism, dogmatic theology, hierarchy and close alliance with the state sufficed for the Pope, Luther and Calvin, but Fox wanted none of those. What appealed to him most was the non-hierarchical pattern exemplified by his spiritual forerunners, the Anabaptists, Christian mystics and his General Baptist friends then living in the Nottingham vicinity. Of all such patterns, none was more useful than those adopted by Menno Simon and his followers at the Schleithem Conference of 1527, as amended by the Dordrecht Conference of 1632, when Fox was but a child.

The prospect of institutionalism raised two key questions: whether it would conform with scriptures and exemplify the teachings of Jesus and his disciples; and whether it would inhibit free communication between God and one's Inner Light. Ancillary queries included: what format would an institution take; by whom and how would decision-making be done; what qualifications would there be for membership; what penalties would be imposed for non-conformance; what recourse would one have who felt aggrieved; would institutionalization lead to excessive hierarchy, bureaucracy and unresponsiveness; and how would Quaker institutions be financed.

Quakerism grew and spread haphazardly during its first decade, but the rudiments of an organized society took form, including a name. Fox did not coin the term "Inner Light" but it appealed to him, or as he was wont to say, it spoke to his condition. Moreover he was familiar with such New Testament phrases as "the light," "the light of men," the "light shineth in darkness," and "I am the light of the world." Also familiar was the phrase "Children of Light" because it had been used previously by Baptists and their progenitors. Given that background, it is not surprising that "Children of the Light" became the first title used by Fox and his followers shortly after his ministry began.

With the passage of time, other titles won acceptance, including "Friends" and the "Religious Society of Friends." The latter title was not used prior to the mid-1660s,[1] perhaps because the term "society" was often associated with "secret societies," then viewed suspiciously by some public officials. The usage of "Friends" hinged upon these words attributed to Jesus in the Gospel of St. John, Chapter 15: "Greater love hath no man than this, that a man lay down his life for his friends," "Ye are my friends, if ye do whatsoever I command you," and "Henceforth I call you not servants . . . but I have called you friends."

Happenings in and around Sedgberg have made that area legendary, even a Mecca for Quakers. The centerpiece is Pendle Hill, a steep but verdant mountain ridge, still grazed by cattle and sheep, from which Fox overlooked surrounding hills, small farms, quaint villages and the nearby sea. A memorial marker now stands where Fox envisaged a large number of people coming together searching for "Truth." Shortly thereafter, he spoke near Brigflatts for three hours to a thousand people. The address was delivered atop Firbank Fell, a moorland ridge, with a crag as pulpit and a natural open-air theater slightly below, a site still fondly remembered as Firbank Chapel. Afterward, Fox addressed large crowds in Sedgberg and neighboring communities, but not without harassment by skeptics and objectors.

Those who came to hear Fox on those occasions were mostly disillusioned Protestant Seekers, Separatists, Independents and others having Puritan backgrounds but who disliked having a State Church, whether controlled by Episcopalians or Presbyterians. What happened in that vicinity was heady stuff for Fox and his intimates. It may have been their first collective sense of power, an essential ingredient for institutionalization.

The triumph at Sedgberg and vicinity mentioned above was due to several factors: helpfulness on the part of small clusters of "convinced" Friends who had heard that Fox was headed in their direction; the region and its people were well known to Fox's traveling companions; Seekers and kindred spirits were numerous; and there were momentous political opportunities occasioned by the King's execution, the end of the Civil War, and Cromwell's eagerness to find a viable substitute for the deposed Stuart Dynasty.

Later that year, Fox stopped at Swarthmoor Hall, the three-story home of Judge Thomas and Margaret Fell, situated near the southern end of the Lake District between the Irish Sea and Morecombe Bay. What prompted his visit at that particular time is unexplained, but in retrospect it could not have been more propitious for Fox and his developing, but still unstructured, movement. That event had great significance for both religious and political reasons, as we shall see.

Thomas Fell and his wife, the former Margaret Askew, whose ages were then 60 and 38 respectively, came from substantial families living in rural northwestern England. Details are scarce, but we know that Thomas followed in his father's footsteps and became an attorney at law. Although traditionally a royalist, he enlisted with the Parliamentary forces during the Civil War and afterwards held numerous public offices, including barrister, justice of peace, Lancaster County member of the Long Parliament, legal officer for several counties, and finally Judge of Assize for the Chester and North Wales Circuit. The term "Assize," as used here, referred to a superior court which met periodically to try both civil and criminal cases.

Having lived in the same rural area most of their lives, the Fells were deeply rooted and familiar with countless politically minded people and their goings-on. Religiously, the couple were Congregationalists; politically they were Independents who had become disenchanted with the parliamentary wrangling which followed the King's execution and Oliver Cromwell's handling of those events. The couple had nine children. Eight survived, of whom seven were girls. The Judge died in 1658, leaving his wife with sufficient funds and properties, including Swarthmoor Hall, to live comfortably and host whomever she pleased.

Eleven years after the Judge died she married George Fox. Before then she had become a Quaker and suffered harsh imprisonment twice in Lancaster Castle for a total of four years or so. She died in 1701 at the age of 81. Of the early Quaker women, none had more experience with politics and public affairs.

The saga of Swarthmoor Hall has often been told.[2] One of the most touching of all events was the arrival and reception of young George Fox, which we bypass here in order to keep our political theme in focus.

Fox's appearance at Swarthmoor Hall, probably without invitation or advance notice, appears presumptuous. Moreover, he had good reasons for being fearful of judges, especially one nearly twice his own age and quite distinguished. It could be, however, that he had been carefully coached in advance by those who knew the Fells were religiously and politically Seekers. Be that as it may, Fox's appearance at Swarthmoor Hall accounts, in considerable measure, for the growth and survival of Quakerism.

Both Margaret and Judge Fell were absent upon Fox's arrival, she briefly and he for several days. Meanwhile, Fox, with Margaret's assent, used Swarthmoor Hall as a base for planning and preaching in the area, a circumstance of incalculable significance to the fledgling Religious Society of Friends.

54

The Judge, though forewarned of happenings at home, was nevertheless gracious toward Fox and two of his preaching companions, Richard Farnsworth and James Naylor, who happened to be present. During the conversations which followed, Fox asked the Judge for permission to hold a public meeting at his home and the request was granted, or as Fox said, he "let the meeting be kept in his home."[3]

That meeting, though small, turned out to be the first of its kind ever held by Quakers at that historic site. The Judge remained respectful of Fox and his followers throughout the remaining six years of his life. Politically speaking, the contributions made by Judge and Margaret Fell were godsends to the youthful George Fox and Quaker beginnings.

Fox laid down no rigid standards for accepting either preachers or others who wished to identify with the Quaker movement. His reputation had left no doubt, however, about the unconventional types of men and women he had in mind for Publishers and Valiants who came and went, often by death. Quite recently, Ernest Taylor prepared a list consisting of sixty-six Valiants, of whom twelve were women, who are discussed in chapter 5.

Oddly for a Quaker, Fox even welcomed former military personnel returning home from the Civil War. Speaking of that phenomenon, Margaret Hirst reported that "from the scattered allusions in contemporary writings a list can be made of more than ninety soldiers and ex-soldiers who became Friends, and no doubt there were many others of whom no record remains." Forty had served as officers.[4] A few had enrolled in the Navy and Parliament; others performed war-related duties.[5]

No Quaker meeting-houses built or specially designed for public worship existed in England until 1672.[6] Before then, religious services were held wherever space was accessible, such as homes, open areas, friendly churches, and less friendly ones after sermons. Regular small meetings usually were held in homes. Customarily, there were no worldly props, music or outward sacraments. Silent worship, interspersed with vocal messages, some of which were quite long, was usual. Spartan settings and procedures resembled those of early Anabaptists, especially the Mennonites. Some Seekers, particularly those in Westmoreland, had previously followed similar procedures.

As Fox wandered about early in his ministry, he must have formulated in his own mind a pattern of church governance which suited his taste. It was not, however, until two decades later—1667-1668—

that scattered meetings coalesced sufficiently to merit institutional status. Given Fox's reclusive disposition, the aftermath of the Civil War, and the ferocity of his critics, it is amazing that the Society not only survived but prospered in terms of numbers and influence, as Hugh Barbour and his colleagues have so ably pointed out.[7]

The pattern chosen by Fox resembled closely the Anabaptist non-hierarchical models, particularly those of early Mennonites and contemporary General Baptists. There were, however, striking differences in both theory and practice which are difficult to summarize. The most obvious was that Central Europeans usually were farmers who tended to colonize in isolated rural areas; Quakers, on the other hand, were likely to prefer singularity and relied less upon agriculture.

Drawing upon the Mennonite Schleitheim (1527) and Dordrecht (1632) Confessions,[8] examples of similarities and differences were as follows. Both Mennonites and Quakers idealized "Primitive Christianity." Both believed that Christ and the New Testament transcended Old Testament law and commandments. Both revered the Bible but the Mennonites usually were more literally inclined than Quakers. Both agreed that the Inner Light and conscience were sacrosanct in the sight of God. Congregational governance and separation of church and state were absolute requirements for both; they also insisted upon simplicity and lay ministry. Both believed male and female human beings had the same status before God, but biblically approved functional differences were permissible.[9] Both rejected the doctrines of predestination, election and original sin. Both disapproved of higher education.

Both used the terms "Monthly Meeting" and "Yearly Meeting" but Quakers added "Quarterly Meeting." Silent worship, with liberty of speech for worshippers, was common to both. A cappella hymn singing during worship services was permitted by Mennonites, but Quakers allowed no singing at all, although occasionally a worshipper would burst out in song. Mennonites limited outward sacraments to three exemplified by Jesus: Baptism (adult only), Lord's Supper (breaking of bread) and feet washing; Quakers honored only inward and spiritual sacraments.

Both disciplined wayward members, but Mennonites may have done so more rigorously than early Quakers. For both, obedience to civil magistrates was required, but only on matters not contrary to the Bible and conscience. Both advocated pacifism, non-conformity with

56

worldliness; plain dress and speech; truthfulness; avoidance of lawsuits; refusal to swear oaths and pay church tithes; and readiness to suffer martyrdom as did Jesus. Both felt obligated to pay taxes demanded by secular magistrates, although some objected to levies dedicated to war-related purposes.

Early Christians were noted for their messianic zeal and took quite literally the command given by Jesus "go ye into all the world, and preach the gospel to every creature."[10] The Protestant Reformation attested to the fact that the Kingdom of God envisioned by Jesus and his "Primitive Christians" was still distant.

Despite disappointing results of the past, Luther and Calvin kept trying by launching crusades to recruit disaffected Catholics and others for membership in the newly established Protestant churches, especially those in Central Europe. Characteristically, emotionalism ran high and threats of eternal damnation for non-conformance were frequent. Indeed, predestination was both implicit and explicit, which meant paradise for an "elected" few, but eternal damnation for all others regardless of piety or good works.

William Penn said of Fox "he was an original, being no man's copy,"[11] a phrase that characterized his preaching as well as his character. His grammar and elocutionary skills were unpolished, but his reputation was such as to attract and hold the attention of both large and small groups for long periods of time, as demonstrated at Firbank Fell and Sedgberg. His speeches usually were impromptu, impassioned, and liberally laced with Biblical allusions and quotations. Like other preachers of his day, he was aware of the sinful inclinations of human beings, but on the whole, his outlook was a hopeful one.

Of all the issues dear to Christian theologians, none has been more troublesome than attempts to explain in brief and intelligible language what is meant by "salvation" and how it can be assured. On such matters, Fox was clearly an amateur and even Robert Barclay (Urie), the only early distinguished Quaker theologian, left puzzling ambiguities.

Fox hinged his theory of salvation squarely upon the Inner Light. For him it was sovereign; conscience, though closely related, was merely an inward monitor of right and wrong; the Light Within, on the other hand, was "something," or "that," of God in every person born into the world. Early Quakers attributed that phenomenon to no particular bodily organ or substance; nor did they attempt to explain it in evolutionary, biochemical, or psychological terms. Even though they had wished to proceed empirically, they were unprepared to do so. Moreover, anatomical and chemical sciences were then in their infancy while biological and psychological sciences were nonexistent.

Given those circumstances, early Friends proceeded intuitively, as did the prophets and mystics of the past, guided and inspired by temperament, acculturation, knowledge, reason, and invisible sources of power. Had they lived in modern times and been more empirically inclined, they might have concurred with this summation:

> Included among the physical and psychological makeup of all human beings is the capability, variously referred to as soul, psyche, divine spark, élan vital, life-force, or creative impulse which makes it possible for men and women to commune directly with and respond to an invisible external force. That capability is for Quakers the God-Christ, or Inner Light.

The verb "to evangelize" was not commonly used in England when Fox began his ministry, but with the passage of time it came to mean preaching Christianity, often in theatrical context, with intent to convert nonbelievers and sinners. For early Quakers, including Fox, that approach presented problems inasmuch as they had been baptized previously and still yearned for something akin to "Primitive Christianity."

Recalling the emphasis placed by General Baptists upon spiritual inwardness as a requirement for membership, Fox accepted that principle which was officially defined in 1676 by London Yearly Meeting in these words:

> All the *faithful* men and women in every country [county?], city, and nation, whose faith stands in the power of God, the Gospel of Christ, and have received this Gospel, the power of God—they have a right to the power of the meeting [i.e., of the particular meeting], for they be heirs of the power and authority of the men's and women's meetings.[12]

Barclay added to that definition "All those persons who were deemed to be such were admitted to the Disciplinary Church Meetings, or in case they were the children of members deemed converted, were

58

'*invited,*' usually by the Elders or Ministers, to attend the meetings for business, with the consent of the Meeting."[13]

Eloquence varied, but the preaching style of Fox and his associates was quite similar. Usually, at public meetings, they relied primarily upon appeals to conscience, persuasion, convincement, utopianism and even martyrdom. Emotionalism often ran high and ecstatic behavior on the part of some listeners was not uncommon. There was no planned singing or other ceremonial actions, such as "altar calls" made famous nearly a century later, during the Great Awakening in North America led by Methodists John Wesley and George Whitfield.

Addressing "The Quaker Mode of Conversion," Richard Vann had this to say:

> Distinctive Quaker thinking about conversion starts from the fact that the Quakers had resolved their spiritual struggles in a way quite unlike the Puritans. Too many of them had already one, or several, conversion experiences which had turned out to be deceptive; too many dreaded the consciousness of sin which the Puritans considered wholesome and necessary. They therefore sought a communion with God so deep that it might be called "continuous conversion"; and they rejected the Baptist or Independent claim to find assurance of salvation in a single flux of grace which could be precisely dated and described for the edification and discernment of other Christians.[14]

Given the novelty of Quaker views and behavior, it is not surprising they were controversial. It was one thing for the curious to overflow public meetings; it was quite another to become a "convinced" Quaker. Friends' journals and other literature mention numerous instances of lengthy agonized seeking, including parental abuse and disownment, for defying conventional wisdom.

With the passage of time, growing numbers and institutionalization, early Quakers placed stress upon regional gatherings for fellowship and discussing matters of mutual concern, particularly sufferings, elementary schooling, assistance for the poor, governing Monthly and Quarterly Meetings, and colonizing in North America. "Camp" and "revival" meetings held by families in tents or wooden structures became commonplace.

Preaching in rural areas and small towns, only a few of which had populations above 10,000 was one thing but doing so in London with a population of 500,000 was something else. Francis Howgill and Edward Burroughs, two of Fox's most capable preachers, were at first in charge but others came and went. James Naylor, probably the most brilliant and popular of the Valiants, assisted and took charge when one or both of his co-workers were away. His ministry was said to be "greatly run after," even by high government officials, titled ladies and army officers.[15] Large preaching services were held at the Bull and Mouth Hall, rented between 1654 and the Great Fire of London in 1666. Funds appear to have been plentiful; services were held at the Hall or elsewhere on Sundays and weekdays; the Hall accommodated upward of a thousand people standing. Interruptions by opponents were frequent.

With such gatherings and the growth of Friends Meetings elsewhere, the Civil War over and Cromwell as Protector, Quakerism appeared to be well on its way, despite relentless harassment by zealous Presbyterian and Episcopalian preachers, allied with sympathetic Justices of Peace. Euphoria was uncommon for somber Quakers, but what little there was quickly disappeared with Naylor's blunder.

James Naylor, of Yorkshire, and the son of a husbandman, was married at the age of 22. He was a bright, well educated, energetic and articulate Puritan who had served as a cavalry officer and lay preacher in Cromwell's army. As an Independent, he undoubtedly had heard of Fox and thought favorably of him when they first met in 1651. From then until Naylor's misfortune the two men were closely linked as Publishers and Valiants, although Fox may have had some misgivings about his stability. Of those recruits, Naylor was the ablest preacher and most helpful theologian until his untimely death in 1660.

The frenetic pace set by Fox and his associates was excruciating and proved to be Naylor's undoing. Legend has it that he was bewitched while imprisoned briefly at Exeter by one of several adoring, but neurotic, female friends. In retrospect, however, he may have had a traumatic seizure, or in less technical parlance an "emotional breakdown."[16]

Be that as it may, a cluster of admirers who had attended a fair at Bristol pantomimed in public view Christ's Palm Sunday triumphal return to Jerusalem. Center stage was Naylor with hands folded sanctimoniously before him while riding a horse. A woman led the animal, a bareheaded man walked ahead, and several women led the procession laying down their scarves and handkerchiefs as they moved along singing "Holy, holy, holy is the Lord God of Hosts. Hosannah in the highest; holy, holy, holy is the Lord God of Israel." Multitudes followed the procession to an inn where the party expected to spend the night. Alerted in advance, few if any of the many local Quakers joined the throng.

Informed of the commotion, local magistrates sent for the entire party. A search of Naylor disclosed letters from women calling him Jesus, the only begotten Son of God, the King of Israel, the Prince of Peace, and similar names. Also found was a brief letter from Fox disassociating himself and other Quakers from such fanciful conduct, which helped spare them from incrimination.

The seriousness of those proceedings eventually brought the case before Parliament for trial. After an investigation, the defendant was convicted of "horrid blasphemy." He escaped the death penalty by vote of ninety-six to eighty-two, but even so the sentence was barbaric by today's standards.

The sentence directed that he be twice set in the pillory; whipped through the streets of Westminster; branded on the forehead with the letter B; tongue bored with a hot iron; ridden through the streets of Bristol on a "bareridged" horse, with face to the tail, then publicly whipped; and finally imprisoned indefinitely.

Naylor accepted the sentence stoically. While incarcerated, he regained emotional stability, wrote numerous tracts dealing with religious subjects, and gradually reconciled with Fox and Friends generally. Released from prison in 1659, he died the following year while in his early forties. That widely reported affair sent tremors among Quakers and other independent religious bodies at home and abroad. Having failed to deter Naylor, Fox directed his energies toward preventing recurrences.

Fox and his followers were often accused of having anarchist tendencies and the Naylor affair, at least in the minds of his enemies, appeared to confirm that hypothesis. Moreover, his previous arrests had been for lesser offenses and his writings showed no genuine interest in, or commitment to, anarchist theory or practice. The thrust of his message, like that of Fox, was obedience to the Inner Light as guided by conscience, but he stopped short of saying a human being was by nature an individual entitled to do whatever he or she pleased.

A major problem early Quakers had was to distinguish clearly between secular and spiritual authority and power. Non-separation of church and state had been so deeply entrenched in Western Europe, whether Catholics or Protestants were legally ascendant, that split loyalties were rare. Indeed, radical freedom-seekers were damned whether they sought liberty from church, state or both. Given that dilemma, early Quakers were trapped by the ancient conundrum requiring them to render obedience to both God and Caesar. As a practical matter, and despite the authoritarian context of those troubled times, they strove to do both simultaneously, and may have contributed significantly to the moderation represented by the Glorious Revolution of 1689 and the rise of democracy during the following century.

The fanatical interest in theology of those times assured seemingly endless collisions between Quaker leaders and their Puritan antagonists. Every thrust demanded a parry. Fox and other early Publishers and Valiants, joined later by youthful William Penn and Robert Barclay (Urie), debated issue by issue, orally and in writing, but never produced a systematic exegesis which might have diminished misunderstanding then and since.

Their most formidable opponents were Richard Baxter (1651-1691) and John Bunyan, mentioned earlier. The former had, during the Civil War, served as chaplain in Cromwell's army, and after the Restoration was imprisoned for eighteen months for libeling the Church of England, then controlled by Episcopalians.

Meanwhile, much of his preaching and writing was done at Kidderminster, a small town located in the vicinity of Coventry and Birmingham. While serving as pastor there he was associated with other pastors of Presbyterian, Independent and Episcopalian churches and used that position to debate and refute the arguments of Catholics, Anabaptists and Separatists. At first, he was bitterly antagonistic toward the Quakers, using such epithets as miserable creatures, seducers, apostates, proud, young raw professors, Papists and upstart sect, but mellowed somewhat later when, in his opinion, they "balanced their mysticism by rational intellectualism."[17] He was not only opposed to Quakers but "had a violent antipathy to lay preaching," perhaps because of its popularity.[18]

Naylor was but one of several early Quakers who troubled Fox and his loyalists. Dissatisfaction appeared as early as 1654 when Fox was likened to the "Pope," ministers were called "Lord Bishops" and accused of preaching "words without power," meeting houses were said to have "pulpits" and "foreign evangelization" was deplored.[19]

62

Among those critics were John Perrott and John Love or Luff who had gone to Rome to persuade the Pope, but the former was placed in a "prison for lunatics" and the latter was executed. Perrott later returned to England, then went to Barbados, Virginia, and Jamaica, where he died. Meanwhile, he had written numerous tracts stressing ultra-individualistic and spiritual mysticism. He and Love were among the first to register complaints about Fox, his numerous preachers and evangelistic crusades.

Among the many complaints were objections to Fox's instructions that male worshippers in Friends' meetings should remove hats during prayers and either stand, as did Presbyterians, or kneel as was customary among Episcopalians. Fundamentally, Perrott's complaint was that Quakers were placing too much emphasis upon being "outwardly" rather than "inwardly" religious. Speaking of that trend, Barclay (Tottenham) points out: "We have here the inroads of the Quietism combined with the views of the Ranters, which struck at the root of all Church order. The party holding those views pleaded liberty of the Spirit and the right of private judgment."[20]

Also brewing was still another schism within the Quaker movement. This time it was led by two former Independent preachers, John Wilkinson and John Story, often referred to as the "two Johns," both of whom had been loyal and dedicated Publishers of Truth. Life was never easy, but it became much harder following the Fifth Monarchy Uprising of 1661, which prompted enactment of the draconian Quaker Act of 1662 and the Conventical Act two years later. Those measures made it hazardous for Friends to assemble, even for worship, inasmuch as paid informers swarmed over England looking for prey and money.

Of the "two Johns," Wilkinson was the older; Story was more aggressive and outspoken than his colleague. Continuous harassments, court trials, fines and imprisonments, with little relief in sight, undoubtedly aggravated the schism. Fox tried to remain aloof from the dispute but to no avail; younger men, notably William Penn, Robert Barclay (Urie) and George Whitehead, bore the brunt of his defense.

The complaints made by the dissidents were numerous and varied. A major one was the rigorous manner in which some Quaker meetings enforced puritanical rules pertaining to such matters as dress, speech, simplicity, taking off one's hat to another person, bowing and scraping to notable people, and taking part in "frivolous" recreations, sports and games. Other complaints included the desirability of having separate Women's Meetings; extravagant displays of wealth; manner of conducting weddings; whether business meetings should be restricted to local members; discourteous behavior during worship services, such as groaning, sighings, soundings and singings; whether or not to pay tithes; fleeing from persecution to escape suffering; and whether the Society had undertaken responsibilities which should have been left to individuals and secular governments.

More fundamentally, the dissidents insisted that only the Inward Spirit of Christ was sovereign, which meant that outward controls by Monthly, Quarterly and Yearly Meetings lacked legitimacy. That point of view resembles the one advocated by pantheistic Ranters, which is addressed by Robert Barclay (Urie) below.

The separatists appear to have had in mind a consensual fellowship without disciplinary powers. Fox may have held that point of view when his ministry began, but changed his mind after observing the "dissenting people," particularly the General Baptists with whom he became acquainted in the Mansfield area. Be that as it may, his slowness to institutionalize suggests reluctance lest the structure become abusive. However, his association with future Publishers, shortly after his release from Derby Prison, convinced him that perfection required at least a firmly structured society of like-minded believers.

Despite countless attempts, formal and otherwise, to end the schism, it continued for over two decades and helps explain the quietism which characterized the Society during the following century. Many separatists became reconciled; most extremists separated from the main body of Friends; but only a few Monthly Meetings seceded.

Aware of schisms of the past and likelihood of others, Robert Barclay (Urie—1648-1690) wrote and published his first of several books at the youthful age of mid-20s, the thrust of which is summarized below. It had been approved by the Yearly Meeting's Second Day Morning Meeting, which consisted of ministers.[21] Barclay's purpose was twofold: to disavow charges that Quakers sympathized with anarchy and refute claims made by Catholic and Protestant churches. His treatise is arranged in ten sections with arguments supported by biblical citations. But for today's readers its syntax is such that comprehension is fallible and paraphrasing is risky. The summary which follows probably is reasonably accurate:

1. The word "Church" as used in the scriptures has reference to a gathering, company or assembly of certain people called together who believe in the same principles, doctrines and points of faith.

2. Jesus Christ appointed and ordained that His church have order and government with the same unity, power, spirit and practices.

3. The Apostles and Primitive Christians, when filled with the Holy Spirit and immediately led by the Spirit of God, practiced and commanded church governance.

4. Refusal of a a member to hear the judgment of the church, or whole assembly, justifies excluding such person by his brethren, as a heathen and publican. God has a special regard for such judgments and orderly procedures; accordingly, there is no encroachment or imposition upon an offender's Christian liberty.

5. The object of church government is both inward and outward. The chief marks of Christianity are care of the poor, widows and fatherless; marriage; removing scandals; and things undeniably wrong.

6. There will be cases and controversies which only can be infallibly judged by the Spirit and Power of God, not by any particular person or persons. Jesus Christ under the Gospels hath ordinarily revealed His will in such cases and controversies through Elders, or General Meeting, whose testimony is neither to be despised nor rejected without cause. Submission in such instances is no detraction from the common privileges of Christians to be inwardly led by the Spirit, seeing the Spirit hath led some heretofore so to do, and yet may. The principle is in no way tainted with imposition, or contrary to true liberty of conscience. Moreover, it differs fundamentally from the usurpation of Papacy, Prelacy, and Presbytery or any other of that nature.

7. Christians should not go to law before the unjust. When two parties differ meum and tuum (mine and thine) it is somewhat hard to please both; except when the power, truth and righteous judgment thereof reached that God in the conscience. When that happens, Christ is fulfilling promises made to man.

8. Nations shall come to be eased and disturbed of that dreadful tribe of lawyers (as well as priests) who by their many times and endless intricacies foment controversies.

9. No one can be accounted to the Church of Christ, or be an officer thereof, who has not been sanctified by the Grace of God and inward revelation, whether they be married, tradesman or servant.

10. When church differences arise, there will be an infallible judgment by the Spirit of God, which may be in the General Assembly, but not limited to a plurality. Neither is infallible. All who are sober and weighty may be present and willingly give their assent as the Spirit leads. If any are disobedient or unclear, and do not all that the Church ought to do, they may be censored or denied spiritual fellowship; but by no means, for matters of conscience, shall such offenders be molested, troubled, or persecuted in any of their outwards.

Despite Barclay's (Urie) prescriptions for harmonizing dissent, still another schism shattered Quakers' equanimity. This time the dispute started in Pennsylvania during the late 1680s and spread to England about the time of Fox's death.

The provocateur was George Keith (1638-1716), a Scotch Presbyterian theologian (though not ordained as such), mathematician, oriental scholar, author and intimate friend of Robert Barclay (Urie). He became a Quaker in 1663, and like most early converts, suffered persecution. Following that ordeal he became a leader, traveled widely, went to Pennsylvania in 1685 to serve as Surveyor General for East New Jersey and later became a schoolmaster. Meanwhile, he accumulated considerable wealth, mostly in land-holdings.

Zealous, moody and hot tempered, he set out to rally Friends around his Calvinistic evangelical views and quickly became engaged in disputes over a long list of controversial topics. High on that list were the transmigration of souls and whether the "Inner Light" was sufficient for salvation without "two Christs," one a spiritual, the other a bodily human Christ. As controversy peaked, he organized a rival faction called "Christian Quakers."

Keith's behavior embroiled him in both religious and political disputes with Pennsylvania Quakers, including Thomas Lloyd, then Deputy-Governor and critic of Governor William Penn, who was at that time in England. Bitterness ensued, whereupon Keith was "disowned" by Philadelphia Yearly Meeting and convicted of slander by the Philadelphia County Court. Returning to England, he continued his crusade for vindication, became an ordained Anglican clergyman, and returned to North America as a missionary for the Society for the Propagation of the Gospel. While on that assignment, he lost no opportunity to excoriate Quakers.

Whether the punishments mentioned were justified remains debatable, partly because substantial numbers of Quakers were sympathetic. Moreover, whether the Philadelphia judges, most of whom were Quakers, were impartial was also debatable. Many of his supporters left the Society of Friends and became Episcopalians or Baptists. Be that as it may, it was Keith's zealotry and ungovernable temper that led to his downfall. In retrospect, his contributions to Quakerism were both positive and negative.

The spirit and flavor of Keith's trial before the Philadelphia County Court is suggested by this extract written by Ethyn Williams Kirby:

> After the indictment was read, the clerk demanded whether Keith pleaded guilty or not. "Before I be demanded to plead to the Presentment," Keith replied, "I desire to be heard in a few Words." Upon receiving the court's permission, he continued: "I would have you to consider, that both ye and we are as Beacon set on a Hill and the eyes of God, Angels and Men are upon us, and if ye do anything against us that is not fair and just, not only these parts hereaway will hear of it, but Europe also; for if we be wronged (if God permit) we think to make it known to the World."
>
> That warning speech provoked the judges, who informed him that they would not tolerate such menaces, and that if he spoke or published any criticism of the sentence which would be pronounced, he must remember that there was a law under which he might be punished. Keith was unabashed. Was he not following the accepted pattern of Quaker life not only in appearing in court for his conscience's sake, but also in defying the judges?[22]

George B. Nash, speaking of the Pennsylvania experience, helps to place the schism in perspective by these observations:

> So combustible was the atmosphere in Pennsylvania in 1692 that it took only a spark provided by a single Quaker metaphysician to spread the flames of civil controversy to the religious sphere. The conflagration that ensued, known as the Keithian schism, enveloped Quaker society for almost two years. Before the fires were extinguished, the Quaker community was deeply riven and the power of the Quaker leaders who gathered

around Thomas Lloyd had been shaken to its roots. . . .
No more dramatic symbol of the failure of the Quaker
polity in Pennsylvania could be found than the Keithian
schism. For more than a decade, since their first arrival
in 1682, Quakers had wrestled with the problem of political disunity and social instability. Now the fires of
contention had spread to the religious community itself.[23]

Never before had English and Pennsylvania Friends been so
wrought up over theology and entangled in secular politics. As Keith
continued his crusade, leading Quakers strove for reconciliation and
did their best to minimize the damage. With that in mind, London
Yearly Meeting prepared and circulated widely a document entitled
"The Christian Doctrine, and the Society of the People Called Quakers Cleared, Etc." That creedal statement was the most authoritative
one issued by Early Friends up to that time. Despite its antiquated
verbiage and numerous scriptural citations, the document is still worth
reading and may have moderated schismatic tendencies.[24]

Of the tactics employed, Kirby says:

> Powerful as the onslaught of Keith and his allies were,
> the Quakers showed themselves extremely able not only
> in warding off attacks but in initiating skirmishes. The
> close organization perfected by Fox continued to prove
> its value . . . Committees were appointed to go through
> the works of leading Quakers and collect references to
> such doctrines as that of the sacraments, while the ablest
> writers were kept at work preparing to prove Keith's es-
> sential unsoundness.[25]

We noted above Fox's hesitation about the pattern his fledgling
society should follow. The schisms mentioned were both shocking and
humbling. Moreover, almost continuous litigation and imprisonment
following the Restoration had wasted precious time and eroded his
health. It was those realities, coupled with numerical growth, that
prompted Fox to focus upon institutionalization during 1667-1668.

Institutional growth is indicated by the following probable dates:
The first official titles, "Children of Light" and "Friends," made their
appearance between 1649 and 1650; Fox headed northward from
Derby Prison in 1651; the triumph at Sedgberg, Brigflatt and

Swarthmoor Hall occurred in 1652; the terms "Publishers of Truth" and "Valiants" came into usage in 1652 and 1654 respectively; the first Monthly Meeting and General Meeting (known later as Quarterly Meeting) met at Sedgberg in 1652; the first General Yearly Meeting met in 1658 at the home of John Crook in Bedfordshire; Fox spent most of the year 1667 and part of the following one setting up Men's and Women's Monthly and Quarterly Meetings, starting in the London vicinity and moving northward; and the first annual Representative General Yearly Meeting was held at London in 1668.[26]

Following is a brief summary of observations and procedures applicable to early Friends Meetings:

1. Monthly Meetings differed widely in numbers and members, strength and activities. Those in northern counties usually were strongest.

2. Monthly Meetings were primary; Quarterly and Yearly Meetings had delegated authority.

3. Monthly Meetings bore the brunt of such matters as accepting and overseeing members; appointing clerks, ministers (lay only), elders, committees and delegates to Quarterly and Yearly Meetings; overseeing worship services, children, the needy and sick, marriages and separations, funerals, properties and finance.

4. Records were kept of members, proceedings, sufferings, wills, births, marriages and separations, deaths and disciplinary actions.

5. Worship was a duty required by law. Silent worship was basic; both men and women were entitled to speak.

6. Both men and women were eligible to preach publicly, hold offices and serve on committees.

7. Separate meetings for women came into existence at various places by the mid-1600s. They did so in response to pressing humanitarian needs occasioned by the absence of men due to traveling and imprisonment; the paucity of schools; large numbers of orphans, poor and sick, especially during and after the Black Death (bubonic plague) of 1665 and Great London Fire of 1666. Their organization and procedures paralleled those of men.

8. Decision-making was to be achieved by reverentially seeking consensus, or as some present-day Friends prefer to say, "sense of the Meeting." Numbers mattered, but the weightiness of concerned members on serious controversial matters appears to have been decisive.

Fox was well aware of the steps taken by the local and regional Meetings mentioned above. He nevertheless thought it desirable for the first General Yearly Meeting to apprise Friends everywhere of desirable standards and practices. With that in mind, and Yearly Meeting approval, he prepared, published and circulated "The Canons of Institutions." Barclay (Tottenham) summarized those Canons which we paraphrase here:[27]

(1) Those who walk not in the truth are to be exhorted by persons appointed by the church, who are to report; (2) Members who follow pleasure, gaming, or are not faithful in their callings or dealings, or are dishonest and "runneth in debt" are to be exhorted and report made; (3) Marriages are not to be contracted in a disorderly manner; they are to be recorded in a book, and at least a dozen witnesses must be present; (4) Widows who marry a second time are to secure the children of the first marriage with a just and equal portion of their property; (5) Widows are to be especially cared for by the church, generally eased, and children apprenticed; (6) Marriages by priests are forbidden; those who do so are to be visited three or four times and repudiated as members unless they "condemn" their conduct; (7) Those who, like the Ranters, wear their hats when Friends pray are to have judgment passed against them; (8) Meetings having a large number of poor are to be liberally assisted; nothing is to be lacking by the church in this matter; (9) Any kind of courtship which does not sincerely intend marriage, draw out the affections of one another or leave one another are to be denounced; (10) All evil speakers, backbiters, slanderers, foolish talkers and idle jesters are to be dealt with; (11) Talebearers are to be reproved and admonished; (12) Cheats and people who borrow money on false pretenses are to be condemned; (13) General Meetings are to be held once a quarter, and differences are to be speedily ended; (14) Children are to be trained up in the fear of the Lord, in soberness and holiness, righteousness, temperance, meekness, gentleness, lowliness, and modest in apparel and carriage; (15) Books for registering births, marriages and burials are to be provided; (16) Brethren who have suffered shall be remembered and praised in ages to come; (17) Payment of

tithes is contrary to the doctrines of Apostles and Martyrs; (18) Prisoners for conscience sake are to be relieved; wives and families are to be supported by the church.

Those Canons had been developing for more than two decades. Though quaint and detailed, the substance of many of them are reflected in today's Quaker Books of Discipline.

As the first General Yearly Meeting met, the Quakers and like-minded dissidents were still paying a heavy price for the violent Fifth Monarchy Uprising of 1661, even though they were innocent bystanders. The Clarendon Code was still in effect, including the Quaker Act, loathed by its victims and other critics. Emigration and banishment were possibilities, but those usually entailed extraordinary zeal, sacrifice, suffering and money. A simpler alternative was to lobby[28] vigorously and relentlessly, as Quakers did, despite their professed disdain for "politics." It is worth noting at this point that they have never stopped doing so.

Shortly after that historic General Meeting, Fox was "at liberty," to use one of his favorite phrases, to visit Ireland, the West Indies and North America. Upon returning home, he and Margaret Fell married and shortly thereafter both were imprisoned, as we shall next discuss.

IV

BELEAGUERED MONARCHS
AND PROTECTORS

England's Revolution and Civil War dominated the political scene when George Fox was growing up in the Midlands. Technically, the Revolution began in 1622 and ended with the Stuart Restoration in 1660. During that period there were two civil wars; one during the years 1642-1646, the other in 1648 which was followed by an interregnum dominated by Oliver Cromwell and his son Richard. The second war was a last-ditch effort by Scottish Royalists to save the King. Our usage of "Civil War" includes both.

The principal actors during that fateful period were King James, the first of the Stuart Dynasty, who died in 1625, the year after Fox was born; King Charles I, who was crowned at the age of 25; and a Parliament dominated by a new bourgeois class generally identified with Puritans, but led by radical Presbyterians.

The British constitution was unwritten then as now. It consisted primarily of historic documents and common-law principles, as applied and interpreted over centuries by monarchs, parliaments and courts. The first such document was the Magna Carta, approved in 1215 when King John was forced by powerful barons to affix his seal to that document.

Meanwhile, Parliament had provided additional constraints upon a monarch's absolutist pretensions. That institution originated in the thirteenth century and assumed modern form during the reign of Henry VIII, with a House of Lords headed by a chancellor and a House of Commons presided over by a speaker. Lords were seated either by appointment or heredity; members of Commons were elected by male voters able to meet highly restrictive qualifications within designated districts. The lords usually could be counted on to support conservative interests; members of Commons were more likely to reflect popular sentiments.

Pre-war Skirmishing Between King and Parliament

Charles I quickly discovered that Parliament was in no mood to become subordinate to the King. Rather, it wanted not merely collateral power but also sovereignty. The King was particularly in need of money and demanded sole authority to levy taxes, which Parliament denied. Adamancy on the part of both parties precipitated the Civil War, but fundamentally both secular and religious issues were at stake.

Although victorious on the battlefields, Parliament was never fully sovereign during the war and "Kingless Decade" which followed, due largely to quarrels with the Army and the assumption of complete control by Oliver Cromwell. The Restoration brought back both monarchy and Parliamentary supremacy, an arrangement confirmed for posterity by the Glorious Revolution of 1688. Meanwhile, Parliamentary expectations were that the restored Kings, Charles II and James II, had coordinate status with special responsibility for diplomacy, ceremonials and administration.

The first crucial test of strength between Charles I and Parliament centered on *The Petition of Right* which came to a head in 1641. Parliament's defense was detailed in a "Grand Remonstrance," to which the King responded vigorously.[1] That episode was unusual inasmuch as the King himself was the alleged culprit. Suspecting the document would be ignored, its sponsors took precautionary steps to avoid that result, whereupon the King unwittingly assented to its provisions. Although champions of the Petition were elated, the King "shewed by word and deed" that he considered it to be "no check on his freedom of action."[2]

The Petition's intent was to remind the King and all subjects that a monarch's authority was less than absolute. Among the complaints listed in the Petition were billeting soldiers and mariners in private residences without prior consent; demanding gifts, loans, benevolences, taxes, or like charges without prior Parliamentary authorization or detention without cause; and the imposition of martial law without Parliamentary approval. Reaffirmed by the Bill of Rights in 1688, the Petition has since ranked among such historic documents as Magna Carta.

Despite the Petition's provision, neither Charles I nor Restoration Kings Charles II (1650-1685) and James II (1685-1688) ever willingly divested themselves of time-honored powers and prerogatives. Theoretically, their monistic concept of sovereignty precluded divisibility absolutely. Among possible alternatives were sovereignty in Parliament alone, King and Parliament conjointly, traditional constitutional precepts, and the people collectively. Complicating decision-making was the fact that Parliament had great powers during the preceding Tudor era, so much so, "there was nothing Parliament could not do."[3]

Parliamentary sovereignty had been discussed repeatedly in England, but never more heatedly than during the debate over the Petition. Addressing that issue, the famous Sir Edward Coke (1552-1634) had this to say:

> The power and jurisdiction of Parliament is so transcendent and absolute, that it cannot be confined, either for causes of persons, within any bounds . . . It hath sovereign and uncontrollable authority in making, confirming, enlarging, restraining, abrogating, repealing, reviving, and expounding of laws, concerning matters of all possible denominations, ecclesiastical or temporal, civil, military, maritime, or criminal; this being the place where that absolute despotic power, which must in all governments reside somewhere, is entrusted by the constitution of these kingdoms.[4]

Civil War and Outcomes

Civil warfare began in 1642 after seventeen years of haggling between King and Parliament. That conflict had far-reaching implications not only for England but also Wales, Scotland, Ireland, Western Europe and the Empire generally, including the embryonic American colonies. The major contestants were Royalists, led by the King, and Parliamentarians, of whom Oliver Cromwell has special interest for this account. Generally speaking, Royalist forces had greatest success in the north and southwest, while Parliamentarians were predominant in central and southeastern regions. Troops were either volunteers or draftees, most of whom were at first ill-prepared for combat.

The Royalists' strategy was to gain as much territory as possible and recover London; Parliamentary forces wandered aimlessly at first then adopted the goal of defeating the King in battle and capturing him in person. The Royalists' defeat was due chiefly to Cromwell's reorganization of the Army. Those changes diminished long-standing class favoritism, created a closely-knit Puritan regiment popularly known as "Ironsides" and a "New Model Army," said by H. N. Brailsford to be "the most astounding creation of the age. There had been nothing like the New Model in the history of our Island, nor had it a successor."[5]

Payments for soldiers, though regularized, proved to be a major sticking point inasmuch as revenues were supplied by counties having suffered least from the war. Shortages were chronic; indeed, on one occasion Parliament came close to repealing the Model. Moreover, shortages dampened morals and prompted mutinous behavior. It nevertheless remained a military and democratic force throughout that troubled period. Disbanded by Charles II in 1662, it served as a paradigm for England's future standing army.

Meanwhile, vestiges of the ancient volunteer militia remained. It was that force which George Fox refused to join in 1649 while a prisoner at Nottingham. There were, however, non-pacific Quakers who did enroll in the militia and other military services. Moreover, there were numerous Anabaptists who did likewise, some of whom were Army generals.[6]

The term "pacifist" was not commonly used at that time; indeed, not until the present century (1905) did it become current.[7] Moreover, Fox's understanding of the term's significance was quite limited, as mentioned above. As for timing, Peter Brock said: "The final crystallization of the Quaker Peace Testimony may be dated to their declaration of January 1661 against the taking up arms, either on behalf of an earthly kingdom or to inaugurate the Kingdom of Christ."[8] That date has considerable significance for the zealous Quakers who had, for more than a decade, successfully struggled for survival and identity in the aftermath of a brutal Civil War.

Calvinists opposed the doctrine that the religion of a ruler had to be the religion of the land. In practice, however, they preferred complete control of both church and state.[9]

That tendency was clearly demonstrated in 1643 when Presbyterian leaders of church and state assembled at Westminster to review their Parliamentary agenda and formulate what became the Westminster Confession.[10] Meanwhile, Parliament had allied itself with Scotland and approved a Solemn League and Covenant, similar to one adopted in 1581 by Scottish Covenanters for the purpose of combating Catholics. The pledge is too long and detailed for full recital here, but the following extracts suggest its principal objectives:[11]

> That we shall sincerely, really and constantly, through the Grace of God, endeavor in all our places and callings, the preservation of the reformed religion in the Church of Scotland, in doctrine, worship, discipline and government against our common enemies; the reformation of religion in the Kingdoms of England and Ireland, in doctrine, worship, discipline and government, according to the Word of God, and the example of the best Reformed Churches; and we shall endeavor to bring the Churches of God in the three kingdoms to the nearest conjunction and uniformity of religion . . .

> That we shall in like manner, without respect of persons, endeavor the extirpation of Popery, Prelacy (that is, Church government by Archbishops, Bishops, their Chancellors and Commissaries, Deans, Deans and Chapters, Archdeacons, and other ecclesiastical officers depending on that hierarchy), superstition, heresy, schism, profaneness, and whatsoever shall be found to be contrary to sound doctrine and the power of godliness . . .

> We shall also with all faithfulness endeavor the discovery of all such as have been or shall be incendiaries, malignants or evil instruments, by hindering the reformation of religion, dividing the King from his people, or one of the kingdoms from another, or making any faction or parties amongst the people, contrary to the league and covenant, that they may be brought to public trial and receive condign punishment . . .

Both houses of Parliament endorsed those proposals with the proviso that a standing committee, composed of representatives from both England and Scotland, monitor performance. Although Cromwell was a devout Puritan, he disapproved of Presbyterian dominance, preferring instead to unify all Protestants.

As Parliamentary forces gained the upper hand, vengeance became rampant. Illustrative of that "reign of terror" were the executions of the Earl of Strafford, a close associate of the King; Archbishop of Canterbury, William Laud; and later the King himself. Moreover, three prerogative courts having special rights and privileges (Star Chamber, High Commission and Council of the North) were terminated inasmuch as they could "punish anything which they regarded as openly moral or sinful, without reference to any rule or definition whatever."[12] It was those courts which judged such horrid offenses as heresy and blasphemy.

Moreover, Episcopal Churches and remaining Catholic sanctuaries were desecrated. Many Anglican Churches lost their ministers; usage of the *Book of Common Prayer* became punishable by fines and imprisonment; tithes were uncollected; tithe-barns and manorial records were burned; riots were common; enclosures were attacked; intolerance, bigotry, censorship and harsh penalties were common. Indeed, that social explosion prompted by Presbyterian leaders and supported by the "common people" was costly not only in terms of money, casualties and devastation but also in national pride and honor. That trauma, though tragic, accounted in considerable measure for the new era of toleration ushered in by the Glorious Revolution of 1688.

Commonwealth, Cromwells, Levellers, and Quakers

As the Civil War approached its ending, public apprehension was widespread. There were prospects of anarchy at home; a restless army whose pay was overdue; Royalists who might attempt to restore exiled Charles II to the throne; unrest in Ireland and Scotland and the ever-present likelihood of involvements in wars abroad. With those prospects in mind, Thomas Pride, acting upon orders issued by a joint Army and Parliamentary committee, purged Parliament of over 100 members (most of whom were Presbyterian) claiming they were Royalist sympathizers. The remaining Rump Parliament, consisting of about fifty members controlled by the Army, arranged for the King's execution and ushered in the "Kingless Decade." Pride himself was one of several who signed the King's death warrant, but Cromwell led the movement for execution.

Governance from then until the Stuart Restoration was both experimental and tenuous, with Oliver Cromwell predominant until his death in 1658. Legally, the presumption was that Parliament was sovereign, but in fact it was subordinate to Cromwell's dictatorship. Parliament was unicameral in form until 1657 when a "House of Lords" was approved unanimously for the purpose of checking and balancing both houses. Parliament had various names: Long, Rump, Nominated or Barebones, Little, and Protectoral, members of which were elected by qualified voters. Officially, Cromwell's titles included "Protector," "Lord General," and "Lord Protector." A Council of State, composed chiefly of Army generals, served as advisors.

There were also some novel features. The first one, established early in 1649, was called the "Commonwealth and Free State" directed by a Council of State. It was acclaimed the world's first national republic, but Parliament met infrequently and bowed obsequiously to a Chief of State, otherwise known as "Protector," who was at the time Oliver Cromwell.

The second feature made its appearance in 1653. On that occasion a new government was proclaimed which was entitled "Commonwealth of England, Scotland, and Ireland and the Dominions Thereto Belonging." Cromwell, after rejecting the title of King, partly because of failing health, was designated Lord Protector for life. A new "Instrument of Government" was included and hailed as the only one of its kind ever operational in England or elsewhere. Actually, however, the Commonwealth turned out to be something else: a military dictatorship, although Parliament did meet from time to time. Speaking of that development, Professor Wilburt Cortez Abbott remarked, "It seems implied that if the people of the British Isles did not precisely enjoy being ruled by military dictatorship, they at least accepted it."[13]

Cromwell assembled his first, and freshly elected, Protectoral Parliament at Westminster Abbey in September, 1654. His speech mentioned current problems at home and abroad; pleaded for spiritual strength; regaled enemies, mentioning particularly Levellers and Fifth Monarchists;[14] outlined the nation's needs; and closed with an appeal for understanding and support.

The year 1655 was a frightful one for Cromwell. His Protectorate had been in existence for two years, his health was precarious, and England was threatened by European Catholic Powers. Meanwhile, at home there were tumults, conspiracies, insurrections and rebellions, many of which were fomented by Royalists, who were then excluded from participating in government despite their overwhelming majority.

78

The response made to those threats was initially developed by major generals who soon became known as "Saints." A dozen or so military districts were established, each of which was commanded by one of the generals. Assisting them were the Army and such county and local officials as justices of the peace, sheriffs, bailiffs, constables, headboroughs, and all other officers and ministers both civil and military.[15] Supporting those officials was a far-flung spy system, including ever-present informers looking for prey, and censorship which was said to be "more stringent than the Star Chamber had ever known."[16]

Managers of that dictatorial regime were instructed as follows:

> They shall in their constant Carriage and Conversation encourage and promote Godliness and Virtue, and Discourage and Discountenance all Prophaneness and Ungodliness; and shall endeavor with the other Justices of the Peace, and other Ministers and Officers, who are intrusted with the care of things that the Laws against Drunkenness, Blaspheming, and taking the Name of God in vain, by swearing and cursing, Plays and Interludes, and profaning the Lord's Day, and such like wickedness and abominations, be put in more effectual execution then they have been hitherto.[17]

Additionally, London and Westminster were required to seek out and suppress all "gaming houses and houses of evil fame."[18]

Whatever Cromwell's motives might have been, his dragonish laws and spy system entrapped not only sinners but also innumerable God-fearing Quakers and like-minded religionists. Indeed, vigilantism flourished throughout the nation (including some colonies) and overwhelmed the already overburdened criminal justice system. The offenses charged were not only those enacted during the Cromwellian Period, but also older ones dating back to the Tudors when Catholics and other religious dissidents were cruelly hounded and punished. Although Cromwell himself was under great pressure because of health and political crises, countless well-intentioned subjects were either grievously harassed or persecuted, as recorded in the following chapter. The system came to an inglorious end early in 1657, about two years after being launched. Even Cromwell was pleased with that result. The laws enacted to launch and support that system remained operative for use as needed.

As the Civil War developed, numerous religious sects and peculiar groups addressed themselves to politico-religious reforms. Of them, none was more vigorous and daring than the Levellers led by John Wilburne (1615-1657). He was known during his youthful years as "Free-born John" because of ancestral rank and quality. His parents and close relatives were staunch Calvinists deeply interested in public affairs, some of whom served in Parliament. It appears, however, that son John did not enroll as a church member until late in life when he became a Quaker. His birthplace was in the rural North Country at Sunderland near the eastern coast.

After attending grammar school, he was apprenticed to a Puritan wholesale clothier situated in London. While at that location, he first savored urban life and the factious disputation then swirling about King Charles I, who had recently offended English opinion by marrying Catholic Henrietta Maria, sister of Louis XIII of France. Following the apprenticeship, Wilburne remained in London, married Elizabeth Dewell, established a home, ran a brewery, joined the Army, became an officer and aide to Oliver Cromwell and fought with his forces during the decisive battle at Marston Moor. He left the Army in April, 1645, and quickly became engrossed in the Leveller movement, which had a life-span of only two short years.

In retrospect, Wilburne is best known for his fierce dislike of arbitrary power, as displayed by his contemporaries James I, Charles I, Parliamentary leaders, Oliver Cromwell and the Church of England. His attitude had been conditioned by an incident which occurred shortly after his apprenticeship. By that time, his rusticity had diminished, he needed funds to support himself and prospective marriage, and was steadily sucked into controversies then raging between King and Parliament. Moreover, he was deeply committed to Calvinism, and as Joseph Frank wrote, he had a "lifelong propensity for martyrdom."[19]

Although Wilburne was not a scholar, he had read the Bible, *Book of Martyrs,* theological treatises of leading Protestant reformers, innumerable political tracts, and particularly the writings of Sir Edward Coke, the most eminent English jurist of that time. Indeed, "To Wilburne . . . Coke supplied exactly what was needed to complete his conception of law and liberty in the state and to support his case against any superiors who ventured to resist his demands."[20]

Wilburne first experienced despotic power personally in 1637 at the age of 22. On that occasion, he encountered a coterie of like-minded men, one of whom was Dr. John Bastwick, who had written a book entitled *Litany* which attacked Anglican Bishops, but it could not be published legally or sold in England. Wilburne agreed nevertheless to have it published in Holland for smuggling back to England and might have benefited financially had he not been betrayed by a trusted friend. Both he and the author were seized and prosecuted before the Court of Star Chamber, noted for its severe sentences. Heavy fines were imposed on both men but Wilburne, because of his open defiance, was made to stand in a pillory, lashed 500 times at the tail of a cart through London's streets, and placed in isolation at Fleet Prison without succor for his wounds.[21]

Despite such cruel punishments, frequent trials and imprisonments, Wilburne was never one to be denied or intimidated without vigorous protest alone or through the Leveller Party. Indeed, centuries of persecution dating back to the Lollards, Anabaptists and beyond had, to borrow a phrase used by Pauline Gregg, "accustomed the young men of Wilburne's generation to very strong meat."[22]

As the Leveller Movement got underway, Wilburne was closely allied with two other able men: William Walwin, a merchant of ample means, nominally Presbyterian, biblically knowledgeable and compared with Wilburne sedate and calm; and Richard Overton, a printer of Baptist upbringing and satirist who delighted in lampooning Independents and Presbyterians.

Speaking of that movement, editors William Haller and Godfrey Davis observed:

> No movement of such kind on such scale organized for such purpose had ever been seen in England. Its leaders were animated by religious convictions and they were experienced in the organization of religious dissent, but the movement was not a religious but a secular one, aiming to secure certain positive rights and benefits by political action. The Levellers constituted a party and in the end became, as Cromwell very well realized, one of the most formidable factors in the situation.[23]

The political party referred to was the first one to resemble those of modern times. It was closely associated with the New Model Army until both were crushed by Cromwell in 1649.

Wilburne disliked the term "Levellers" because it suggested "social levelling," which if successful would create a "classless" society, probably result in fratricidal conflict and take considerable time. Speaking to that subject, Wilburne said:

> We profess . . . that we never had in our thoughts to level mens estates, it being the utmost of our aimes that the Commonwealth be reduced to such a passe that every man may wish as much security as may he enjoy his property.[24]

Alternatives to the terms "Levellers" and "levelling" were not easily come by. The inference was that something other than England's present social order was urgently needed. What they hoped for was a more egalitarian society and democratic political system, which in retrospect anticipated modern constitutional government.[25]

Despite continuous harassment, Wilburne and his associates flooded Parliament and the public generally with what today would be called "propaganda." Speaking of newspapers, Professor Pease said they "were at best ephemeral, and sprang up, decayed, and changed titles frequently . . . " He went on to say that "tracts were preferred and included everything from the broadside, petition, or ordinance, or the four-page squib, to the weighty theological or political tract running to four hundred pages." Moreover, "The literature supposedly passed through the hands of licensers before being printed, and from 1645 to 1653 unlicensed books issued in streams from illicit presses, and voiced the most outspoken criticisms of the ruling powers. The newspapers were even more difficult to censor than the tracts."[26]

The most famous Leveller tract was entitled *An Agreement of the Free People of England,* signed by Wilburne and others on May 1, 1649, about four months after King Charles I was executed.[27] Briefly summarized, its proposals were as follows:

♦ Establish a "Supreme Authority in England and Territories" consisting of 400 "Representatives of the People" chosen by manhood suffrage.

- Substitute a written constitution for the existing unwritten one.
- Abolish monarchy.
- Separate powers of government.
- Provide binding safeguards for individual rights, including conscientious objection to military and naval service.
- Separate church and state.
- Outlaw monopolies and socialize the economy.
- Permit no one except Parliament to declare war.
- Authorize each county to select its own officials.
- Require that trials be judged by twelve-member citizens.
- Choose jurors from districts of residence.

Debate in Parliament over that tract was of historic proportions and feelings ran high. Modifications were discussed at length, but basically the proposals were too extreme for those intolerant times. Even some Independents and Baptists withdrew their support. Meanwhile, Wilburne and Cromwell became implacable foes.

Cromwell's reasons for crushing the Leveller Movement were undoubtedly well known at the time, but not until about five years later did he publicize his action. He did so on that occasion before the first session of the Parliament of the Protectorate in 1654, with these words:

> What was the face that was upon our affairs as to the interest of the nation? to the magistery? to the ranks and orders of men, whereby England hath been known for hundreds of years? A nobleman, a gentleman, a yeoman? [That is a good interest of the nation and a great one.] The magistery of the nation, was it not almost trampled under foot, under despite and contempt by men of levelling principles?
>
> I beseech you, for the orders of men and ranks of men, did not that levelling principle tend to the reducing all to equality? Did it think to do so, or did it practice toward it for propriety [property] and interest? What was the design, but to make the tenant as liberal a fortune as the landlord? Which I think, if obtained, would not have

lasted long! The men of that principle, after they had served their own turns, would have cried up interest and property then fast enough.[28]

With those remarks, Cromwell displayed not only his own personal biases but also those of the Parliamentarians to whom he was speaking. Among them were "lords," earls, a baron, numerous knights, well over a hundred bearing military titles, many government officials, a few regicides, and over thirty judges serving on the High Court of Justice.[29]

The Levellers' defeat was a fatal blow to Wilburne personally and his many avid supporters. The King had been executed; Royalists were enraged and plotted revenge; the Army was in disarray; economic distress was widespread; Parliamentary governance was at a transitional state; and Wilburne was charged with high treason, allegedly for his part in fomenting rebellion in the Army.

The trial was held at Guildhall, in London, before a Court of Oyer and Terminer presided over by a panel of two judges assisted by an all-male jury. The courtroom was filled, largely with the defendant's supporters, while Wilburne pleaded his own defense for two days. Meanwhile, tensions ran high in the courtroom and riotous outbursts were feared. The jury's verdict was acquittal, whereupon partisans cheered and celebrated well into the night. More important from a legal point of view was the jury's insistence that facts as well as law were pertinent to the verdict.[30]

That freedom was nevertheless tenuous given Wilburne's propensity for crusading and infuriating protagonists. Finally, in 1651-1652, one of his many petitions angered Parliament sufficiently to impose a heavy fine and condemn him to death if he should be found in England at the end of thirty days. That Parliamentary verdict was clearly vengeful and contrary to fundamental law. Although declared so by civil courts, Cromwell made sure Wilburne would never again meddle in politics.

Wilburne was first detained in London Tower then shipped to Jersey, one of England's Channel Islands off the coast of France, where he was confined at Mount Orgueil Castle and later at Dover Castle, located southeast of London in County Kent. Meanwhile, his wife successfully appealed for desperately needed funds and Wilburne, counseled by Quaker Luke Howard, affiliated with that Society until his death two years later. Meanwhile, he was granted brief leaves of absence to visit relatives, close friends and nearby Quaker gatherings. He died outside prison walls.

His death occurred from lingering ailments. Funeral services were held at the ancient Bull and Mouth situated in London where Friends customarily held meetings. Interment was at Bunhill Fields, a Quaker cemetery adjacent to Spinning Wheel Alley, now Liverpool Street.[31] Ironically, Wilburne, a staunch Calvinist who never joined his parental church, a soldier who fought with Oliver Cromwell's victorious dragoons at the Battle of Marston Moor, and one who had suffered endlessly for democratic ideals, was among the earliest converts buried at Bunhill Fields.[32]

Apparently George Fox, whose ministry had barely begun when the Leveller Movement started, never met Wilburne nor is his name mentioned in Fox's *Journal*. It is well known, however, that some of the earliest Quakers actively supported the Levellers' agenda despite their apolitical inclinations. Professor Pease estimated that there were 10,000 Levellers in London, many others in nearby shires and unknown numbers more distant. As many as 30,000 pamphlets were printed on one occasion.[33]

For a movement once despised and touted as a failure, it is amazing that Wilburne and the Levellers' Party have since been acclaimed for their contributions to democracy. Speaking of that phenomenon, Joseph Frank made this appraisal:

> The central purpose of the Leveller Party was to establish a constitutional democracy in England. In the seventeenth century that purpose failed. When in the nineteenth and twentieth centuries it was at least partially realized, the Levellers had long been forgotten. Yet they formed a link in the chain of England's evolution toward democracy; by helping to channel the nascent and amorphous democratic sentiment of the seventeenth century in the direction of those ideological stations through which it moved in the three following centuries, the Levellers made their major contribution to the history of modern ideas. When examined from the vantage point of these three centuries, this contribution can be broken down into four constituent elements, which, though overlapping and interlinked, can be labeled optimism, secularism, rationalism, and pragmatism.[34]

Their crusade may have "failed," as suggested above, but their efforts, coupled with those of Quakers and other seekers, may have been fruitful as early as the Glorious Revolution of 1688.

The Diggers were an offshoot of the Levellers led by Gerard Winstanley (1609-1676).[35] He was born in Wigan, Leicestershire, England, of socially prominent parents who were Independents, a circumstance which prevented him from attending a university even though he had been baptized in an Anglican Church.[36] Instead, he was apprenticed to a clothmaker and later became one himself. His career varied from then on to bankrupt debtor, indefatigable pamphleteer, champion of the working classes, crusader for utopian communalism and a Quaker.

Apparently, Winstanley was strongly influenced by the radical Familists, or Family of Love, founded in 1541 by either David George (also known as Joris) or Henry Nicholas, both of whom were born in the early 1500s.[37] Centered in Holland, the Familists gained a considerable following there and elsewhere on the Continent. They first surfaced in England during the mid-1500s and by 1579 there may have been 1000 members. The sect became extinct in the mid-1700s.

Winstanley's views and objectives are well illustrated by the following incident and his pamphlet entitled *Utopia: The Law of Freedom*. The former took place in 1649 shortly after King Charles I was executed. On that occasion a group known as the "Diggers" gathered on St. George's Hill, near Cobhand in Surrey County. Their intention was to occupy and plant gardens on an "enclosed" hillside, a practice once permitted for the benefit of serfs, which was phased out gradually by the enclosure acts of 1235 and 1285. Irate neighbors and landowners protested then destroyed the community. Some Diggers returned again and again until forcibly evicted, tried and punished.[38]

Winstanley's *Utopia* is quaintly written and difficult to digest. Berens provides the following essence of his theology:

> Reason is the Ruling Spirit of the whole Creation, is God, Spirit of Righteousness, who is ever seated within the hearts of men combatting the lusts of the flesh, the promptings of the brute animal nature of mankind . . . Reason, in short, is the spark of the Divine man, the Spirit of Light that swells within and may rule the mind and actions of every man. Conscience is but the promptings of Reason, inspiring men to right action, to

deal justly and brotherly and live in peaceful and harmonious association with their fellows . . . And similarly it is the ruling of the spirit of Jesus Christ, the Inward Light, within the hearts of man, not the sufferings of a man Jesus Christ, which is the essential condition of individual and social salvation.[39]

Those precepts anticipated the writings of a poor nineteenth century American, Henry George (1830–1897), whose *Progress and Poverty* sold millions of copies in many parts of the world. Moreover, Winstanley's theses, though speculative, pointed in the direction of populist governance, cooperatives, communalism and socialism. Indeed, to quote Eduard Bernstein, "he represents the most advanced ideas of his times."[40]

Whether George Fox and Winstanley ever met is unclear; neither the latter's name nor the Diggers are mentioned in Fox's *Journal*. Inasmuch as both men were apocalyptically and mystically inclined, Rufus Jones said they "bore the marks of direct influence from Jacob Boehm, founder of a small sect called 'Boehemists.'" He doubted, however, "whether Winstanley in any degree influenced Fox. There is to my mind no sign of it."[41]

Despite Jones' doubts, Winstanley held numerous views similar to those of Fox. One, for example, dealt with the Inner Light, the most basic of all Quaker doctrines. His comments were:

And because among the variety of mankind ignorance may grow up, therefore this Original Law is written in the hearts of every man, to be his guide and leader; so that if an Officer be blinded by covetousness and pride, and ignorance rule in him, yet an inferior man may tell him when he goes astray. For Common Preservation and Peace is the Foundation-Rule of all Government: therefore if any will preach or practice Fundamental Truths, or Doctrine, here you may see where the foundation thereof lies.[42]

The Digger Movement spread widely in England but gradually faded away, as explained by Berens:

Winstanley's writings met with the fate that awaits all thought much in advance of the times in which it is given to the world. They have been ignored and forgotten; and till very recently even his memory had vanished from the minds of his fellow-countrymen, to whose emancipation he unstintedly devoted his life. Nor can we be surprised at this, when we consider the circumstances. There can be no doubt but that his earlier writings were the quiver whence the early Quakers derived many of their arrows, their most pointed and consequently by their opponents most hated doctrines.[43]

Although both Winstanley and Fox were mystically inclined, Rachel Hadley King was of the opinion that the latter was less likely to "slip over into rationalism, humanitarianism and secularism."[44] Rufus Jones, after noting that Winstanley was fifteen years older than Fox, had this to say:

But it needs to be said that Winstanley was no passive Quietist, withdrawn from storm and stress of practical life. He is most like Fox in his strenuous determination to turn his visions into deed . . . His great "openings" all have reference to action and deed. His business in the world, as it was "revealed" to him, was to break yokes and set men free. Whatever one may think of his economic and social theories, one cannot fail to feel a thrill of sympathy with a man who flings himself, as Winstanley did, into a task of so changing the social conditions that "all mankind might have a quiet subsistence and freedom to live upon earth."[45]

Early Quaker writings show little interest in either "levelling," as advocated by John Wilburne and Gerard Winstanley, or what we call "Communalism." The most authoritative statement this author has found bearing upon those concepts is in Robert Barclay's *Apology*,[46] which deals primarily with "Salutations and Recreations," such as flattering titles, hat wearing, knee bending, gaming, swearing and fighting.

Barclay's comments on what he calls "levelling" are comparatively brief and treated as "mutual" and "natural relations," not political and economic systems. His words were:

> I would not have any judge, that hereby we intend to destroy the mutual relation that either is betwixt prince and people, master and servants, parents and children; nay, not at all: we shall evidence, that our principle in these things hath no such tendency, and that these mutual relations are rather better established, than any ways hurt by it. Next, let not any judge, that from our opinion in these things, any necessity of levelling will follow, or that all men must have things in common. Our principle leaves every man to enjoy that peaceably, which either his own industry, or his parents, have purchased to him; only he is thereby instructed to use it aright, both for his own good, and that of his brethren and all to the glory of God: in which also his acts are to be voluntary, and no ways constrained. And further, we say not hereby, that no man may use the creation more or less than another; for we know, that as it hath pleased God to dispense it diversely, giving to some more, and some less, so they may use it accordingly.

Barclay went on to admonish the rich and comfort the poor. The former should use their abundance moderately and help the needy, while those of lesser ranks should be "content with their condition . . . knowing they have received abundance, as to the inward man; which is chiefly to be regarded." Moreover, the poor have an advantage over the rich and noble "as to the inward and spiritual fellowship of the saints" and "become the brethren and companions of the greatest and richest; and in this respect, let him of low degree rejoice that he is exalted." That doctrine may have conformed in some respects to the teachings of Jesus, but politically speaking it approved an upper-class society while under classes had comparatively little access to power. Barclay, it should be noted, neglected to say how that might be done with reasonable dispatch without politicizing both lower and upper classes.

The earliest Quakers were, for the most part, much too harassed and unsophisticated to dwell upon such profound and dangerous theories, but, as noted above, many of them were sympathetic to the views of Levellers and Diggers. And in more liberal times ahead many Quakers played active roles, especially after the French and American Revolutions. Even so, genuine democracy was far distant.

John Bellers (1654-1725), a London cloth merchant, economist and social reformer, was the first of many notable Quakers to move in that direction. He wrote extensively on both spiritual themes and pragmatic reforms; indeed "he was interested in improving the whole community, besides each man's spiritual worth."[47]

The same author listed Beller's proposals for improving society under the following headings:

> Education to fit people for life, hospitals to keep them well, colleges of industry to keep them employed, reformed prisons and criminal law to deal with the morally sick, reformed elections to ensure good statesmen, and lastly, a European Senate to keep the peace—virtually a germ idea of the League of Nations.[48]

His Colleges of Industry attracted considerable attention then and since by scholars, philanthropists and champions of the working classes. Karl Marx and Friedrich Engels made several references to Beller's writings in their famous *Capital, A Critique of Political Economy*. Bellers prefaced one of his many brief pamphlets with these perceptive remarks:

> The Poor without Employment are like rough Diamonds; their Worth is unknown.
> Whereas regularly labouring People are the Kingdom's greatest Treasure and Strength, for without Labourers there can be no Lords; and if poor Labourers did not raise much more Food and Manufacture than what did subsist themselves, every Gentleman must be a Labourer, and every idle Man must starve.[49]

The account continued by listing the advantages of Colleges of Industry in these words:

> 1. That the poor will have a constant employment.

2. That they will have a constant vent, for what manufactures or food they will raise.
3. That they will have plenty of food, clothing, and all other necessities for themselves and their children.
4. That they may be good education for the children.
5. That there will be a considerable profit for their founders that shall so employ them.

The summary ends by saying: "The scheme I offer for fully answering these five great ends, which are all that the poor want, or the rich can reasonably desire."

Despite Beller's benefactions and fame, he, like so many Quakers of that early period, was on two occasions arrested, prosecuted and fined for offenses which today appear frivolous. Apparently, however, he was never imprisoned.[50]

Fox had numerous contacts with minor officials, but at no time did he have a personal relationship with an English monarch, as did William Penn during the reigns of Charles II and James II. He did, however, have four meetings in London during the "Kingless Decade" with Lord Protector Oliver Cromwell and occasionally corresponded with him. They first conversed in March, 1655.[51]

Fox, then about 31 years of age, had been arrested at Leicester for participating in a tumultuous gathering of Quakers and priests, who probably were Presbyterians and Independents. He was taken by a military officer to London and permitted to justify his conduct to Cromwell in writing. With his freedom at stake, and aware that he was writing to a much older and prestigious man, Fox drafted his letter with great care and denied "carrying or drawing of any carnal sword against any, or against thee, Oliver Cromwell, or any man . . . And this I am ready to seal with my blood." With that declaration he used the equivalent of an oath without mentioning either the word "oath" or "swear," as was his custom, but apparently neither the officer in charge nor Cromwell made an issue of those omissions.

On the following morning Fox was ushered into Cromwell's residence, whereupon he again defended himself, saying "we quarrelled with the priests . . . and I told him I did not quarrel with them, but they quarrelled with me and my friends." The *Journal* went on to record that Cromwell approved of what Fox was saying and concluded with these touching remarks:

And many more words I had with him [i.e., Cromwell]. And many people began to come in, that I drew a little backward, and as I was turning he catched me by the hand and said these words with tears in his eyes, "Come again to my house; for if thou and I were but an hour in the day together we should be nearer one to the other," and that he wished me no more ill than he did his own soul. And I told him if he did he wronged his own soul; and so I bid him harken to and hear God's voice that he might stand in the counsel and obey it, and if he did not hear God's voice his heart would be hardened. And he said it was true. So I went out, and he bid me come again.

Fox's custodial officer followed and released him, or as Fox said "I was at liberty and might go whither I would." Meanwhile, the Protector had invited him to dine with his gentlemen but he refused. He then asked that the Protector be told "he would not eat a bit of his bread, nor drink a sup of his drink." Upon learning of Fox's remarks, the Protector was reported as saying:

> There was a people risen, meaning us, that could not win either with honour, high places, or gifts, but all other people he could. For we did not seek any of their places, gifts nor honours, but their salvation and eternal good, both in this nation and elsewhere.

Fox's second visit occurred in 1656 after spotting the Protector in a park and following him home accompanied by Edward Pyott. Upon their arrival Cromwell had a distinguished guest, John Owen, the Vice-Chancellor of Oxford. Fox spoke about the sufferings of Friends and stressed the "Light of Christ who had enlightened every man that cometh into the world." Cromwell differed, saying there was no Inner Light of Christ Jesus, only a natural one. He then displayed irritation and left the room, whereupon Fox and Pyott went elsewhere to preach.

The third visit was made the following year; his fourth is related below. Earlier he had written Cromwell about sufferings in both England and Ireland, after which he and Fox met in a park. Fox was concerned over talk about making the Protector a King and told him "they that sought to put him on a crown would take away his life, and bid him mind the crown that was immortal," whereupon Cromwell expressed thanks and "bid me go to his house." Fox later sent similar warnings by mail.

In addition to the four incidents referred to above, Fox and Cromwell were indirectly involved later in 1656. On that occasion Fox and his companions went to Scotland with plans to spread Quaker Gospel throughout a land where Presbyterians reigned and religious dissenters were unwelcome. Upon hearing that news, Cromwell's Council, headed by General George Monck with headquarters in Edinburgh, ordered Fox to present himself. He did so, but the reception was cool.

Upon entry he was asked to take off his hat but refused, saying "I had been before Oliver Cromwell with my hat on," whereupon the doorkeeper took it off. Fox was then asked what business he had in mind and how long he might stay, to which he replied "my time was not to be long, yet in my freedom I stood in the will of him that sent me." Displeased, the presiding officer ordered him to "depart in the nation within seven days." Fox left peaceably and with several co-workers continued their journey, preaching as they went.[52]

Fox overstayed the seven days, and despite the advice of friendly people, defied the order saying:

> So the noise of their warrants [to arrest him] was all over. And I told them, "What! Do you tell me of their warrants against me? If there were a cartload of them I do not heed them, for the Lord's power is over them all." For they were now afraid to meddle with me.

The *Journal* continued:

> And since a great increase there is, and great there will be, in Scotland. For when I set my horse's feet atop of the Scottish ground I felt the Seed of God to sparkle about me like innumerable sparks of fire, though there is abundance of thick cloddy earth of hypocrisy and falseness that is atop, and a briary, brambly nature which is to be burnt up with God's Word, and ploughed up with his spiritual fruit to the glory of the heavenly, glorious

and omnipotent Lord God Almighty. But the husbandman is to wait in patience.

How long Fox and his co-workers disobeyed the Council's order is
uncertain. The *Journal* account suggests that the crusade was quite
successful, but whether such boastfulness and disrespect for public
officials conformed with St. Paul's admonition to respect and obey
"higher powers" is questionable.

As mentioned above, Fox had four personal visits with Cromwell, three of which have been reported. His fourth one took place at
Hampton Court, his favorite residence, located a short distance from
London. The visit was brief and sad, as indicated by the following
account:

> And the same day, I took a boat and went to Kingston,
> from whence I went thereafter to Hampton Court, to
> speak with the Protector about the sufferings of Friends.
> I met him riding into Hampton Court Park, and before I
> came at him he was riding in the head of his lifeguard. I
> saw and felt a waft of death go forth against him, and he
> looked like a dead man. When I had spoken to him of
> the sufferings of Friends and warned him as I moved to
> speak to him, he bid me come to his house.

Fox returned the following day but "the doctors were not willing
I should come to speak to him. So I passed away, and never saw him
more." Cromwell's death occurred on September 3, 1658, less than a
month after his favorite daughter Elizabeth died and during one of the
worst storms in English history. Three hours later his son Richard
was proclaimed Protector.[53]

Cromwell's death at Whitehall marked a major turning point in
English history, despite the grossness which followed. Emulating the
pomp and ceremony of royalty at home and abroad, the rituals were
solemn and lavish; his life-sized wax effigy was prominently displayed for viewing by honored guests; and the long procession
through London's streets was, for the most part, respectful. His body
was supposedly placed in "Oliver's Vault" at Westminster Abbey but
whether that actually happened has been debated endlessly.

Be that as it may, about two years later the Convention Parliament, then controlled by Royalists who were anticipating an early

return of Charles II, ordered court commissioners to condemn ten regicides to death and twenty-five to life imprisonment; three were arrested in Holland and sentenced to death in London, but some were never captured. The Convention Parliament also ordered that the bodies of three former regicides, one of whom was Cromwell's, be disinterred, hanged, beheaded and otherwise desecrated "in the sight of people till sun set, and buried at the gallows' foot."[54] That gruesome spectacle took place opposite Whitehall on the date and at the place where King Charles I was similarly disgraced.

Whether Fox witnessed the funeral procession is uncertain, but Quaker Edward Burroughs did and was so appalled that he exclaimed "Oh abominable! Oh idolatry! Oh folly and vanity."[55] The *Journal* records the following account:

> Now was there a great pudder [pother] made about the images of *effigies* of Oliver Cromwell lying in state, men standing and sounding with trumpets over his image after he was dead. At this my spirit was greatly grieved, and the Lord I found, was highly offended. Then did I write the following lines and sent them to reprove their wickedness and warn them to repent:
> Oh friends, what are ye doing? And what mean ye to sound before an image? Oh, how am I grieved with your abomination! Oh, mad people, how am I wearied! My soul is wearied with you, saith the Lord; will I not be avenged of you, think ye, for your abominations? . . . And how are ye turned to fooleries, which things, in times past, ye stood over! . . . The sober people in the nations stand amazed at your doings, and are ashamed, as if ye would bring in Popery.[56]

To whom Fox was writing is uncertain, but at issue for the Quakers were idolatry, vanity and simplicity.

Cromwell's death distressed most Quakers and like-minded men and women. He had witnessed the growth of radical Quakerism from zero to well over 30,000 members, and Fox would never again "be bidden to come to his house." Whether the personal attention shown by the Lord Protector to Fox, Margaret Fell and other Quaker Valiants was genuine, tactical, or both is questionable. Nor was his apprehension unreasonable, given the rapid growth of that intransigent

Society and the fact that England had still not fully recovered from her most serious crisis since the Roman Conquest of 1066 and threatened invasion by the Spanish Armada in 1588. Be that as it may, Cromwell's close affiliation with the military and penchant for dictatorial resolution of conflict kept religious dissenters doubtful of his intentions.

Despite Cromwell's authoritarian tendencies, he had many notable attributes and accomplishments. He was a happily married gentleman-commoner of Welsh ancestry and Calvinist faith who had eight children, seven of whom were girls. He spent a year at Cambridge University and later studied law at one of London's Lincoln's Inns; served in Parliament from 1628 onward, during which time he stood firmly with the Puritan Party throughout the Civil War; distinguished himself as a military commander and strategist; and served as Protector, Lord General and Lord Protector during most of the "Kingless Decade." Whether anyone else might have salvaged the Levellers' democratic aspirations is food for thought.

There can be no doubt, however, that within his Calvinist frame of reference, he could be tolerant and merciful. Indeed, to quote Professor C. H. Firth:

> Cromwell's was the most tolerant government which had existed in England since the Reformation. In practice, he was more lenient than the laws, and more liberal-minded than most of his advisers. The drawback was, that even the more limited amount of religious freedom which the laws guaranteed seemed too much to the great majority of the nation. Englishmen—even Puritans—had not yet learnt the lesson of toleration.[57]

Speaking of Cromwell's religion, Antonia Fraser wrote:

> Throughout life, his religious views showed signs of being completely objective, and he had personally chosen the Independent structure originally for the reason that the looser bonds would give fuller play to his temperament, rejecting in turn Anglicism and Presbyterianism. Certain facets remained sparkling in his beliefs, including his dislike for those who wanted to jacket their comrades' spirit of uniformity, instead of fighting the com-

96

mon enemy. . . . That meant that the external forms which the practice of religion might take never meant as much to him as it did to many of his contemporaries.[58]

With the above comments as background, Cromwell's primary aim was to maintain a united Puritan Party, consisting of Presbyterians, Independents and Baptists,[59] on matters pertaining to both church and state.[60] From his point of view, it was not faith, ritual, and discipline that mattered, but whether parishioners adhered to the main principles of Christianity, which included respect for magistrates, obedience to law and peaceable behavior. Attaining that objective, however, had been made extraordinarily difficult by the expulsion of Anglicans during the Civil War and "Kingless Decade." Compounding that dilemma was the rapid rise of Quakers and like-minded dissenters.

More particularly, Cromwell's tolerant disposition is illustrated by the following observations gleaned from several sources:

In Parliament his speeches were characterized by unfailing moderation and good sense.

During the Saints' moral crusade, he preferred reliance upon education and religion to rigorous law enforcement.

While Cromwell himself welcomed Jews who had been expelled from England in 1290 by King Edward I, haggling by critics delayed legal readmission until after the Reformation.

Although he was one of the regicides who signed the King's death warrant, he remained ambiguous about the hereditary principle. He rejected it, however, for himself and his family.

He apparently spared Quaker John Naylor from capital punishment and otherwise demonstrated his sympathy.

He had several personal encounters with George Fox and released him from custody on one occasion.

He ameliorated persecution for many Quakers and like-minded dissidents. He may also have had a moderating influence on criminal law and proceedings.

The following summation reflects Cromwell's attitude and accomplishments:

> He led Puritanism to military victory and glory, over-threw Anglicans—if only for a time—broke through the divinity that hedged in a king, and set up a brief personal dictatorship. That was the sum of his worldly achievement, that and his insistence on "toleration"—which did not extend to Catholics or Episcopalians, only to a limited extent to Presbyterians, and not at all to Unitarians. Recognition of his own ascendancy was, in fact, the measure of that toleration. But greatest of all was that, whatever he accomplished or failed to accomplish, he set himself among the immortals of history.[61]

Although honorable and popular, Richard Cromwell lacked political experience and inherited his father's troubles. Shortly after his inauguration, Parliament was recalled; a resolution was adopted saying the Commonwealth must not be governed by a single person; Richard, unable to control the Army, resigned; and General Monck, who had previously commanded the Scotch Army, was made Commander of the English, Scotch and Irish Armies. A Convention Parliament, so called because it was not summoned by a sovereign, was assembled; the order to kill several regicides was given despite Charles' preference for leniency; the Long Parliament was finally terminated; and the Restoration, arranged by General Monck, took place in April, 1660.[62]

Writing to Fox about that historic event, Richard Hubberthorn said:

> This day did King Charles and his two brethren James and Henry come into this city [London]; Charles is of a pretty sober countenance, but the great pride and vanity of those that brought him in is inexpressible; and he is in danger to be tempted to those things, which he in himself is not inclined unto. The great excess and abomination that hath been used this day in this city is inexpressible.[63]

Stuart Restoration and Persecution

The Convention Parliament met in April, knowing full well that sovereignty was the crucial issue. With that in mind, and aware of the checks and balances pioneered during the Protectorate, both Houses declared that "according to the ancient and fundamental laws of the Kingdom, the government is, and ought to be, by Kings, Lords and Commons." Charles' prompt acceptance followed, whereupon a conjoined sovereign relationship came into existence known as "King-in-Parliament," despite its ambiguities. As confirmed later by the Glorious Revolution of 1688, that conjointure had gradually become "an omnipotent trinity of King, Lords and Commons" and a fundamental rule for English subjects ever since.[64]

Although disdainful of secular politics, Fox and his close associates kept abreast of governmental affairs affecting their religious interests. Meanwhile, their distaste for intellectualism and worldliness kept them from tapping such scholarly works then available as James Harrington (1561-1612), Thomas Hobbes (1588-1679), Sir Edward Coke (1552-1634), John Locke (1631-1704) and John Milton (1608-1674), all of whom strove to understand and improve political systems wherever interest was shown. Quaker disinterest in such matters is confirmed by the absence of any of those names in such Quaker classics as Fox's *Journal* and Barclay's *Apology*. Disinterest also accounted for the paucity of Quaker statesmen; only William Penn and another Englishman, John Bright (1811-1889) merit that distinction, although countless others have since distinguished themselves in related fields of endeavor.

Of the scholars mentioned above, Hobbes has special pertinence for this account. He had tutored Charles Stuart during his youthful years abroad and followed his career closely. With such attention, the Civil War, his father's execution and his own exile for more than a decade, it is not surprising that the restored King believed and acted as he did. Although cheerful and physically impressive, he was also "indolent, fickle, untrustworthy and absolutely devoid of reverence."[65] Politically, he was Hobbesian and Machiavellian to the core, as illustrated by his effective use of "the influence of the Crown." That prerogative enabled him to distribute such favors as pensions, offices and honors to gain political ends, one of which was to dispense with Parliament during the last four years of his reign.[66]

Hobbes, a rationalist, materialist, empiricist and political absolutist, is best known for his classic *Leviathan,* said by a recent scholar to be "the greatest, perhaps the sole, masterpiece of political philosophy written in the English language."[67] Many critics, however, consider him arrogant, atheistic and inhumane. His basic premise was that men are naturally selfish, individualistic and constantly at war among themselves. Indeed, every man is his brother's wolf.

The latter parts of *Leviathan* dwell at length upon "A Christian Commonwealth" and "The Kingdom of Darkness." Hobbes' theology was basically Protestant and, as one might expect, highly critical of the Catholic Church. Of "Christian politics," he said it "dependeth upon supernatural revelations of the will of God."[68] Even so, "we are not to renounce our senses and experiences; nor, that which is the undoubted Word of God, *our natural reason.*"[69]

That empiric declaration had special pertinence for such mystics as Quakers, although *Leviathan* showed no interest in their Society. The realism displayed in the following quotation suggests the fundamental difference between Hobbes and the Quakers:

> When God speaketh to man, it must be either immediately; or by mediation of another man, to whom he had formerly spoken by himself immediately. How God speaketh to a man immediately may be understood by those well enough to whom he hath spoken; but how the same should be understood by another, is hard, if not impossible to know. For if a man pretend to me, that God hath spoken to him supernaturally and immediately, and I make doubt of it, I cannot easily perceive what argument he can produce, to oblige me to believe it. It is true, that if he be my sovereign, he may oblige me to obedience, so, as not by act or word to declare I believe him not; but not to think any otherwise than my reason persuades me. But if one that hath not such authority over me, should pretend the same, there is nothing that exacteth either belief, or obedience.[70]

Shortly before the Restoration two major declarations favorable to Quakers were made. The first one, prompted by Richard Hubberthorn, a devotee of Fox, was made by General George Monck who managed Charles' return. It stated "I do require all officers and soldiers to forbear to disturb the peaceable meetings of Quakers, they doing nothing prejudicial to the Parliament or commonwealth of England."[71] The second was issued by the soon-to-be-King: "We do declare a Liberty to tender consciences, and that no man shall be disquieted, or called in question, for differences of opinion in matters of religion, which do not disturb the peace of the kingdom . . ."[72] The King demonstrated sincerity shortly after his coronation by setting free about 700 Quakers imprisoned during the Protectorate.

Soon after that happy event the King would have welcomed Fox for an interview had he not been in prison, but Richard Hubberthorn substituted for him. Present at that friendly meeting were the King, a few Lords of the Privy Council, and Hubberthorn. The questions and answers were astonishingly frank but too long for recitation here. Rather, all but a few questions must suffice:[73]

1. Is it true, those who have ruled over you have been cruel, and have professed much which they have not done?

2. But why can you not swear? For an oath is a common thing amongst men to any engagement.

3. But can you not promise before the Lord, which is the substance of its oath?

4. But how do we know from your word that you will perform?

5. Pray, what is your principle?

6. A Lord asked how long we had been called Quakers, or did we own that name?

7. Do you own the Sacrament?

8. How know you that you are inspired by the Lord?

9. One of the Lords asked, How do you know that you are led by the true spirit?

10. How do you own magistrate, or magistry?

11. The King said "That is enough." A Lord asked "Why do you meet together, seeing everyone of you have the church in themselves?"

12. How did you first come to believe the Scriptures were Truth?

Hubberthorn answered all questions asked briefly and concluded by saying, "So the King promised that we [the Quakers] should not any ways suffer for our opinion or religion; and so in love passed away." The two most controversial issues were oath-taking and the Inner Light; the least disagreement dealt with magistery because both parties agreed it should be honored. Despite that friendly encounter, bitterness and persecution resumed with the Puritan Parliament, re-established Anglican Church and disgruntled Presbyterians leading the way. Ironically, Hubberthorn died in Newgate Prison less than two years after his cordial interview with the King.

The restored King, then thirty years of age, was at first jubilant, but euphoria ended in less than a year. That sudden change was brought about by a small group of mystical Anabaptists who called themselves Fifth Monarchists and took seriously King Nebuchadnezzer's dream of a kingdom set up by God which would never be destroyed. Daniel, a Jew who lived in the sixth century B.C., was directed to rule the province of Babylon. He too had apocalyptic visions—four of them—which provided background for the Book of Revelation (known to Roman Catholics as Apocalypse), and other New Testament passages such as those cited below. Revelation was written late in the first century A.D., presumably by the Disciple St. John.[74] Included in the King's visions, as translated by Daniel, were four kingdoms, which succeeded one another: Assyrian, Persian, Greek and Roman Empires. The "Fifth Monarchy" was to be the last of five kingdoms.

From what has been said above, prophetic revelations of cosmic cataclysms, whereby evil powers are destroyed and the righteous saved, have ancient origin. Such messianism flourished, particularly in times of crises, and especially during the post-Reformation period when warring, persecution and fanaticism were endemic. During England's Civil War period, such fears and hopes led by Anabaptists, including the Fifth Monarchists, soared. The latter preached not only the imminence of Christ's Kingdom, but also the use of force to usher it in.

The Monarchists resorted to violence from time to time, most recently during the Protectorate, in 1657. On that occasion they plotted to assassinate Oliver Cromwell, but the scheme was aborted, thanks to the comprehensive "spy system" installed by the "Saints" described above. They struck again early in January, 1661, with intent to kill the King. The coup de main failed, leaders were hanged or imprisoned and the movement dwindled but left a legacy of fear throughout the nation. To quote Trevelyan, the episode "caused a furious persecution of the pacific Quakers, who were haled to prisons by thousands."[75] Isabel Ross added "The Rising gave occasion for magistrates to arrest and imprison Friends all over the country. In a few weeks 4,230 were in jail. In some counties no men Friends were left free. In Cambridge the prisoners included widows and fatherless children. But the Meetings were continued, even if only two or three were left to carry on."[76]

Both Sewel's *History* and Fox's *Journal* record that episode in considerable detail.[77] Fox was in London at the time and a major suspect. Sewel provided these details:

> It was in the night when these people [the Monarchists] made a rising; which caused such a stir, that the King's soldiers sounded an alarm by the beating of drums. The trained bands appeared in arms, and all was in an uproar, and both the mob and soldiers committed great insolences for several days; so that the Quakers though altogether innocent, became the object of fury of the enemies, and many were haled to prison out of their peaceable meetings.[78]

Sewel went on to say:

> This insurrection of the Fifth Monarchy men caused great disturbance in the nation; and though the Quakers did not at all meddle with those boisterous people, yet they fell under great suffering because of them; and both men and women were dragged out of their houses to prison, and some sick men off their beds by the legs; among which was one Thomas Pachyn, who being in a fever was dragged by the soldiers out of his bed to prison, where he died.[79]

Soon after the uprising, Fox and eleven associates presented the King with a lengthy disavowal entitled "A Declaration from the harmless people of God, called Quakers, against all plotters and fighters of the world."[80] About the same time, Margaret Fell, widow of the prestigious late Judge Thomas Fell, spoke directly to the King and

Council on at least two occasions with considerable success. The disavowal was pertinent not only to the uprising but also the Quakers' "Peace Testimony." Indeed, the only official document of first-rate importance on the subject of war in the Restoration period is the declaration against plots prepared by Fox and Hubberthorn at the time of the Fifth Monarchy rising, and republished by the Morning Meeting in 1684. That document is known to Quakers as "The Declaration of 1660."[81] The tragic Monarchist uprising and the indiscretion of James Naylor were probably the most serious crises faced by early Quakers.

Most Quakers, as well as Fifth Monarchists, were well versed in the scriptures, including the apocalyptical passages of the Bible, which predicted the world would someday come to a convulsive ending; the dead would be resurrected; Jesus would return; and the dead would be judged, some to be consigned everlastingly to Heaven, others to Hell. It should also be noted that no major church has set a date for those spectacular events to occur, although some individuals and groups, known as Adventists, have done so.

The sequence of happenings, as detailed in the Revelation account, is difficult to follow and comprehend. Apparently, the Devil was bound for a thousand years, whereupon he became ruler of Hell and was "tortured day and night forever." Confusion arises over when the "thousand years" began and ended. The phrase is repeated four times, but why a "millennium" was chosen is unstated.[82]

Early Quakers, although aware of those scriptural passages, were generally inclined to stress their practical and spiritual significance rather than revelatory mysteries. There can be no doubt, however, that the passages cited in the Books of Daniel and Revelation portray God as an almighty warrior ever-ready to avenge enemies and wrongdoers. But little is said of such gentler traits as love, mercy and forgiveness. Although both Fifth Monarchists and Quakers read the same or similar accounts it is clear that the latter preferred gentler values. Both, however, dared to suffer dearly for their convictions.

With the nation frightened by the Monarchist uprising and prisons full, the King and Parliament took steps to assure conformity by enacting four statues known as the "Clarendon Code," named for the Lord High Chancellor, Edward Hyde Clarendon: Corporation Act of 1661; Act of Uniformity, 1662; Conventical Act, 1664; and the Five Mile Act, 1665. The Quaker Act (1662) was aimed directly at the Society of Friends. Brief commentaries follow:

Corporation Act: The object was to exclude nonconformists from sharing in national and local government. Among its provisions were those forbidding taking up arms against the King under any circumstances, and stipulating that no one could hold office in a corporate town who did not take the Anglican sacraments and also renounce the Presbyterian Solemn League and Covenant which bound believers to conform with stated canons of faith and ecclesiastical rules.

Act of Uniformity: Aimed at assuring loyalty and conformity by Anglican clergymen and schoolmasters. A revised *Book of Prayer* must be read in Anglican Churches and schoolmasters must conform with its provisions; both clergymen and schoolmasters must declare the illegality of taking up arms against the King. Noncompliance was made punishable by deprivation of rights and benefits. Those provisions prompted many clergymen to suffer severe hardships.

Conventical Act: Applied to all dissenters and made illegal assemblies of more than four persons, exclusive of their families, for religious worship where Anglican forms were not held. First and second violations were punishable by imprisonment, the third by banishment. Persons returning after banishment were punishable by death. Similar provisions were in the Quaker Act mentioned above.

Five Mile Act: No nonconformist minister could teach in any school, or come within five miles of any city or corporate town without taking an oath acknowledging it was unlawful to bear arms against the King or endeavor to alter the government of the Anglican Church or the State. The law's effect was unexpectedly severe in London during the Great Plague of 1665 when many Anglican clergymen fled the city but replacements from the outside were legally forbidden to enter. The Great Fire in London a year later made matters worse.

NOTE: Quaker and Conventical Acts were renewed in 1670. Moreover, informers were entitled to one-third of fines imposed and judges were directed to construe the law strictly against the accused. Those provisions accounted for much Quaker persecution, as detailed in the following chapter.

Chancellor Clarendon, for whom those dragonish laws were named, fell from grace five years later. Charged with such offenses as corruption, treachery during the Civil War, and unjustly imprisoning opponents, he took the King's advice and fled to France where he died several years later.

Despite Charles' great power, he had to reckon with the political implications of the King-in-Parliament formula, which required viable political parties for successful governance. Factionalism had long been the rule, but embryonic parties surfaced during Charles' reign. It was not until the reign of Queen Anne (1702-1714), however, that "parties triumphed over patronage in the management of Parliament."[83]

Of the embryonic parties, there were four principal ones: Court or Tory, representing upper classes generally and more particularly Royalists and Lords; Country or Whig, supported by landed gentry whose constituents favored Civil War objectives, including Parliamentary supremacy and toleration; and two minor parties known as Liberal and Conservative. The Levellers' Socialist Party provided an example, but nothing did more to coalesce factions than the "Exclusion Bills" of 1680 and 1681, supported by Whigs and disapproved by Tories. The intent of those bills was to prevent Catholic Duke of York, Charles' brother, from becoming King. That effort failed due to Charles' strenuous opposition and connivance. One consequence of that melee was that Papists were excluded from public life.[84]

James II, formerly the Duke of York, was fifty-two years of age and, like his elder brother, spent over a decade in exile. Much of that time he was affiliated with the Armies of France, Spain and Holland. The Restoration brought him back to England where he married, became Lord High Admiral and served in the Dutch Wars, during which England established her supremacy over the English Channel and granted proprietary rights to captured Dutch settlements in North America, known later as New York and Albany. He converted to Catholicism, probably in 1668, and married again after his first wife died, this time to a well-connected French Catholic. Meanwhile, he had approved his daughter Mary's marriage to William of Orange, the son of the late Charles I. William and Mary were both Protestants and later became King and Queen of England.

Although James was less profligate than his brother, he was more obsessional and lacking in judgment. Shortly after becoming King, his legitimacy was challenged by one of Charles' sons, James Scott, Duke of Monmouth. On that occasion, Monmouth landed on the southern coast, moved westwardly toward Taunton in County Somerset, gathered a small army of peasants, had himself crowned King and met James' forces, who were primed for vengeance.

Monmouth's men held their ground until gunpowder ran out, whereupon they were overwhelmed and treated barbarously. Captured and taken to London, Monmouth begged the King to spare his life, as the axman severed his head. Those who were not slaughtered were tried at Taunton by the Court of Assize, known since as the "Bloody Assize," presided over by Baron George Jeffries. Of those tried, about 300 were hanged, nearly 800 were transported as forced laborers to Barbados, while many more were whipped and imprisoned. There were numerous Quakers in the Somerset area but only a few were active in the rebellion, though not with arms. William Penn was deeply concerned for the victims and "begged twenty of the King, presumably to go to Pennsylvania." Judge Jeffries was later imprisoned and died in the Tower of London. That ugly episode poisoned the atmosphere and set the stage for the Donnybrook which followed.[85]

Relationships between the King and Parliament were at first amicable, but they clashed before the year ended and the latter never met again during James' reign. From then on, Parliament was not only ignored but humiliated by the King's determination to restore the Roman Church abolished by Henry VIII more than a century before.

With Parliament disassembled, James launched an all-out crusade to restore Catholicism. Among means to that end, he appointed several Catholics to the Privy Council which served as an advisory body to the King and smaller groups of officials, whether or not Parliament was in session; established a Court of Commissioners for Ecclesiastical Causes similar to the one which was abolished near the end of the Civil War; appointed favorites to the universities, army and municipal corporations; and preempted Parliament's prerogatives by suspending oaths and tests required for civil and military officers. Moreover, encouraged by his friend William Penn, the King granted free "exercise of religion in any manner whatsoever" and pardoned all who were imprisoned for conscience's sake, including not only Catholics but also Protestants and about 1,200 Quakers, who were the most severely persecuted of all religious dissenters of Protestant and Anabaptist persuasion.[86]

Toleration and Bill of Rights

James' behavior created intense hostility throughout England and its colonies, but his pardon pleased the Catholics, Quakers and other religionists who had borne the brunt of persecution. To complicate matters, a Catholic heir to the throne was born (James Francis Edward). James' death in 1701 prompted the Act of Settlement which terminated the Stuart Dynasty. James Francis Edward protested but was attainted (i.e., stripped of all civil rights) and all efforts to reverse that decision were unsuccessful.

After James fled from England, Parliament took charge and paved the way for the Glorious Revolution of 1688. Several steps were taken: the Convention Parliament deposed James II and confirmed William of Orange and Princess Mary as joint sovereigns. The Toleration Act followed, which liberated subjects from religious constraints imposed by earlier monarchs and parliaments. There followed the famous Declaration of Rights. Meanwhile, William and Mary had arrived in England without an army or bloodshed.

As finally approved, the Declaration of Rights became the Bill of Rights to assure legality. That document was quite long and began with a list of James' offenses summarized above. The Toleration Act, supplemented by the Bill of Rights detailed below, has since been fundamental, not only in England but also her many dependencies ever since. Following are the rights guaranteed:

> That the pretended power of dispensing the laws or the execution of laws by regal authority without consent of Parliament is illegal.

> That the pretended power of dispensing with laws or the execution of laws by regal authority as it hath been assumed and exercised of late is illegal.

> That the Commission for erecting the late Court of Commissioners for ecclesiastical causes and all other commissions and courts of like nature are illegal and pernicious.

> That the levying of money for or to the use of the crown by pretense of prerogative without grant of Parliament for a longer time or in other manner than the same is or shall be granted is illegal.

> That it is the right of the subjects to petition the King and all commitments and prosecution for such petitioning are illegal.

> That the rising or keeping a standing army within the kingdom in time of peace unless it be with consent of Parliament is against the law.

> That the subjects which are Protestants may have arms for their defense suitable to their conditions and as allowed by law.

That the election of members of Parliament ought to be free.

That the freedom of speech and debates or proceedings in Parliament ought not to be impeached or questioned in any court or place out of Parliament.

That excessive bail ought not to be required nor excessive fines imposed nor cruel and unusual punishments inflicted.

That jurors ought to be duly impanelled and returned and jurors which pass upon men in trials for high treason ought to be freeholders.

That all grants and promises of fines and forfeitures of particular persons before conviction are illegal and void.

And that for redress of all grievances and for the amending strengthening and preserving the laws Parliament ought to be held frequently.[87]

In retrospect, that list of Rights marked both the end of an historic constitutional era and the start of a fresh one. We summarize here several developments of the recent past:

- ◆ Ascendance of Protestant pluralism and the degradation of Roman Catholicism
- ◆ Growing ascendance of Parliament and constitutionalism, including the King-in-Parliament formula with the latter ascendant on legislative matters
- ◆ Constitutional and political experimentation as represented by the Commonwealth Period
- ◆ Decline of the ancient divine-right-of-kings doctrine
- ◆ Growing constraints upon the powers and duties of the Official Church of England
- ◆ Gradual unification of England, Wales, Ireland and Scotland
- ◆ Expansion and development of the British Empire, including the North American colonies.

V

IDEOLOGICAL CONFLICTS AND PERSECUTION WITHIN ENGLAND

This chapter demonstrates that the Quaker Movement was inextricably "political" despite protestations to the contrary. Stated in legal terms, there could be no *imperium in imperio*, that is, an empire within an empire. Accordingly, lesser bodies, whether or not religious, were legally subordinate to *imperio*.

There can be no doubt that early Quakers were commonly perceived as troublesome, unpopular and a threat to England's body politic. Fox's views were at that early date embryonic and quickly embroiled him in bitter controversy over issues spawned by the Puritan Revolution and Civil War. Whether he had anticipated those hazards or ignored them during his apprenticeship and early ministry, his genius, seriousness and contentious disposition served as catalytic agents which inevitably provoked hostility and persecution.

Fox had an obsessive interest in the Bible, a photographic memory and prompt recall of its salient contents. Early Quakers hinged their cause primarily upon five controversial premises: Fox's idealistic version of "Primitive Christianity"; the Inner Light; Truthfulness and Integrity; Pacifism; and Caesarism. We comment upon those premises below.

Primitive Christianity

The term "Primitive Christianity" is much too imprecise for accurate definition. Whether Fox ever used the term is improbable. It is likely, however, that he gradually became aware of its meaning from Bible reading and especially conversing with General Baptists and other seekers during his pilgrimage. Be that as it may, the focus of his ministry was upon the "Apostolic Pattern" set by Jesus himself and his disciples.

That pattern had the appearance of sixteenth-century anarchism led by Menno Simon and his like-minded followers in Germanic and Swiss sectors of the Continent. Given the cultural outlook of Western Europe at that time, persecution and warfare were common. Early Quakers encountered similar circumstances in post-Civil War England, including the American Colonies. Although their zealotry threatened the status quo, personal and institutional integrity may have spared them from a bloodbath. Luckily, only a few Quakers were executed and less than four hundred died in England's prisons or from wounds.

Inner Light

Underlying the Quakers' concept of the Inner Light was their belief that God provided three dispensations: paradise in the Garden of Eden; Old Testament Hebraic Law; and the Regnancy of Jesus Christ eternally in all living souls.[1] Speaking of the latter, Fox said "All old things are passed away and all things became new."[2]

Among the "old things passed away" was the premise that every person born into the world was inherently sinful and foredoomed to Purgatory or Hell unless God predestined otherwise. Early Quakers disavowed that presupposition. Rather, they believed that all persons had within themselves two seeds: one of God, the other of Satan, but each individual had freedom to choose which of the two would have precedence. "We confess, then," said Barclay (Urie), "that a seed of sin is transmitted to all men from Adam, although imputed to none, until by sinning they actually join with it . . . ."[3]

Fox agreed that people had within them the nature of swine, dogs, wolves, serpents, other beasts and creatures, but they also had "invisible and immortal" seeds that could, if properly nurtured, enable them to walk in the Light. His plea was "Oh, therefore mind that which is eternal and invisible, and him who is Creator and mover of all things."[4] That was to say, there is no such thing as "original sin" (a term unmentioned in the Scriptures); rather, everyone has an intense and often urgent inclination to behave sinfully. Free will is the rule; not foreordained sinfulness, as stated by Martin Luther and John Calvin.

Early Quakers had great difficulty in explaining and justifying their concept of the Inner Light. Skeptics often charged them with blasphemy, which was then a serious criminal offense defined as contempt or lack of reverence for God, or claiming the attributes of deity. How they asked can Christ be within a human being predestined by God to sinfulness because of the Fall of Adam and Eve?

The principal passages at issue are found in the Gospel of St. John, Chapter I, paragraphs 1-9:

> In the beginning was the Word [meaning Christ], and the Word was with God, and the Word was God. The same was in the beginning with God. All things were made by him; and without him was not any thing made that was made. In him was life; and the life was the light of men. And the light shineth in darkness; and the darkness comprehended it not. There was a man sent from God, whose name was John. The same was a witness of the Light, that all men through him might believe. He was not the Light, but was sent to bear witness of that Light. That was the true Light, that lighteth every man that cometh into the world.

Controversy over those words has been endless, but less bitterly so with the passage of time. Pragmatically speaking, early Quakers were so biblically engrossed that spiritual reality was often obscured. With that in mind, the following comments may provide clarity: For Quakers, the Inner Light was sovereign. Conscience, though closely related, was merely an inward monitor of right and wrong. The Light Within, on the other hand, was "something," or "that," of God in every person born into the world. That phenomenon had no particular bodily organ or substance; nor was it explained in evolutionary, biological or psychological terms. Even though early Quakers wished to proceed empirically, they were unprepared to do so. Moreover, anatomical and chemical sciences were then in their infancy while biological and psychological sciences were nonexistent.

Given those circumstances, early Quakers proceeded intuitively, as did the prophets and mystics of olden times, guided and inspired by temperament, acculturation, knowledge, reason and invisible sources of power. Had they lived in modern times, they might have concurred with this summation:

112

Included among the physical and psychological makeup of all human beings is the capability, variously referred to as soul, psyche, divine spark, élan, life-force, or creative impulse which makes it possible for men and women to commune directly with and respond to an invisible external force.

That capability is for Quakers the God-Christ, or Inner Light. Thus defined, the Inner Light requires maximum freedom short of societal anarchy, within both church and state. But the gap between "maximum freedom" and "societal anarchy" is always variable and widely so in Fox's time. That concept contributed significantly to then nascent democracy, including the Glorious Revolution of 1688.

Truthfulness and Integrity

Among the politically significant issues prompted by those two virtues were legal requirements for swearing and oath taking. Used together, they became solemn attestations of truth. Their first appearance in the Bible is at Genesis 26:3 where the Lord is quoted as saying "and I will perform the oath which I swear unto Abraham Thy father." Leviticus 19:12 adds substance with these words: "Ye shall not steal, neither deal falsely, neither lie to one another. And ye shall not swear my name falsely, neither shall thou profane the name of thy God: I am the Lord."

Matthew's version is radically different:

> Again you have heard that it hath been said by them of old time. Thou shalt not forswear thyself, but shall perform unto the Lord thine oaths; but I say unto you, swear not at all: neither by heaven; for it is God's throne; nor by the earth; for it is his footstool; neither by Jerusalem; for it is the city of the great King. Neither shalt thou swear by thy head, because thou canst not make a hair white or black. But let your communication be, Yea, yea; Nay, nay; for whatsoever is more than these cometh from evil. (5:33-37).

Fox conceded that forswearing had been customary in olden times, but insisted a new dispensation had been ushered in by Christ who said "swear not at all." That new standard was widely accepted not only by Quakers but also countless other "Primitive Christians," including Anabaptists.[5]

That Fox paid dearly for his refusals to forswear is illustrated by the following episode. He was at first charged with plotting, as were other dissidents including Catholics and Presbyterians, to take up arms against King Charles II. He was finally tried, however, for refusal to swear to an Oath of Allegiance and Supremacy, one of the most heinous legal offenses of that time.[6]

Fox was under great stress for several reasons: His health was fragile; this was his eighth imprisonment; he had been prevented from visiting his mother before her death; the proceedings started late in 1673 and lasted over two years. The sentence was forfeiture of all goods and chattels and life imprisonment. Appeals by Friends and Fox's wife, Margaret, to the King were unsuccessful but an application for review, on grounds of procedural error, to the Court of King's Bench sitting in London was successful. Thereupon Fox was pardoned by Lord Chief Justice Hale. Conscientious affirmation was not then a permissible alternative to oath swearing in England, although it became so two decades later, in 1695.

Speaking of that agonizing event, Craig Horle made these observations:

> The protracted and complex efforts to liberate this prominent Quaker leader, while utilizing traditional Quaker arguments and strategies, also revealed an increasing willingness by Friends, Fox included, to employ legal counsel, to pay the fees necessary for copies of the indictments, mittimuses, and writs, and to combat the law with legal weapons. Yet at the same time, Friends had often operated at cross purposes, and had demonstrated serious tactical confusion, the result of which may have been to lengthen, rather than shorten, Fox's incarceration. More than any other incident, this case focused Quaker attention dramatically on the need to provide appropriate legal counsel and strategy for those Friends who wished to utilize it, and to create a centralized committee to coordinate legal and lobbying efforts . . . That committee would be the Meeting for Sufferings, the prototype of a modern legal defense organization.[7]

Pacifism

Although the word "pacifism" is of recent origin, its behavioral significance dates back to primitive times, as suggested by the following remarks attributed to Jesus:

> Ye have heard that it hath been said, An eye for an eye, and a tooth for a tooth: But I say unto you, that ye resist not evil; but whosoever shall smite thee on thy right cheek, turn to him the other also. And if any man will sue thee at the law, and take away thy coat, let him have thy cloak also. And whosoever shall compel thee to go a mile, go with him twain. Give to him that asketh thee, and from him that would borrow of thee turn not thou away. Ye have heard that it hath been said, Thou shalt love thy neighbor and hate thine enemy. But I say unto you, Love your enemies, bless them that curse you, do good to them that hate you, and pray for them which despitefully use you, and persecute you . . . (Matthew 5:33-45)

Those words were prompted by one of the most basic human instincts: *vengeance*. The Hebrews had stressed law and justice as guidelines; but Jesus proposed substitutes which were radically different: *love, forgiveness, generosity* and *readiness to suffer*. Jesus did not disparage law and justice, but clearly implied there were higher standards. Moreover, His mandates were couched in positive terms, not negative ones as are the Ten Commandments.

Although Jesus's mandates were straightforward and clear, they became obfuscated by Biblical exegesis, changing times, institutionalization and especially the alliance of church and state in 324 A.D. Despite that development, there have been countless Christians, primitive and otherwise, who believed strongly that the Sermon on the Mount meant what it said, lived by it, managed their lives accordingly and suffered passively. Among them were the Anabaptists and Quakers.

Fox's commitment to pacifism developed gradually, but when and where he was introduced to that point of view cannot be pinpointed. Available data suggest no such inclination by his parents and other near relatives, although there is some likelihood that his mother may

115

have been influenced in that direction by tales of the Mancetter and other martyrs. Puritanism suggests no obvious clues. His baptism and childhood attendance at the Fenny Drayton Anglican Church, growing familiarity with Presbyterianism, and what little we know about his apprenticeship suggest no pacifist influences. It is more likely that his pacifism derived from repetitive reading of the Sermon on the Mount and similar biblical passages, seemingly endless disputation during his pilgrimage, and cordial relations with such "dissenting and separate" people as the General Baptists, spiritual heirs of the Germanic Ana-baptists.

Pacifism has reference to peaceful behavior as opposed to mili-tancy. Jesus, in the Sermon on the Mount, contrasted and approved the former rather than the latter. But how is one to know what is, or is not, Christlike behavior in a large, diverse and complex universe? Fox's answer was that all persons can know Christ experientially through the Inner Light aided by conscience; and for Quakers that view has changed little with the passage of time, although behavioral responses vary widely as illustrated by choices made by recent consci-entious objectors to war.

Whether early Quakers measured up to the high standards set forth in the Sermon on the Mount is not easily determined. Fox be-lieved that "lusts" cause wars, as stated in the *Epistle of James,* which fundamentally may be true, but practically it overlooks peaceful alter-natives short of human perfection.

Moreover, how does one go about determining who is an "enemy," and how does one "love" him or her? Early Quakers of-fended countless honorable people who were irked by their plain speech and dress; refusal to doff hats, even to high governmental of-ficials; swear oaths; pay church tithes; bear arms and interrupt preaching services; but did they do so "lovingly"? Would they have been more Christlike if they had proceeded patiently over time, as did such saints as Augustine (354-430), Francis of Assisi (1182-1226), Thomas Aquinas (1225-1274), Meister Eckhart (c. 1260–c. 1328) and Jacob Boehme (1576-1624)? Be that as it may, Fox chose to model his crusade squarely upon the pattern set by Jesus and his disciples, knowing full well the risk of martyrdom.

Quaker growth raises the question of what catalytic force pro-duced that result? Was it "love" or other factors, including *fear?* The answer, though speculative, may have been due to Fox's inordinate sensitivity as a youth and young man, but more particularly to the anguish and melancholia he displayed by abruptly terminating his apprenticeship and wandering about until his "heart did leap for joy" and he knew God's work "experientially." Moreover, he took seriously the apocalyptic prophecy foretold in the Book of Revelation and exhibited by other enthusiasts, including the Fifth Monarchy Men. Such anxiety was not limited to Fox but shared by many of his followers and other contemporaries. Those fears and fantasies undoubtedly had a significant bearing upon Quaker growth.

Following is the most comprehensive and authoritative declaration of Quaker pacifism. It was prompted by the Fifth Monarch Uprising of 1661 when Quakers were officially suspected of complicity. Quaker lobbyists stationed in London hastily, but carefully, prepared their response and submitted it to the King and Council. That declaration is quite long and written with apocalyptic fervor, as indicated by the following extracts:

> Our principle is, and our practices have always been, to seek peace and ensue it and to follow after righteousness and the knowledge of God, seeking that good and welfare and doing that which tends to peace of all. We know that wars and fightings proceed from the lusts of men (as Jas. IV:1-3), out of which lusts the Lord hath redeemed us, and so out of the occasion of war. The occasion of which war, and war itself (wherein envious men, who are lovers of themselves more than lovers of God, lust, kill, and desire to have men's lives or estates) ariseth from the lust. All bloody principles and practices, we, as to our own particulars, do utterly deny, with all outward wars and strife and fightings with outward weapons, for any end or under any pretense whatsoever. And this is our testimony to the whole world . . . .
>
> For this we can say to the whole world, we have wronged no man's person or possessions, we have used no force nor violence against any man, we have been found in no plots, nor guilty of sedition. When we have been wronged, we have not sought to revenge ourselves, we have not made resistance against authority, but wherein we could not obey for conscience's sake, we have suffered even the most of any people in the nation. We have been accounted as sheep for the slaughter, per-

secuted and despised, beaten, stoned, wounded, stocked, whipped, imprisoned, haled out of synagogues, cast into dungeons and noisome vaults where many have died in bonds, shut up from our friends, denied needful sustenance for many days together with other like cruelties.

Therefore consider these things ye men of understanding; for plotters, raisers of insurrections, tumultuous ones, and fighters, running with swords, clubs, staves, and pistols one against another, we say, these are of the world and this hath its foundation from this unrighteous world, from the foundation of which the Lamb hath been slain, which Lamb hath redeemed us from the unrighteous world, and we are not of it, but are heirs of a world in which there is no end and of the kingdom where no corruptible thing enters. And our weapons are spiritual and not carnal . . .[8]

Caesarism and Higher Powers

Equally controversial was political absolutism. That issue was prompted by a conversation between Jesus and scheming Pharisees who asked whether it was lawful to pay tribute to Caesar, whereupon Jesus is quoted as saying "Render unto Caesar the things which are Caesar's; and unto God the things that are God's." (Matthew 22:15-21).

The second passage is from St. Paul's famous letter to the Romans, extracts of which say:

Let every soul be subject unto the higher powers. For there is no power but of God; the powers that be are ordained of God. Whosoever therefore resisteth the power, resisteth the ordinances of God; and they that resist shall receive to themselves damnation. For rulers are not a terror of good works, but to the evil. Wilt thou then not be afraid of the power? Do that which is good, and thou shall have praise of the same. For he is the minister of God to thee for good. But if thou do that which is evil, be afraid; for he beareth not the sword in vain; for he is the minister of God, a revenger to execute wrath upon him that doeth evil. Whereupon ye must needs be sub-

118

ject, not only for wrath, but also for conscience sake.
For this cause pay ye tribute also; for they are God's
ministers, attending continually upon this very thing.
Render therefore to all their dues; tribute to whom tribute is due; custom to whom custom; fear to whom fear;
honour to whom honour. Owe no man any thing, but to
love one another; for he that loveth another hath fulfilled
the law . . . (13:1-10).

Sovereignty was the fundamental issue posed in the above biblical
quotation. Controversy over that subject dates back to antiquity when
mythology and polytheism were commonplace. It was not until about
1000 B.C. that Moses wrote the Genesis account of Creation, which
until recently was thought to have occurred in 1404 B.C. Whether
intended or not, the brevity and imprecision of Moses' account fostered dualistic concepts of sovereignty which continue to confound
both temporal and spiritual rulers.

That account suggests the universe is dominated by two opposing
principles, one of light and goodness, the other of darkness and evil.
The first chapter of Genesis states unequivocally that "In the beginning God created the heaven and the earth" and "God said let there be
light; and there was light." Furthermore, "God saw the light that it
was good; and God divided the light from the darkness." The third
chapter reported the killing of Abel and the Fall but nothing is said
about who planned and engineered those events. The inference was
that God commanded light and goodness, but someone else was com-
mander-in-chief of darkness and wickedness. Unmentioned, however,
were such words as "Lucifer," "Beelzebub," "Satan," and "Devil."
Indeed, those terms did not appear in the Old Testament until centuries later and it was not until the Christian era that their usage became
common.

Nor was a specific name given to the region called darkness and
evil. Presumably, it became known long after the Genesis account
was written as the Hebrew Sheol or Tophet, Greek words for Hades,
and still later Gehenna and Hell. The Sheol or Tophet of the ancient
Jews was a gloomy place for departed souls to wander about, but not
for punishment. The terms "Hades," "Gehenna," and "Hell," on the
other hand, referred to a place of fiery torment for the dead. The latter concept was largely developed by Christian theologians.

The word "Caesar" was a family name for Roman dictator Caius Julius Caesar, used as a title for succeeding emperors until A.D. 138. Herod, the Roman King while Jesus lived, was one of those successors. Whether Jesus's remarks had reference to Herod in particular or to Caesarism in general is speculative. Be that as it may, His words identify and distinguish two coexisting realms: a temporal one over which an absolute monarch reigns; the other a spiritual one ruled by God. Whether a monotheistic God of Love possessed of monistic sovereignty would bifurcate His universe, as suggested by Jesus's remarks, remains a theological conundrum.

Jesus's reference to Caesar, spoken at a time when absolutism was the rule, appears to say that whoever possesses temporal sovereignty is answerable to no one on earth, while a subject is obliged to distinguish "things" under Caesar's jurisdiction and "things" that are God's and render obeisance accordingly. That appears tantamount to saying Caesars have unlimited power over both temporal and spiritual affairs inasmuch as only they could legitimately make law and enforce it with courts and carnal weapons. Meanwhile, subjects are left in a quandary over where God's jurisdiction begins and ends.

Jesus's schooling is not detailed in the Gospels, but it appears to have been centered in home and synagogue. Hebrew traditions placed great emphasis upon history, law, and customs set forth in the Old Testament; it is reasonable, therefore, to assume that Jesus was taught to respect not only Roman Caesars but also a long list of absolutist Hebrew Kings dating back to the Genesis account of Creation. Hellenism had by that time affected Palestine, but neither the Gospels nor Pauline writings indicate awareness of Aristotle's differentiation between monarchy, aristocracy, anarchy and democracy, written in the fourth century B.C. That account, based upon then existing Mediterranean politics, remains available in Aristotle's classic *Politics*.

Given Jesus's upbringing, his advice to the scheming Pharisees is understandable, but as a practical matter it helped buttress absolutism for centuries and even today lends legitimacy, at least in Christendom, to a state's assertion of power, whether done in autocratic or democratic context. The dilemma posed goes far toward explaining the frequency of wars, rebellions, martyrdom, conscientious objection and even anarchy.

St. Paul's usage of the term "higher powers" doubtlessly included the "Caesar" mentioned by Jesus. The word "higher" suggests there must have been "lower" ones as well, but no mention is made of the latter. Nothing is said about constitutional legitimacy, qualifications for office, manner of selection, terms of office, scope of jurisdiction and what today are known as "bills of rights," "impeachment," and "separation of powers." The inference was that rulers were subject to no worldly powers, only to God.

Paul's words "There is no power but of God" and "The powers that be are ordained by God" appear, in retrospect, to be unequivocally authoritarian. Coupled with Jesus's reference to Caesar, they acknowledged a sanctified relationship between God and temporal rulers, church and state. Nothing is said about non-rulers, but the inference is that they had less status. Paul's views, as expressed above, undoubtedly reflected first century Caesarism well known to him through his missionary travels and persecution. Nurtured for centuries, chiefly by Catholic theologians, they have ever since had a bearing upon secular politics, but less so with the rise of democracy during the eighteenth century.

Fox's published works are replete with admonitions to honor "higher powers" and so are those of William Penn and Robert Barclay (Urie), both of whom were quite knowledgeable about secular politics. Such deference was common not only to those men but also to Quakers generally, notably and quaintly so during court trials and imprisonments. Indeed, their pacifism made most of them model litigants and prisoners.

Jesus's deference to monarchical sovereignty had other far-reaching implications. Both Moses and Jesus issued commandments, but who could legally compel a Caesar to obey them? Whether Jesus was aware of that dilemma is conjectural. Be that as it may, the Gospels nowhere condemn rulers for wrongdoing, even though their conduct is hideously brutal. Herod's massacre of infant male children is an example; the killing of John the Baptist is another. Jesus appears to have been respectful of Pontius Pilate and his Jewish adversaries throughout his own trial and crucifixion. Moreover, He is quoted as saying "woe unto" Jewish scribes, Pharisees and hypocrites, but never to a Caesar. His response was one of pacific submission to constituted authorities, a tactic, though legal, accounts in large measure for not only His own martyrdom but countless others.

Disputations over how best to manage and control power are probably as old as the human race. Secular monism appears to have gradually displaced excessive pluralism as monotheism superseded pluralist paganism. In both instances public attitudes toward the goodness and badness of human beings were important considerations.

How to control the tyrannical exercise of secular and ecclesiastical power, whether closely allied or separated, has been a problem since ancient times and remains so. The tactics used ranged from numerous forms of barbarism to humane constitutionalism. The former included, among others, assassination, as happened to Julius Caesar; revolution and civil war, which prompted the execution of King Charles I; and international war, which doomed German Chancellor and Führer Adolph Hitler. Historically, most Christians have taken a dim view of human nature and acted accordingly. The Protestant Reformation nevertheless set in motion tendencies which moderated tyranny somewhat and bolstered constitutionalism in England sufficiently to produce the Glorious Revolution of 1689.

The command of St. Paul not to resist "higher powers," backed by the threat of damnation, raises similar questions. Did not Jesus resist Jewish "higher powers"? What about defiance by Luther, Zwingli, and Calvin of the Pope, who at that time had considerable temporal as well as spiritual authority? Have ordinary people no legal or human rights? Are the early Quakers, who infuriated many rulers, now in Hell? Are Calvinistic Presbyterians who opposed Charles I and prompted his execution now being tortured in Hell with the Quakers? Assuming the biblical passages quoted above were valid when Caesars and Popes ruled arbitrarily, were they equally so in Fox's day? For today's recent and present dictatorships? For today's genuine democracies? Are not meekness, long-suffering, martyrdom, and other pacifistic behavior forms of resistance? Could it be that St. Paul overstated himself or his words were mistranslated? Recent revisions, such as those made by the Standard Edition of *The New English Bible,* simplify and clarify, but the substance of St. Paul's words remain about the same.

The early Quakers agreed that "higher powers" should be honored. They also accepted the dualistic distinction attributed to Jesus between temporal and spiritual rulers. They applauded the reference to loving and righteous behavior. But many early Quakers did not hesitate to confront, pressure, or provoke "higher powers" at both national and local levels aggressively, persistently, and stubbornly. Purists still question whether those Quakers' objectives justified their means.

122

The Quaker campaign under Fox's leadership, with headquarters first at Swarthmoor Hall and later in London, was the first of its kind in England. There is, of course, no way of measuring empirically the impact of those organized efforts, but that they played a significant role in moderating political absolutism, expanding religious freedom, fostering humanitarianism, and otherwise nurturing nascent democracy, probably is a reasonable assessment.

Early Quakers were well aware of the biblical passages reviewed above, but their premises and options were radically different from those of contemporary Protestants and Catholics. Those differences hinged upon historical perspective, biblicism, and hierarchy. For Quakers, the Old Testament had profound historical, prophetic, and literary significance, but the coming of Christ marked the beginning of a totally new era.

Henceforth, they insisted the Old Testament was subordinate to the New, especially the words attributed to Jesus, except as otherwise prompted by the Spirit of God. Obviously, therefore, a literal interpretation of the Scriptures could never be the definitive rule. Moreover, by organizing Quaker Meetings without hierarchical structures similar to those of Protestant and Catholic Churches, they could, hopefully forever, avoid obfuscating the Spirit of God.

Barclay had this to say about the Scriptures:

> . . . they are only a declaration of the fountain, and not the fountain itself; therefore they are not to be esteemed the principal ground of all truth and knowledge, nor yet the adequate primary rule of faith and manners. Yet because they give a true and faithful testimony of the first foundation, they are and may be esteemed a secondary rule, subordinate to the Spirit, from which they have all their excellency and certainty: for as by the inward testimony of the Spirit we do alone truly know them, so they testify, that the Spirit is the first principal leader.[9]

That broad view of the scriptures has remained controversial ever since, even among many Quakers.

Where "state churches" have existed in Christendom, bouts over where sovereignty resides inevitably prompt rivalries; not only for power, status, prerogatives, ideologies and policies but also over such mundane things as administrative procedures, funds and properties.

Indeed, drawing an unmistakably clear line between the jurisdictions of Caesar and God has proven to be an impossibility.

The Universal Catholic Church at times attained supremacy, notably in areas where feudalism had been endemic during and after the Middle Ages. Protestantism helped set in motion countervailing forces, of which the English Civil War was an example, tending toward democracy but never ending tyranny, as demonstrated quite recently by Nazi Germany. In that instance the state was sovereign; the state church had been Lutheran for several centuries, but ruthless autocracy prevailed.

The phrases "separation of church and state" and "separation of powers" were seldom used in England and elsewhere when absolutism was the rule. Acceptance spread with the slow and painful growth of democracy. Charles Lewis Montesquieu, the French lawyer and political philosopher, writing more than a century after England's Civil War, did much to popularize the phrases mentioned in his famous book entitled *The Spirit of Laws*.[10] His concepts of separation were nowhere more fully embraced than by American colonials when adopting their Declaration of Independence in 1776 and Constitution in 1789. The latter document featured separated legislative, executive, and judicial powers with an appended bill of rights headed by religious guaranties.

The Quakers' attitude toward war rested squarely upon Matthew's command to "resist not evil," a point of view heavily relied upon previously by Anabaptists and their followers notably the Germanic Mennonites and Swiss Brethren. Given that background, the emphasis was upon "resistance" rather than positive good will, but in fact they did both. Presently, the word "pacifism" is widely thought to be more positive and flexible; hence it is preferred in this volume.

The Quakers' intent was to enthrone conscience, as directed by the Inner Light, and constrain fallible "higher powers," then generally known as "magistrates." Addressing that subject, Robert Barclay (Urie) declared:

> . . . no man, by virtue of any power or principality . . . hath power over the consciences of men is apparent, because the conscience of man is the seat and throne of God in him, of which God is the alone proper and infallible judge, who by his power and Spirit can alone rectify the mistakes of conscience, and therefore hath re-

served to himself the power of punishing the errors therefore as he seeth meet . . .[11]

Barclay went on to say that no magistrate had authority to meddle with God's prerogatives.

Fox demonstrated his pacifist convictions as early as 1647 when beaten after church services by angry parishioners for interrupting a preacher before he had done. He was congenitally provocative, perhaps excessively so, but beatings continued and there is no evidence that he resisted physically.

His first pacifist declaration of military significance registered in the *Journal* occurred at Derby Prison in 1652. That episode is detailed above, but his refusal was genuinely based upon Jesus's teaching. So was his presentation to Oliver Cromwell in 1655 for engaging in a "tumultuous gathering." Moreover, he welcomed ex-soldiers who fought against Royal forces during the Civil War and others who remained in the armed forces or joined later. But, as Braithwaite observed, no genuine Quaker could long remain a soldier ready to kill and submit to rigorous military discipline.[12] Despite such overtures, it was not until the famous declaration of 1662 mentioned above that Quakers officially and unequivocally committed themselves to religious pacifism.

While Fox gradually became what today would be known as a "pacifist," "conscientious objector," or "war resister," he appears not to have been openly hostile to the Army, Navy, Militia and their bureaucracies then operating in the British Isles and overseas, perhaps because they represented "higher powers." It is worth noting also that Fox, though of eligible age and able-bodied, did not volunteer nor was he levied (drafted) during the Civil War or afterwards. Nor did he pay close attention to foreign affairs then deeply committed to imperial aggrandizement, mercantilism, and endless warfare, including the devastating Thirty Years War, of which England was a participant. As that war ended in 1648, Fox was pilgrimaging and starting his ministry. Moreover, the offer made to him at Derby Prison was not for alternative humanitarian service, a choice which today is frequently available, but for enlisting in the Army and actively participating in the Worcester fight. Fox and his colleagues did, however, keep plugging for personal and collective Christlike perfection.

Even so, given the diverse backgrounds of early Quakers, including their largely rural location, levels of education, antipathy toward higher education, brevity of the Quaker Movement and the novelty of aggressive religious pacifism, Quaker governance was often tenuous, overbearing and susceptible to schisms. Meanwhile, persecution had a winnowing effect which may account for the existence and survival of institutionalized Quakerism.

Among the absolute requirements stated by Jesus and St. Paul, one of them was paying tribute to "higher powers." The word "tribute" did not necessarily mean money, although Jesus implied as much by displaying a coin impressed with Caesar's image. Early Quakers interpreted that admonition literally, although many of them balked at paying tithes to a state-related church. They objected to such levies, claiming the Light of Christ within every living soul ought not to be distrained. Taxes, on the other hand, usually were dutifully paid, either with money or whatever else was legally required.

How dutiful the Quakers were is illustrated by the following abstracts written by William Penn and Fox respectively:

> I am Caesar's friend: I seek none of these kingdoms from him; nor will I sow sedition, plot or conspire his ruin; no, let all men render unto Caesar the things that are Caesar's; that is My doctrine; for I am come to erect a kingdom of another nature than that of this world, to wit, a spiritual kingdom, to be set up in the heart; and conscience is My throne; upon that will I sit and rule the children of men in righteousness . . . I never imposed My help, or forced any to receive Me; for I take not My Kingdom by violence but by suffering.[13]

> To the earthly we give the earthly: that is, to Caesar we give unto him his things, and to God we give unto Him His things. And so in the other Power's days we did not forget on our parts, though they did fail on theirs . . . Which, if Friends should not do and had not done— give Caesar his due, and custom and tribute to them that look for it, which are for the punishment of evil-doers— then might they say and plead against us. How can we defend you against foreign enemies and protect every one of their estates and keep down thieves and murderers?[14]

Those comments indicate that the words of Jesus and St. Paul quoted above were interpreted literally. Moreover, they acted on the premise that "higher powers" could do no wrong, regardless of qualifications, methods of appointment or election. In retrospect, it seems impossible to reconcile such absolutist views with the Inner Light, Quaker principles and nascent democracy. The truth of the matter seems to be they accepted absolute monarchical rule hoping that individual and collective spiritual perfection would someday, perhaps quite soon, eventuate either in this world or after death. Indeed, as late as the American Revolution which began in 1775 many Quakers, though generally opposed to war and neutral in the conflict, preferred Royalists to commoners, despite the complaints registered against King George III in the Declaration of Independence.[15]

Persecution

As the Civil War ended, England's constitution remained an unwritten one that embraced England, Wales and distant dependencies in a unitary frame of reference. Under that arrangement, Cabinet officers usually had responsibility for managing matters of national concern, often with local collaboration. Prisons were primarily a national responsibility. Gaols, otherwise known as jails, were nominally the Crown's responsibility, but for the most part County Sheriffs were in charge. At both levels, sheriffs, courts, justices of the peace, bailiffs, constables, headboroughs and other public officials had law-enforcement responsibilities, for which the financial costs were substantial. Fines, sequesters, distraints, confiscations and other legal processes helped pay the costs. Self-help required of prisoners, families, friends and others, though burdensome, helped lower operating costs. The levies mentioned often reduced Quakers and many others to penury.

Despite much research, the numbers of Quakers officially persecuted remains uncertain. Two primary sources detail sufferings at considerable length: Norman Penny's *Extracts* cited below and George Besse's *A Collection of the Sufferings of the People Called Quakers*.[16]

Several accounts provide figures showing the numbers of Quakers imprisoned, but for differing time periods. Braithwaite's figures show that prior to the Restoration of 1660 "an old Quaker tract" stated 3170 persons had "suffered imprisonments, putting in stocks, whippings, loss of goods, and other abuses . . ." He added that as of April, 1659, only twenty-one had died, "compared with at least 300 during the Restoration Period."[17]

Sharpless reported that William Penn and two others presented a petition to King and Parliament in 1680 saying 10,000 had been imprisoned and 243 had died there. The report also stated that large numbers of estates had been confiscated, allegedly because Quakers were Papists in disguise; exorbitant fines had been imposed in other cases, and as many as 4,000 were in jail at one time later.[18]

Writing nearly two centuries later, and after examining countless original documents, Barclay (Tottenham) stated that 13,562 Quakers suffered imprisonments between 1661 and 1697. He went on to say that 198 had been transported overseas and 338 died in prisons or from wounds. Furthermore, said he:

> This account of suffering was aggravated by the confiscation of property, and spoiling of their goods to an enormous amount, and *to an extent which disorganized the trade of the kingdom.* It is admitted on all hands, that the Christian non-resistance and patient suffering of the Society which was in the providence of God, moulded by George Fox to some extent from the Puritan gentry, as well as to the yeomen, artisans, and the Independent and Baptist soldiery, formed a spiritual army which had no small share in winning for England the religious liberty which she now enjoys. It had been fought without carnal weapons by religious men and their religion but suffered in the conflict.[19]

To summarize the figures mentioned before and after the Restoration by Braithwaite and Barclay, it appears that a total of 16,732 were imprisoned and 359 died. A number of others were sentenced to die and suffered acutely but for various reasons were not executed. Five were executed overseas, however: four in Boston and one in Rome. Countless others suffered or died after release as a consequence of incarceration.

In retrospect, England's persecution of early Quakers, though horrible, was comparatively moderate when one recalls the countless instances of genocidal behavior scattered throughout present and past centuries. On a more positive note, Oliver Cromwell reopened the door for Jews driven from England centuries before.

England's correctional system, though undoubtedly horrid, appears to have been less brutal than in times past. Professor Cross related that widespread lawlessness during the fourteenth century prompted the establishment of county officials known since as Justices of the Peace. He went on to say:

> Punishments were barbarous, aiming at retribution and vengeance rather than prevention of crime. Prisoners were thrown, sometimes naked, into horrible dungeons, dark, damp, indescribably filthy, often partly filled with water and swarming with rats and vermin; and their usual fare was moldy bread and stagnant water. Lesser offenders were put in the stocks. Torture was common to make the accused confess, or to make him submit to jury trial. The horrible practice of breaking on the wheel, where a man was stretched out and his limbs broken with an iron bar, was not unknown; hanging was most common and, as towns and local lords had this right, gallows were often seen, gruesome spots on the landscape. In cases of treason a man was cut down while his body was still warm, he was drawn and quartered, and his bowels were taken out and burned . . . What with royal regulation, town and guild, and church regulations, the individual had very little freedom.[20]

During the sixteenth century public opinion began to turn against the usage of torture by such contrivances as thumbscrew, scourge and rack; moreover, it appears that Quakers were not subjected to them during the latter half of the following century. However, non-capital punishments remained severe in England as illustrated by those inflicted upon James Naylor and John Wilburne. Moreover, as late as 1681, when Charles II granted William Penn a royal charter for governing Pennsylvania, there was a long list of capital crimes, both high and petty.

After Justices of the Peace were authorized, the judicial system changed gradually, but basically the pattern remained much the same when Quakers arrived on the scene. Each justice performed pretrial tasks but two were required to hold "Petty Sessions" for trying minor criminal offenses. All justices within a county assembled quarterly in courts known as "Quarter Sessions" to deal with more serious offenses. Still graver and more difficult cases were adjudicated by "Assizes," held in every county at least twice yearly. Additionally, there were specialized courts, including the highest of all in the mid-1600s, the Privy Council, composed of Lords or appointees by the House of Commons, whose decisions were normally reviewable by monarchs.

All judges, including justices of the peace, were selected from upper classes, appointed for life, and served without compensation. Overall administration was centered in the office of Lord High Chancellor. Meanwhile, grand and petit juries, both of French origin, made their appearance. The avalanche of litigation involving Quakers was handled chiefly by justices of the peace sitting in Petty and Quarter Sessions. The time, effort, and financial costs to both the Quakers and general public were enormous. Recognizing the justices' critical importance, some early Quakers actively supported "the appointment of justices, of persons whom they knew to be inclined toward fairness."[21]

Prosecutions were conducted differently in England than in Western Europe. The English system was said to be "accusatorial," meaning that responsibility for accusations, investigations, and prosecutions rested in most instances upon private accusers. Moreover, the costs were borne by the accusers rather than the state. In Western Europe, where Roman Law provided the background, the system was said to be "inquisitorial" with responsibility for prosecutions and costs resting upon the state and performed by public law enforcement officers.

Theoretically, under the accusatorial system innocence was presumed until guilt was established by private prosecutors in neutral courts, but in mid-1600 England prejudice was common, particularly when such inflammable issues as religion were involved. Moreover, private accusations and prosecutions often were recklessly made by ill-informed people lacking the financial resources and legal training required to assure fairness. The Continental inquisitorial system could be, and often was, equally or more biased. Both systems have since been drastically modified, but their rudiments remain. The American Colonies followed the English practice, but supplemented it with public prosecutors early in their development.

Quakerism began in small localities, such as Fenny Drayton, Nottingham and Derby, surrounded by larger areas. Politically, aristocrats dominated both, but in the former there remained a modicum of local control which began during the period between the settlement of Anglo-Saxons (449 A.D.) and the Norman Conquest (1055 A.D.). The local units which came into existence during those centuries were shires, hundreds, townships and parishes.

As population grew, some local units were incorporated as boroughs and towns, terms which were often used interchangeably. They were governed by councils with members elected either by voters or chosen by co-optation, i.e., choice by sitting members. Usually such units were "close corporations" governed by burgesses, otherwise known as "freemen," in whom were vested special property, trading and fiscal rights as well as a monopoly of governing power. Government by such units were almost always oligarchical and often corrupt. Magistrates and constables were police arms of boroughs and towns.

By the mid-1600s, England's population was about 5,000,000. London accounted for an estimated 500,000 and as late as the Restoration, in 1660, there were only four towns with more than 10,000 people. London, a municipality incorporated in the twelfth century, had attained great wealth, power and influence, and become the undisputed center of English Renaissance culture. It suffered later by struggles with Stuart Kings over issues that precipitated the Civil War; the bubonic plague of 1665 carried by rat fleas which took about 75,000 lives; and the great fire of 1666 that virtually destroyed the municipality.

Feudalism had declined, but differences in class status and wealth remained. Moreover, half the population were laborers or small farmers whose rank was akin to peasants living on and tending holdings owned by noblemen, usually in return for services rendered. There were no public schools and illiteracy was widespread among all but the upper classes. Bigotry, cruelty, crudity and superstition were endemic.

The performance of trial courts varied widely, but many obviously operated unprofessionally. The famous criminal trial, reported in *Bushell's Case,* is illustrative.[22] The Quaker defendants were twenty-six-year-old William Penn and William Meade, an older man and linen draper with a fair knowledge of law who later married one of Margaret Fell's daughters.

The charge was for violating the Conventical Act of 1664 by aiding and abetting a tumultuous assembly on London's Grace Street. A large crowd had assembled outside the Quaker Meetinghouse because it had been closed by soldiers, but nothing "tumultuous" happened. The trial took place at Old Bailey before a Court of Quarter Sessions, with Mayor Sir Samuel Starling presiding, a Recorder who served as chief spokesman, and eight other judges. The jury consisted of twelve middle class men, selected at random from jury rolls of the City of London. Edward Bushell unofficially led the jury.

Although both Penn and Mead kept their composure throughout the trial, it got off to a bristling start over their refusals to remove hats. The hats were forcibly removed, but after a recess, the Recorder put them back on and fined the defendants for contempt of court. Both men asked for fair hearings and those were promised, but baiting by the Recorder continued, whereupon they were placed in baildock, a locked cage in a corner of the room and recessed below floor level with open top, which permitted the two men to hear and shout replies. While so confined, the defendants were formally accused and indicted. The men continued to protest loudly enough to be heard, whereupon they spent the night in a "stinking hole without meat, drink, or other accommodations," including a "chamber pot."

Later, the jury was ordered to return a guilty verdict, but Bushell and three others refused. Polled again, the jury would not budge. Rather, and despite threats by the Mayor and Recorder, the jury would go no farther than to say: "We the jurors hereafter named, do find William Penn guilty of speaking and preaching to an assembly, met together in Gracious Street, the 14th of August last 1670, and that William Mead is not guilty of the said indictment."

Outraged, the Recorder said to the jury: "I am sorry Gentlemen, you have followed your own judgments and opinions rather than the good and wholesome advice that was given you: God keep my life out of your hands. But for this the Court fines you forty marks a man and imprisonment till paid." Penn and Mead were also jailed until fines imposed during the hat incident were paid.

The decision was later overruled by Writ of Habeas Corpus in the Court of Common Pleas. In doing so, Chief Justice Vaughan asked: "But if the Judge, from the evidence, shall by his own judgment first resolve what the law is, and order the jury penally to find accordingly, what either necessary or convenient use can be fancied of juries, or to continue trials by them at all?" Although reversed on appeal, because the Court of Common Pleas lacked jurisdiction in criminal matters, *Bushell's Case* established the right of trial by juries to decide controversies freely and solely upon their merits, and by so doing set precedents that helped end centuries of struggles between judges and juries in both England and the United States.

Following are selected quotations which illustrate the gist and flavor of that historic trial:

> *Penn:* The question is not, whether I am guilty of this indictment but whether the indictment is legal. It is too general an answer to say, it is the common law, unless we know both when, where and what it is. For where there is no law, unless there is no transgression; and that law which is not in being, is so far being common, that it is no law at all.
>
> *Recorder:* You are an impertinent fellow. Will you teach the Court what law is? It's Lex no Scripta, that which may have been studied thirty or forty years to know, and would you have me tell in a moment.
>
> *Penn:* Certainly if the common law be so hard to understand, it's far from being very common; but if the Lord Coke, in his *Institutes* be of any considerations, he tells us that common law is common right and that common right is the great Charter-Privileges . . .
>
> *Penn:* I appeal to the jury who are my judges, and this great Assembly whether the proceedings of the court are not arbitrary, and void of all law, in offering to give the jury their charge in the absence of the prisoners: I say it is directly opposite to, and destructive of the undoubted right of every English prisoner . . .
>
> *Mead:* Are these according to the rights and privileges of Englishmen, that we should not be heard, but turned into baildock for making our defense and the jury to have the charge given them in our absence: I say, these are barbarous and unjust proceedings.
>
> *Clerk:* Look upon the prisoners at the bar. How say you? Is William Penn guilty of the matter whereof he stands indicted in the manner and form, or not guilty?
>
> *Foreman:* Guilty of speaking in Gracious Street.
>
> *Court:* Is that all?

Foreman: That is all I have in commission.

Recorder: You had as good say nothing.

Mayor: Was it not an unlawful assembly? You mean he was speaking to a tumult of people there?

Foreman: My Lord, this was all I had in commission.

Recorder: The Law of England will not admit you to depart, till you have given in your verdict.

Jury: We have given in our verdict, and we can give in no other.

Recorder: Gentlemen, you have not given in your verdict, and you had as good say nothing: Therefore go and consider it once more, that we may make an end to this troublesome business.

Clerk: What say you? Look upon the prisoners. Is William Penn guilty in manner and form as he stands indicted, or not guilty?

Foreman: Here is our verdict. We the jurors hereafter-named do find William Penn to be guilty of speaking or preaching to an assembly, met together in Gracious Street, the 14th of August last 1670, and that William Mead is not guilty of the said indictment.

Recorder: Till now I never understood the reason of the policy and prudence of the Spaniards in suffering the Inquisition among them; and certainly it will never be well with us, till something like the Spanish Inquisition be in England.

Penn: I demand my liberty, being freed by the jury.

Mayor: No; you are in for your fines.

Penn: Fines for what?

Mayor: For contempt of court.

Penn: I ask if it be according to the fundamental laws of England that an Englishman should be fined or amerced, but by the judgment of his peers of jury . . .

Recorder: Take him away; take him away; take him out of the court.

Observer: They haled the prisoners in the baildock, and from thence they were taken to Newgate for non-payment of their fines and so were the jury.

Bushell's Case had far-reaching consequences, not only in England but throughout the British Empire, as demonstrated by the famous *Zenger Trial* held in New York City in 1735. The plaintiff was William Bradford, printer of the *New York Gazette;* the defendant, John Peter Zenger was a printer for the *New York Weekly Journal,* said to be the first politically independent one on the continent.

A battle royal followed between Governor William Cosby, a supporter of Bradford, and Zenger's staff, whereupon Zenger was charged with publishing seditious libels and imprisoned until the trial began. Fundamentally, the issue was whether in libel suits juries could determine not only *law* and *facts* but also whether the published materials were *true* or *false.* Relying heavily upon the Penn-Meade victory, the Zenger jury, after taking truthfulness into account, quickly returned a not guilty verdict. That decision was widely acclaimed by champions of freer speech and press and later enshrined in the First and Fourteenth Amendments of the American Constitution adopted in 1787.[23]

The Civil War was nearing its end when Fox began his ministry in 1647 and shortly thereafter he ran afoul of the law. Meanwhile, affairs of state were in transition with Oliver Cromwell preeminent. He was moderately tolerant of Quakers, but by mid-1650 his Council felt compelled to suppress radical behavior. From then on during the "Kingless Decade" suppression was the rule.

Penny's *Extracts* list sufferings inflicted upon Quakers by local authorities. Of twenty-six charges against them we list eleven most frequently used and show the numbers prosecuted from high to low:

Speaking in churches	2756
Trespasses	2177
Contempts	1428
Refusal to pay court fees and fines	1096
Nonpayment of tithes	1080
Refusal to swear oaths	832
Refusal to give securities	813
Refusal to remove hats	589
Traveling on First Day (Sunday)	389
Vagrancy	383
Nonattendance at National worship Services and holding unauthorized services	363

Behind those figures lie not only grief and tragedy but also pathos, as illustrated by the following abstracts. The first one has been altered for easier reading and understanding:

> Thomas Harrison Esquire Sheriff of ye said County (Yorkshire) to ye Gaoler or Keeper of ye Castle at Yorke Greeting. I command that you the body of Robert Maniford by me taken you detayne and safe keepe so that I may have his body before Ye Justices of the common bench at Westminster from ye day of Easter in one month to Answer Charles Keane Clerke in a plea of Trespass. Given under the seal of My office the 28th day of April 1658 by ye sherriffe.[24]

This second sample is a Mittimus, or warrant of a commitment to prison:

> To the Keeper of his Majesty's Gaol, within the City of Worcester. I hereby send you the Body of *Edward Bourne,* who was this evening apprehended while he was preaching at an unlawful Conventicle or Meeting, under Pretence of exercising Religion, contrary to the Liturgy of the Church of England, openly in a street called Fryar's Street, in the Parish of St. Helen's within the said city, where were present several persons, above the number of twenty, contrary to the late Act of Parliament in that case made and provided, which by notorious Evidence and Circumstance of the Fact it proved against him. These are therefore, in his Majesty's Name, by Virtue of the said Act, to will and require you to take into your Custody the body of the said Edward Bourne, and him safely to keep till he shall be thence delivered by due Course of his Majesty's Laws: Whereof fail not at your Perils. Given under my Hand and Seal this 17th Day of *March,* in the 34th Year of the Reign of *King Charles the Second* over *England, Annoque Dom.* 1681.[25]

Following Bourne's imprisonment, he had this to say in a letter to George Fox:

I am now a Prisoner here in City-Prison, where I am satisfied I am in my Place, being called Thereunto of the Lord, for whose Word's Sake I suffer Bonds, which he makes easy for me, in his affording me The Enjoyment of his Sweet, and Glorious, and Heavenly Presence.[26]

A third sample has reference to a warrant issued by a petty-constable in Westmoreland County:

Whereas I have received a Warrant from his Majesty's Deputy-Lieutenants of this County, for the suppression of all numerous and unlawful Meetings, by Virtue of a certain special Order from his Majesty: These are to require you to give public Notice within your Constable-wick, that from the 11th of this Instant January, there be no numerous Meetings of *Quakers, Sectaries,* or other disaffected Persons, in any secret or unusual Places, upon any Pretence whatever, as they will avoid the Penalties and Forfeitures which by the Laws of this Nation are to be imposed upon such Offences. Dated the 5th Day of January 1660. [The document was signed by Tho. Riggs, High-Constable.][27]

Immediately following the above quotation were remarks saying that pursuant to the warrant 116 Quakers were imprisoned for refusals to swear oaths.

We summarize below random offenses and penalties from Besse's collection. Monetary values are states in pounds (£) and shillings (S):

John Brown, for *refusing to swear* when summoned to serve on jury, was fined 20 S. and committed to Ailsbury Gaol where he lay twelve weeks. *Buckinghamshire, 1658.*

Deborah Harding, *after the Priest of Dirsley had ended his sermon would have given a Christian exhortation to the people,* but they fell into an uproar, some crying kill her, others strike her down, others tear her in pieces; the magistrates, to secure her from the rabble, sent her to prison. After some time an uncle of hers in-

137

terceded on her behalf; they would have discharged her by winking at her escape through a back door, but when she refused to comply they sent her to Glocester Gaol. *Glocestershire, 1656.*

For absence from national worship, the following fines were levied at £30 a month:

38 men for eleven months	£8360.
2 wives for the same time	£220.
111 men for three months	£6660.
40 wives for the same time	£1200.
Total	£16440.

Bristol, 1683.

At the beginning of the year, several persons were insulted in their houses by soldiers of the County Militia, *who under pretense of searching for arms,* entered into houses, eating and drinking what they could find and carrying away what they pleased. *Glocestershire, 1660.*

In November of this year, Henry Howland had three cows and one steer taken from him for *permitting religious meetings in his house. Glocestershire, 1665.*

After the accession of King William and Queen Mary to the throne, a *poll tax* was levied by Act of Parliament, wherein preachers were charged for their stipends or pay. Several people called Quakers were *assessed as preachers,* but as they received no stipend or pay, they thought it a dishonor to their profession of a free ministry to make such payments, and for that reason they refused and several suffered distresses of their goods. *Glocestershire, 1689.*

William Jennings, elected Beadle (a minor Parish official) of Southampton, and *refusing to take an oath* at the entering upon the office, was sent to prison and confined there about three months. *Hampshire, 1678.*

A widow, named Rawling, for a *demand of 10 S. for tithe,* suffered distress of horse and cattle to the value of £50. *Bedfordshire, 1664.*

For *being at the same Meeting,* the following distresses were made: Thomas Sutton £5., John Bullock £7, William Lamann £6, William Metcalf £8, Mary Read 12 S., Robert Rotham 14 S. *Bedfordshire, 1670.*

Thomas Tyack was sent to prison *for tithes* and continued in prison above eight year. *Cornwall,* 1675.

Nicholas Emmatt, *for absenting national worship,* was committed by the Sheriff and imprisoned for four years. *Cornwall,* 1675.

Isaac Pennington, about three weeks after release from his last imprisonment for *refusing to swear,* was again apprehended by soldiers sent from Sir Philip Palmer who took him out of his bed and conveyed him directly to Ailsburg Gaol, where, without any legal cause, he was kept a year and a half in rooms so cold and damp, and unhealthy, that he contracted sickness of several months continuance. During that long confinement he was never called for either Sessions or Assize, but by some illegal means remained on the Calendar to remain in prison. At length, having been removed by Habeas Corpus to the King's Bench Bar, the Court, surprised to find a man kept so long in prison for nothing, set him at liberty. *Buckinghamshire,* 1666.

For *holding a Meeting,* consisting mostly of children between the ages of 12 and 14. Because most of the men and women were in prison, the children kept up their meetings regularly. On July 23rd five boys were put in stocks two hours and a half. On the 30th, in the afternoon, about fifty children were at the meeting when an officer with a twisted whalebone stick, beat many of them unmercifully, striking them violent blows on their heads, necks and faces; few of them escaped without some marks of his fury. *Bristol,* 1682.

James Potter, for *reading a paper of Christian advice to the people after a sermon in the steeple house* was committed to Winchester Gaol till the Assizes; where the cause of his commitment appeared insufficient and he ought to have been released; but the Court took occasion against him for *appearing with his hat on,* fined him £5 and sent him again to prison, where he lay two years and two months longer. *Hampshire and Isle of Wight,* 1653.

William Gill, William Valler, and Elizabeth Streater, for *refusing to pay toward the charge of the County Militia,* were imprisoned at Winchester fifteen days, and afterwards had their goods distressed to the value of £1, 5 S. *Hampshire, 1660.*

Thomas Willis, *taken at a Meeting*, was by the Mayor of Southampton committed to prison, where he died after about seven months of confinement, contentedly laying down his life for his constancy of religion. *Hampshire, 1662.*

The wife of Samuel Burgis was buried in a burying ground of the people called Quakers, at Baghurst. The Priest of that Parish, whose name was Woodward, informed a Justice, procured a warrant, came with several attendants, and took account of their names. A woman spake a few words at the grave, whom he charged his attendants to take into custody, which they refused: This angered him and he gave them many threats. Upon his report to the Justices, they laid a fine on several of the Friends *for being at a conventicle,* and shortly after they suffered distress of their goods to the value of £25, 6 S. *Hampshire, 1670.*

Robert Reeves had his lands of £13, 10 S. per annum seized by force of the *statute against Popish Recusants. Hampshire.. 1681.*

Taken for tithes, from John Valler and James Potter, hay and corn to the value of £18 and 14 S. *Hampshire, 1678.*

Ralph Charles suffered twelve weeks imprisonment for *refusing to contribute toward repairing the steeple house.* Others were fined for the same reason. *Hartfordshire, 1656.*

John Bresbone *for going to a Meeting,* had a horse, bridle and saddle taken away worth £5. *Hartfordshire, 1656.*

Richard Hubberthorn and others were *taken out of a Meeting,* bound hand and foot, and so carried and laid in the open fields in a cold winter night to the hazard of their lives. Ralph Barnes and John Barnes were *taken from a Meeting* at Warrington Heath, and committed to Lancaster Gaol. *Lancashire, 1652.*

On the 16th of June several persons were coming out of a Meeting and found the passages beset with

armed men, who would not suffer them to depart till
some Justices of the Peace came, who tendered them the
Oath of Allegiance, as a means of discovering Papists
and upon their *refusal to take* it sent them to Lancaster
Gaol. *Lancashire,* 1660.

Class Status of Early Quakers

Much has been written in recent years about the socio-economic
aspects of early Quakerism. Even such scholars as Karl Marx (1818-
1883) and his associate Frederick Engels (1820-1895) paid attention to
that phenomenon.[28] Of the early Quakers, John Bellers was the first to
dwell seriously upon such matters and by so doing anticipated England's industrial revolution of the 1800s.

The earliest Quaker statistics showing a modicum of occupational
data were prepared for seeking release from imprisonment. The most
comprehensive of those were assembled by then-existing Quaker
Meetings and reported by Besse and Penny. With the passage of time,
both Meetings and Parishes kept occupational and related records
which became available for research.

Although such data were commonly used by Friends Meetings, it
was not until recent times that scholars inquired about Quakers' class
status. Ernest E. Taylor's provocative book entitled *The Valiant
Sixty*[29] was among the first to address that issue. The following chart
suggests the socio-economic character of that volume:

The Valiant Sixty

Ayrey, Thomas	Yeoman (Husbandman)	Birkfield
Adam, Thomas	Yeoman	Warmsworth
Atkinson, Christopher	Yeoman	Kendal
Audland, Ann	Wife of Shopkeeper	Preston Patrick
Audland, John	Linen Draper (Farmer)	Preston Patrick
Banks, John	Glove Maker (Fell-monger & Husbandman)	
Bateman, Miles	Husbandman	Underbarrow
Benson, Dorothy	Wife of Yeoman	Sedbergh
Benson, Gervase	Yeoman (Husbandman)	Sedbergh
Bewley, George	Yeoman (Gentleman)	Haltcliffe Hall
Birkett, Miles	Miller	Underbarrow
Blaykling, Anne	Sister of Yeoman	Draw-well
Blaykling, John	Yeoman (Husbandman)	Draw-well
Braithwaite, John	Shorthand Writer	Newton-in-Cartmel

141

Briggs, Thomas	Husbandman	Newton, Cheshire
Burnyeat, John	Husbandman	Crabtree Beck
Burrough, Edward	Husbandman	Underbarrow
Camm, John	Yeoman (Husbandman)	Preston Patrick
Camm, Mabel	Wife of Yeoman	Preston Patrick
Caton, William	Secretary	Swarthmoor Hall
Clayton, Richard	Yeoman	Gleaston-in-Furness
Dewsbury, William	Shepherd (Clothier)	Allerthorpe
Farnsworth, Richard	Yeoman	Tickhill
Fell, Leonard	Husbandman	Baycliffe
Fell, Margaret	Gentlewoman	Swarthmoor Hall
Fisher, Mary	Servant	Selby
Fletcher, Elizabeth	Gentlewoman	Kendal
Fox, George	Shoemaker (Shepherd)	Drayton
Goodaire, Thomas	Yeoman	Selby
Halhead, Miles	Husbandman	Underbarrow
Harrison, George	Gentleman	Sedbergh
Hebden, Roger	Tailor	New Malton
Holme, Thomas	Weaver	Kendal
Holme, Elizabeth	"Lower Ranke"	
Hooton, Elizabeth	Wife of Yeoman	Skegsby
Howgill, Francis	Farmer (Tailor)	Grayrigg
Howgill, Mary	Sister of Tailor	Grayrigg
Hubbersty, Miles	Husbandman	Underbarrow
Hubbersty, Stephen	Husbandman	Underbarrow
Hubberthorne, Richard	Yeoman (Soldier)	Yealand Redmayne
Kilham, Thomas	Gentleman	Balby
Lancaster, James	Husbandman	Walney Isle
Lawson, John	Shopkeeper	Lancaster
Lawson, Thomas	Gentleman (Schoolmaster)	Lancaster
Naylor, James	Butcher	Bolton Forest
Parker, Alexander	Husbandman (Soldier)	Ardsley
Rawlinson, Thomas	Gentleman	Graythwaite
Rigge, Ambrose	Schoolmaster	Grayrigg
Robertson, Thomas	Yeoman	Grayrigg
Robinson, Richard	Yeoman	Countersett
Salthouse, Thomas	Husbandman	Dragglebeck
Scaife, John	Day-Labourer	Hutton
Simpson, William	Husbandman	Sunbricke
Slee, John	Husbandman	Mosedale
Stacey, Thomas	Yeoman	Cinder Hill
Story, John	Husbandman	Preston Patrick
Stubbs, John	Husbandman (School-master & Soldier)	
Stubbs, Thomas	Soldier	Pardshaw
Taylor, Christopher	Schoolmaster	Carlton
Taylor, Thomas	Schoolmaster (Beneficed Minister)	Carlton
Waugh, Dorothy	Servant	Preston Patrick
Waugh, Jane	Servant	Preston Patrick

142

Whitehead, George	Schoolmaster (Grocer)	Orton
Whitehead, John	Soldier	Holderness
Widders, Robert	Husbandman	Over Kellett
Wilkinson, John	Husbandman	Preston Patrick

Of these sixty-six Friends fifty-four were men and twelve women. Of the men Friends the occupations of fifty are fairly clear as follows:

Gentlemen	12	Craftsmen and shopkeepers	8
Yeomen	13	Schoolmasters	4
Husbandmen	17	Soldiers	2
Wage Earners	1	Other Professions	2
Millers	1	Not ascertained	4

Richard Vann's analysis of Taylor's data is shown as follows:[30]

Occupation/Status	#	%	Occupation/Status	#	%
Gentlemen	6	11.1	Agriculture	36	66.7
Professional	8	14.8	Gentlemen	5	9.3
Schoolmasters	6	11.1	Yeomen	15	27.8
Secretary, short-			Husbandmen	13	24.1
hand writer	2		Steward, Laborer,		
Soldiers	2	3.7	Shepherd	3	
General Trade	4	7.4	Trade in Food	2	3.7
Drapers	2		(Miller, Butcher)		
Fellmonger,			Clothing Production	2	
shopkeeper	2		(Weaver, Shoemaker		

For other scholars who addressed the class issue, we rely briefly upon Richard T. Vann[31] and Alan Cole,[32] both of whom gathered statistical data from Quaker Meetings and Parish registers. They concluded, however, that those materials were too limited for scholarly usage.

Vann argued quite firmly that "All writers dealing with the earliest period of Quakerism have emphasized the relative poverty of most of the early Friends." Alan Cole concluded that early Quakers were "mainly drawn from the urban and rural *petite bourgeoise.*" Frederick Tolles agreed that recruitment of members from the lower classes was one of the distinctive marks of the [Quaker] sect. He went on to say, however, that within a half-century the lower classes had risen to "class respectability."[33] Reflecting on those comments, Vann concluded:

Given the fragmentary quality of the evidence, we should not place an exaggerated confidence in the percentage distribution among Friends as compared with the samples of the general population; but it can be said with assurance that Quakerism at the beginning drew adherents from all classes of society except the very highest and the very lowest, ranging from the lesser gentry to a few totally unskilled laborers. . . . The clearest trend is the gradual disappearance of landed gentry among Friends.[34]

VI

WILLIAM PENN'S MATURATION
AND COLONIAL GOVERNANCE

Penn's Upbringing, Maturation, and Imprisonments

William Penn's father (1621-1670) was of Welsh ancestry. His wife, Margaret, born in London in 1644, was the daughter of John Jasper, a well-to-do Dutch merchant who had numerous Irish landholdings, the values of which had depreciated markedly due primarily to Catholic and Royalist rebellions.[1] The father had joined the Navy wrested from King Charles I during the Civil War and was well aware of Oliver Cromwell's fame as a cavalier. After that conflict, both men became preeminent in their respective offices, Cromwell as proprietor and Penn, also known as Sir William Penn, as admiral.

Their compatibility was severely strained when the Admiral blundered at sea in 1654 during an encounter with the Spanish Navy in the West Indies. His orders were not only to seize lands and treasure ships, but also to break Spain's colonial monopoly and retaliate for damages caused by the Inquisition. In doing so, he accidentally lost one of his ships and a hundred men, but nevertheless conquered the Island of Jamaica. Machiavellian to the core where naval matters were concerned, he may also have left the scene and returned to London without prior authorization.

Upon returning home the Admiral and a colleague were sent to London Tower, allegedly for complicity with Charles II and other royalists, then in exile. Shortly thereafter, he and his family left reluctantly for Ireland. Meanwhile the father's income lessened, due in large measure to Cromwell's delay in providing land rentals; he was, however, compensated for services rendered at nearby Kingsdale.

The family spent about four years in southeastern Ireland located twenty-six miles west of Cork. Their home was a castle named

145

Macroom which doubled for a fort named Shanagary. The father also served, in absentia for the most part, as Governor of Kingsdale, a port and market town protected by a company of foot soldiers. Son William had previously been tutored in a small London village and taught by strong-minded Puritans at Chigwell Free Grammar School. He was tutored later at Macroom and learned much about that part of Ireland, but whether an itinerant Quaker named Thomas Loe preached there appears to be untrue.[2]

Anticipating the Stuart Restoration of 1660, the Penns returned to London, not only to resume the father's naval career but also to provide schooling for their three children. William, the oldest, was then about sixteen and undoubtedly had college in mind, as well as the coronation of Charles II, where he would be presented by his father with much pride and pageantry.

Shortly after the coronation Penn enrolled as a gentleman commoner at Christ Church, one of seven colleges at Oxford University. Apparently, he did quite well as a student and showed a penchant for manly sports, religion and politics. Moreover, he was impressed by such liberal professors as John Locke, then lecturer in Greek, rhetoric and philosophy, who was later dismissed by Charles II for his liberal inclinations. Later, both Locke and Penn shared common interests including the development of North American colonies. Meanwhile, both Oxford and Cambridge mixed "learning with religion and politics."[3] Indeed, there had been close liaison throughout the Civil War and Restoration periods between church, state, politics and universities. Moreover, revised statutes mandated that the latter conform to strict Puritan standards.

As might be expected of cautious university officials during troubled times, they became increasingly annoyed over Penn's nonconformist inclinations, whereupon he was expelled near the end of his second year. Apparently, that penalty was imposed because of his unwillingness to conform with Puritan orthodoxy and college standards, such as joining other students to protest wearing the traditional surplice, a loose white ecclesiastical vestment worn on special occasions. There were other infractions as well, such as attending unauthorized worship services rather than those held in Oxford's Chapel.[4]

Penn was particularly impressed by such outside lecturers as John Owen, formerly Dean of Oxford's Christ Church and Chancellor of the University. He had lived through two previous tumultuous decades, meanwhile shifting from Anglicanism to Presbyterianism to

146

Congregationalism. He was deposed in 1660, the year Penn entered the University. Whether he met or was taught by Thomas Loe at Oxford is uncertain; but they did meet later at Cork, Ireland, and occasionally thereafter.

Penn returned home in disgrace, knowing full well the high expectations his parents had, especially the proud and hot-tempered Admiral. Beatings and expulsion from the household followed, whereupon his father sent him to France, hoping to divert his fanaticism; become familiar with the French Court, the paramount center of culture and political influence during the reign of King Louis XIV; and hopefully become a "fine gentleman."[5] On one occasion, while wearing his sword, he was challenged by a total stranger and might have been killed had Penn not outmaneuvered him. Reflecting upon that episode, Penn said:

> I ask any man of understanding or conscience, if the whole ceremony were worth the life of a man, considering the dignity of the nature, and the importance of the life of man, both with respect to God his creator, himself, and the benefit of civil society?[6]

Following his stay in Paris, Penn spent about two years at the Huguenot College of Saumur in Anjou, directed by the famous liberal Calvinist and orator Moïse (Moses) Amyraut. While there he studied theology, became proficient in French and acquired "a working knowledge of Latin, Greek and the writings of early church fathers."[7] Upon concluding his studies, he toured Italy briefly, during which his father, whose anger had subsided, called him home. Arriving in August, 1664, he studied law at Lincoln's Inns of Court until the Bubonic Plague broke out. Meanwhile the Dutch War began and his father engaged him as an aide. His travel and studies had made him a gentleman quite different from what his father originally had in mind.

While at Paris and Saumur, Penn became aware of the endless intrigues on the part of prominent refugees who had fled England during the Civil War and Commonwealth period, including future Stuart Kings, Charles and James, who loathed Oliver Cromwell and rejoiced over his death, which made the Restoration possible. Sir William Penn held similar views and benefited from that turn of events. Son William was also pleased, at least with the Restoration, and had a warm relationship with both Charles II and his brother James, who was then titled the Duke of York.

Penn returned to Ireland in 1666 to attend to properties restored by Charles II. While there he encountered Thomas Loe, who was then an itinerant Quaker preacher, and was overwhelmed by his sermon and kindly companions. It was on that occasion that Penn gave up his sword and cast his lot with Quakers. By doing so he was imprisoned briefly, due to his prestigious family, while his associates served longer terms.

Following that event, Penn plunged headlong into Quaker affairs, then in great turmoil because of unprecedented persecution. How long before then he felt inclined to write and publish is uncertain, but within two years three polemic tracts made their appearance, one of which was entitled *The Sandy Foundation Shaken,* which caused him serious trouble, partly because he lacked an official license to publish the tract.[8]

On that occasion he disputed publicly with the prominent Presbyterian preacher, Thomas Vincent, who challenged Penn's "damnable" views on the "Holy Trinity" set forth in the tract mentioned above, for which he was arrested and imprisoned at London Tower for blasphemy. Penn's comments, in retrospect, were one-sided, excessively polemic and of little lasting consequence, but the public was aroused and he became widely known to Quakers as well as the general public. Penn later, but while still in the Tower, modified his views but the damage had been done. Such intense scriptural argumentation was due not only to the issues at stake but also to severe penalties. To make matters worse, that episode took place during the aftermath of London's Bubonic Plague and Great Fire. Meanwhile, Penn continued writing tracts until his health failed. The most impressive one was probably *No Cross, No Crown,* published in 1669. The total list exceeded well over a hundred.[9]

Penn's incarceration lasted about nine months and may have been shortened by his father's prestigious reputation, serious illness and influential friends. Sir William had retired in 1665 and died at the age of 49 shortly after his son's release. The two men had previously become fully reconciled and since William was the eldest male child in the family he inherited the father's considerable estate by right of primogeniture. Fortunately, his mother had ample assets of her own.

Altogether, Penn was imprisoned on six occasions (depending on how they were counted), all but one of them in London: at Cork, Ireland, for aiding Quaker prisoners; London Tower for blasphemy; Newgate Prison, for holding a meeting (Conventicle) that precipitated the famous Penn-Mead trial at Old Bailey; Newgate for violating the Conventical Act of 1671; London Tower (briefly) and confinement at home similar to what today would be called "house arrest," prompted by a Jacobin plot on suspicion of high treason shortly after the accession of William and Mary; and Fleet Street Prison for nonpayment of a contested debt secured by Colonial Pennsylvania. All terms were quite short compared with those of innumerable other Quakers, including George and Margaret Fell Fox.[10] None, however, was more embarrassing and exhausting than the fifth which involved Philip and Bridget Ford, as sketched below.

The New World offered hope for religious liberty despite its hazards and loneliness. In most instances, the earliest arrivals were religious congregations seeking respite from persecution. Of all the colonies, those having aristocratic and bigoted tendencies were least tolerant, but none were more so than Massachusetts and Connecticut, where Puritanism had become entrenched. Rhode Island, on the other hand, allowed complete religious freedom. Barbados, "then in the heyday of its prosperity," was the principal stopping point for Quakers en route from England to the North American Colonies.[11] The first Quakers to land on American soil were women, Mary Fisher and Ann Austin, who arrived in Boston in July, 1656.[12]

The dislike for Quakers by strict Puritans in Massachusetts is nowhere more evident than the following enactment of October, 1656:

> Whereas, there is a cursed sect of *heretics* lately risen up in the world, which are commonly called Quakers, who take upon them to be immediately sent of God, and infallibly assisted by the Spirit, to speak and write blasphemous opinions, despising government, and the order of God in the Church and Commonwealth, speaking evil of dignitaries, reproaching and reviling magistrates and ministers, seeking to turn the people from the faith, and gain proselytes in their pernicious ways . . .

The law went on to provide punishments for ship masters bringing in "blasphemous heretics"; banishing Quakers from the colony; importing or concealing "Quaker books or writings concerning their devilish opinions"; anyone who defends "the heretical opinions of the

Quakers, or any of their books or papers"; or reviling "the persons of magistrates or ministers, as is usual with the Quakers." Among the penalties imposed were banishment, fines, imprisonment and whippings.[13]

Among Fox's travels outside the British Isles, the most rigorous and significant were to the West Indies and North America. His trip began in 1671 and ended in 1673. Fox and his traveling companions stopped at Barbados and Jamaica, then headed for the nearest American colonies, but not before burying their intrepid companion, Elizabeth Hooton, in Jamaica. It was she with whom Fox had affiliated early in his ministry. The party traveled by horseback and boat through several colonies, preaching as they went to Indians as well as others, despite weather, primitive roads, bridges, and amenities. Their visits, though primarily religious in character, had considerable political significance for the sparsely-settled colonists surrounded by wilderness.

Of the New England colonies, Rhode Island was the mecca for religious dissenters. Roger Williams (1603-1689), a Baptist and protégé of the renowned jurist Sir Edward Coke, had gone to Boston in 1631 and served as teacher and minister in nearby communities. Strong-minded and outspoken, he expressed radical religious and political views, for which he was banished from Massachusetts Bay Colony by the oligarchic Puritans then in control. He settled nearby in what became Rhode Island. A land-grant issued in 1644 by England and reaffirmed as a royal colony in 1663, made him Founder and guaranteed absolute liberty of conscience.

That haven of freedom welcomed not only radical Baptists but also such unpopular religionists as Quakers and Jews. Moreover, Williams was a trusted friend of the Indians, despite their restiveness which culminated in the French and Indian War (1699-1763). The chief obstacle for Quakers was their objection to continuous preparations for war, but they nevertheless settled in considerable numbers and adapted. Indeed, Rufus Jones reported that "for more than a hundred years Quakers were continually in office, and for thirty-six terms the Government of the Colony was occupied by members of the Society."[14] The Founder himself had been elected Governor in 1654 and served three terms.

Despite Williams' liberal inclinations, he disliked Quakers, perhaps for reasons similar to those of his co-religionist John Bunyan. Anticipating Fox's arrival, a formal debate was planned, but he felt compelled to depart before the date scheduled. Meanwhile, Williams prepared an agenda which included fourteen propositions, examples of which were:

The people called Quakers are not true *Quakers* according to holy scriptures.

They (the Quakers) do not own (believe in) the holy scriptures.

The people called Quakers (in effect) hold no God, no Christ, no Angel, no Devil, no Resurrection, no Judgment, no Heaven, no Hell, but what is in man.

The Quaker Religion is more obstructive and destructive to the conversion and salvation of the souls of people than most religions this day extant in the world.

The sufferings of Quakers are no true evidence of the Truth of their religion.[15]

Great crowds gathered for the debates lasting four days. Leading Quakers—John Stubbs, John Burnyeat, and William Edmundson—battled elderly Williams. The current Colonial Governor served as moderator. Williams' tactics infuriated his opponents and Quaker retorts were equally vituperative. In retrospect, many of the issues seem petty and much of the discussion ill-tempered, but such debates among religious groups were then common and quite popular. This one, however, may have been the first in the New England area involving only two major religious bodies.[16] Following those debates, both contestants published their views: Williams entitled his *George Fox Digged Out of the Burrowes* while Fox preferred *A New England Firebrand Quenched*.

Fox made two other trips abroad, the first to Holland and Germany in 1677, the other to Holland seven years later. Of the dozen or so who joined the party, Fox was the leader and assigned tasks. The other most prominent companions were William Penn, Robert Barclay (Urie), Isabel (Fell) Yeamans and George Keith, whose wife assisted members of the party. Their objectives were to become acquainted with kindred spirits, preach whenever possible, assist Monthly, Quarterly and Yearly Meetings, plead for help in moderating persecution at home and abroad, and establish a base in Central Europe for future missionary activities.

Their spirits were buoyed when Penn, Barclay and perhaps others visited Elizabeth, Princess of the Palatinate, a granddaughter of King James the First of England and cousin of Robert Barclay. She welcomed her guests graciously and talked at length about Quakerism despite its unpopularity among Catholics and members of other faiths in that vicinity. She never married, was deeply interested in religion, spiritually inclined and impressed with Quakers' emphasis upon the inwardness of Christ and tenderness toward mankind, although she never became a member of that faith. Fascinating correspondence followed between herself, Fox, Penn and Barclay until shortly before her death in 1680. Rufus M. Jones said of her she was "a combination of philosopher and saint." She might also have been the first to interest Penn in colonizing New Jersey and Pennsylvania.

The second trip to Holland in 1684 was shorter and the party smaller. The principal reasons for going there were to attend Yearly Meeting, check up on developments and feature Fox, whose fame was by that time legendary and his health fragile. Fox also made contacts with Jews, hoping thereby to enlist their support for Quaker objectives.

Altogether, Penn made three trips to the Continent, the last in 1686. Speaking of results, William I. Hull had this to say:

> The fruits of these visits were not many converts to Quakerism, but many thousands of colonists in America, where the Dutch Quakers founded Germantown in 1683, and the German religious exiles settled far and wide in Pennsylvania. The great migrations of Germans to Pennsylvania began in the year 1709 . . .[17]

Many other Quakers traveled widely; indeed, some went as far as Russia, Turkey, Egypt, Jerusalem and China. More would have done likewise had they not been denied passage by ships' captains. Their intentions were to persuade any and all who would listen, including kings and other potentates. As persecution intensified, large numbers either visited or settled permanently in North America.

Meanwhile, the slavery issue made its appearance. Negro slaves were introduced in North America via Virginia in 1619. Humanitarians protested, but it was not until 1714 that Pennsylvania forbade such trade. Penn, though nearing death, had the satisfaction of knowing his colony was among the first to outlaw a practice he detested. Despite that effort, 4,000 slaves were brought to the colony in 1730; mostly by English, Welsh and Scotch-Irish owners. Those numbers increased to about 10,000 by 1790.[18]

It was German Mennonites mentioned above who first admonished Quakers for holding slaves. Daniel K. Cassell explains what happened:

> On the 18th of April, 1688, Gerhard Hendrick, Dirk Op den Graeff, Francis Daniel Pastorius and Abraham Op den Graeff sent to the Friends' Meeting the first public protest ever made on this continent against the holding of slaves. A little rill there started which further on became an immense torrent, and whenever thereafter men trace analytically the causes which led to Shiloh, Gettysburg and Appomattox, they will begin with the tender consciences of the linen weavers and husbandmen of Germantown.

The author went on to say, the protest was forwarded to the nearby Friends Meeting and then to the Yearly Meeting, but "To the Quakers belong the credit of having successfully carried the work further, also the same for witchcraft."[19] The Yearly Meeting's approval occurred in 1696.

As stated above, the first Quakers to land on American soil were women, Mary Fisher and Ann Austin, both of whom had sailed from Barbados to Boston Bay, arriving in July, 1656. The population of Massachusetts was then about 21,000 and Boston had become the principal municipality in that region. The latter was governed by an elective "General Court" consisting of twelve able but bigoted Puritans, chosen at town meetings, a form of local government since cherished in New England.

The two ladies were promptly suspected of heresy, fined, searched from head to toe for evidence of "witchcraft," and after five weeks of imprisonment, banished to the West Indies from whence they had come. Returning to England, their ministry continued but Ann Austin's labors were shortened by London's horrible Bubonic Plague of 1665. She was buried at Bunhill Fields, London's first Quaker burial place.

As other Quakers arrived in Boston, they too were treated harshly by members of the General Court. Some chose banishment but others

153

preferred to rely upon God and passive resistance, as did Jesus. Marmaduke Stevenson was the first Quaker hanged on Boston Commons; then followed William Robinson, Mary Dyer and William Leddra, a resident of Barbados but formerly a native of England. Of the last three, the two men were Quakers and Dyer was an Antinomian who believed that faith alone was necessary for salvation. Both Robinson and Dyer had been spared previously at the last moment and banished from the colony. Upon reflection, however, they chose to return to Boston and suffer martyrdom.

Those four hangings alarmed Fox and other Quakers, whereupon they intervened with recently-restored Charles II. The King was receptive and dispatched the famous "King's Missive" to all colonial governors ordering the release of Quakers then imprisoned or sentenced to death. The expectation was that such persons would be sent back to England for readjudication, but with persecution raging there, the criminal justice system overloaded and Quakers strenuously resisting, that requirement had little effect. Of the twenty-eight Quakers released in Boston, one of them—Wenlock Christison—was spared from hanging.

Rufus M. Jones, reflecting upon that historic event, gave this report:

> The authorities of the Colonies had . . . anticipated royal interposition and had already changed their policy of dealing with the Quakers, but nonetheless this "missive" from the King marks an epoch in the history of colonial Puritans. They might congratulate Charles the Second . . . but in their hearts they knew that a dangerous turn of the tide had set in, and that the enemy of their faith [Charles II] and their ideals was now their sovereign. They no longer had behind them the great moral and spiritual England of the Commonwealth, and they were never again to have an entirely free hand in working out their lofty vision of a New England, which in their dreams was to be a New Jerusalem—a Republic of the Saints of God. They had fought their Armageddon and it was a drawn battle. It was now unmistakably evident that the Colony must henceforth be *shared* with these unwelcome Quaker guests.[20]

The Missive was not only a "godsend" for Quakers and kindred spirits, but also a prelude to spectacular colonization opportunities that lay ahead.

After the youthful Stuarts, Charles and James, fled from England to Western Europe because of their father's execution, they soon became aware of the machinations going on within Royal Courts, wars and commercial rivalries, especially those involving North America. Meanwhile, settlements were established in the West Indies and along the North American Atlantic coast, not only by England but also by Spain, France, The Netherlands and Sweden. Data bearing upon England's North American colonies are shown on the following chart:

COLONIAL GOVERNMENT	NAME AND FOUNDER	DATE FOUNDED
CHARTER (SELF GOVERNING)		
Governors chosen by freemen for 1-year term.	Rhode Island, Roger Williams Grantor: Charles I	1636
Legislature bicameral: both houses elected by freemen for 1-year terms.	Connecticut, Emigrants from Massachusetts Grantor: Charles I	1636
Judges appointed by governor in council.		
Crown could not veto laws, but cases could be appealed from highest colonial court to King in Council.		
PROPRIETARY		
Proprietor owned colony but acknowledged sovereignty of King of England	Maryland, Lord Baltimore Grantor: Charles I	1634
Governor appointed by proprietor	Delaware, Swedes Grantor: Charles I	1638
Legislature bicameral (except in Pennsylvania). Upper house appointed by proprietor, lower house elected by freemen. Laws (except those of Maryland) were subject to approval and veto by Crown. Judges appointed by Governor and Council. Appeals could be taken to King in Council.	Pennsylvania, William Penn Grantor: Charles II	1681

Crown controlled directly by commissions and instructions to colonial government	Virginia, London Company Grantor: Charles I	1607
Governor appointed by Crown and acted as King's deputy. Legislature bicameral (except in Georgia). Upper house appointed by King, lower house elected by freemen. Upper house acted as Governor's Council. All laws subject to approval and veto by Crown.	New York, Duke of York Grantor: Charles II	1664
	New Jersey, Berkeley and Carteret Grantor: Charles II	1664
Judges appointed by Governor. Appeals could be taken to King in Council.	North Carolina, a separate colony Became a royal colony Grantor: George II	1712 1729
	South Carolina, a separate colony but later a royal colony Grantor: George II	1719 1729
	Georgia, James Oglethorpe and 19 associates Grantor: George II	1732

NOTE: Government data are approximate.

When the Restoration occurred in 1660, England and New Netherlands were rival powers, both of whom had extensive land holdings in North America. They fought a costly war in 1662-1667 which effectively terminated Dutch rule, not only in what had been New Netherlands but also in a former Swedish colony located on the left bank of the Delaware River. The Swedes had settled there in 1638 and purchased land on both sides of the river. John Printz became Governor of New Sweden and established himself on an island later known as Tinnicum, located near present-day New Castle. Surrounded by friendly Indians, Lutheran missionaries were the first to introduce them to Christianity.

All that came to naught, however, in 1655 when the Dutch dispatched an armada of seven vessels with several hundred men, who not only destroyed the fortresses but also "laid waste the houses and plantations, killing the cattle and plundering the inhabitants of every thing they could lay hands on."[21] Officers and prisoners were returned to New Amsterdam while the Dutch remained in possession of the area. The inhabitants surrendered peaceably and ended "the only colony Sweden had ever possessed."[22] The defeated colonists were either absorbed by England or transported to Europe. English armed forces avenged that assault in 1664, thereby reaffirming England's claim south of what became Philadelphia.

The Dutch Reformed Church (of Presbyterian persuasion) was one of several institutions seriously affected by the Stuart victory. Ironically, it had zealously persecuted nonconformists, including Quakers, while Continental Holland was at that time extraordinarily tolerant.[23] The church mentioned lost establishment status, but it still survives in New York City.

Colonizing East and West New Jersey

Having defeated the Dutch, Charles II granted a royal charter to his brother, the Duke of York, dated March 20, 1664. Thereupon the Duke conveyed what became New Jersey to Lord John Berkeley and Sir George Carteret, who were friends of the Stuarts. The grants were:

> Bounded on the east part of the main sea, and part by Hudson's River, and hath upon the west of Delaware Bay or river and extendeth southward to the main ocean as far as Cape May at the mouth of the Delaware Bay, and to the northward as far as the northernmost branch of said bay or river of Delaware, which is in forty-one degrees and forty minutes of latitude, and worketh over thence in a strait line to Hudson's river—which said tract of land is hereafter to be called by the name, or names of Nova Cesarea, or New Jersey.[24]

Upon receiving those lands, the proprietors framed the first constitution, which, among other features, provided for equal privileges and freedom of conscience. Philip Carteret (1639-1682), a cousin of Sir George Carteret, arrived from England in 1665 to become Governor. Elizabethtown became the capital, land was bought from the Indians and efforts were made to entice settlers. That constitution remained effective until the Dutch were vanquished. Another one was adopted in 1675 and a year later New Jersey was divided into East and West New Jersey.

Complicating those developments were the high-handed tactics employed by Major Edmund Andrus (1637-1747). He was then Governor of New York, serving on behalf of the Duke of York. Later, as Captain General and Governor in Chief, he ruled the consolidated colonies and while doing so diminished the authority of each of them until James II was deposed. Thereupon he was imprisoned briefly in England, after which he became Governor of Virginia and Guernsey, one of England's Channel Islands lying southwest of France.

The division of New Jersey prompted lengthy boundary disputes. George Keith, a Quaker and close friend of Robert Barclay and William Penn, was at that time Surveyor General and ran the first boundary line diagonally from Little Egg Harbor, located southeasterly along the Atlantic coast, to what is now the Delaware River Gap. That line proved to be highly controversial and several attempts were made to satisfy critics, but as a practical matter its relevance diminished when the two Jerseys reunited, as mentioned below. That point turned out to be well above the Gap near where Northeastern Pennsylvania, New York and New Jersey coincided (40° 41'). It, too, was controversial until adjudicated much later. Similar disputes arose over the northeastern borders between New Jersey and the upper reaches of the Hudson River.[25]

In 1685, Quakers bought Carteret's share and persuaded governmental officials to establish an organization entitled "The Board of Proprietors of the Eastern Division of New Jersey," popularly known as "Twenty-Four Proprietors." Penn initiated that project and Robert Barclay, the Apologist, served as Governor in absentia for life. Thomas Rudyard, a London merchant, became the first secretary. The Proprietors needed large sums of money from land sales and other sources, if for no other reason than to pay off personal debts and help resettle Quakers impoverished by persecution. Penn was particularly interested in having Barclay, a Scotsman, involved inasmuch as there were many of his nationality living in areas which were poor. Even land was often given to poverty-stricken people. Circumstances were such that the Scottish proprietors dominated the Board. Indeed, there were five Scotsmen, all of whom played prominent roles, and two others—Governor Robert Barclay and Surveyor General George Keith—were of the same nationality.[26]

Additional details were provided in the Board's minutes:

The journal consists of 168 folio pages commencing on April 9, 1685 and ending October 27, 1705, in which as separate meetings were held, counting successive days, of which there were 50 such sessions. According to the resolution passed in March, 1685, the council met monthly until March of the following year, each meeting having been a two-day session. Thereafter, meetings were held every two months until March 10, 1686 when monthly sessions were resumed up to August 1687. Gatherings were convened on the second Tuesday of each month until the Revolution of 1688. When there was no government in the Province, no meetings of the Council of the Board were held between August 7, 1688 and December 1689. There was another lapse of two years and four months—between May 20, 1690 and September 16, 1692—during which time there were no meetings. Thereafter, sessions were called as occasions arose, the intervening intervals running from two to twenty-four months between meetings.

The Council held their sessions at Elizabeth until July 8, 1686, with the exception of an extraordinary one held at "Amboy Perth" on November 27, 1685. Thereafter, all such gatherings were held in the capitol of the Province.[27]

Altogether, there were fifty two-day sessions spread out over twenty years. Five members attended all sessions; the others did so when possible; the average was eight. Governor Barclay died after serving only five years. Royalty, the Colonial Governor and other high officials appeared occasionally. Lord Neil Campbell or one of his heirs presided. John Barclay, a brother of the Governor, was one of those who attended all sessions. Most members were rewarded with land dividends for services rendered, the first in 1692 with 10,000 acres, the second in 1698 with 5,000 acres, and the third in 1672 with 2,500 acres. An additional 1,000-acre dividend was given to each following a purchase made by Indians.[28] The Board held its last meeting in 1705 but surrendered its powers three years before that date, whereupon the two Jerseys were reunited and became a royal colony of the usual type. The Board's demise was caused by too many proprietors, confusing land titles, poor administration, excessive division of shares, resentment over Board authority and disturbances in both provinces.

As East New Jersey got underway, West New Jersey developed more slowly because of distance and isolation. Moreover, Berkeley was growing old and disillusioned, due chiefly to his inability to collect quitrents. With William Penn as mediator, John Fenwick and Edward Byllinge, both of whom were Quakers, bought Berkeley's shares. They and other Friends were the first to arrive in Western New Jersey on an English ship via the Delaware Bay and River. They docked in 1675 near what became the semi-independent town of Salem, which also served as the seat of government until Burlington became the capital two years later.

Burlington was situated on the Delaware River, twenty miles northeast of where Philadelphia would soon be located. Penn would later establish *Pennsbury Manor* across the river, near what is now the Borough of Bristol. Penn also assisted in drafting a constitution for West New Jersey which anticipated those of Pennsylvania and Delaware. Fundamental to those charters were principles which their framers hoped would end tyranny and ensure more freedom than ever before, especially of religion and conscience. Penn knew those principles well from experience and reading such polemicists as James Harrington and John Locke.[29] It was those precepts which accounted for the harmonious relationships between Quakers and Indians. They also help explain why West New Jersey was the first Quaker colony ever to exist.

Meanwhile, in 1676, Byllinge and a host of other signifiers adopted a new constitution entitled "The Concessions and Agreements of the Proprietors, Freeholders, and Inhabitants of the Province of New Jersey, in America." Penn was one of those who played a leading role. The divisional line agreed upon was stated as follows:

> We have all that side of Delaware River from one end to the other; the line of partition is from the east side of Little Egg Harbor, straight north through the country, to the utmost branch of the Delaware River; with all powers, privileges, and immunities whatsoever. Ours is called *New West Jersey;* his is called *New East Jersey.*[30]

Great care was taken to conform that document with the fundamental laws of England, including such provisions as religious freedom and

160

jury trial with the right to challenge. Indeed, never before had an English colony been granted such a panoply of democratic rights and privileges. That achievement anticipated the Glorious Revolution of 1688 by more than a decade.

Such impressive support, followed by widely-circulated publicity, prompted many Quakers, as well as others, to emigrate and purchase as much land, as five-to-ten thousand acres per buyer. Approximately 875,000 acres were purchased by the time Proprietor Penn arrived in 1681.[31] Many of those landowners became influential not only in farming and business but also in politics and Yearly Meeting affairs. Indeed, the latter two were often indistinguishable.

William Penn's relationships with Charles II and the Duke of York were such that all three of them were interested in lands formerly claimed by the Dutch in North America. Charles owed a debt of £16,000 to the deceased Admiral Penn for provisioning his fleet. That obligation was satisfied in 1681 when son William, sole heir of his father, was granted the huge colony west of the Delaware River, which would soon become Pennsylvania.

Colonizing Pennsylvania

Charles II signed Penn's Charter on March 4, 1681, after lengthy discussion with the Privy Council for the Trade and Plantations, otherwise known as the "Lords of Trade." Both legal and policy matters were taken into account, including poorly defined and controversial boundaries. The charter resembled those of medieval times, modified to assure firmer control of colonial affairs. Religiously inclined as he was, Penn included such standards as toleration, morals, justice and brotherly love. Moreover, the large numbers of criminal offenses formerly punishable by death were reduced to two: murder and treason.[32] Furthermore, the Charter had "the first amending clause in any written constitution."[33]

After receiving his charter, Penn finished writing the First Frame of Government, prefaced by remarks which are still widely read and admired, an abstract of which is quoted below. Before Penn left England, the Duke of York added Delaware to Penn's Charter, primarily to assure access via the Delaware River to the Atlantic Ocean. Penn's triumphal landing at New Castle, Delaware on October 27, 1682 marked the beginning of a new era, not only for the Quakers' "Holy Experiment," but also for western expansion. Shortly thereafter, the

161

First General Assembly met at Chester, located a short distance southwest of Philadelphia. Much of that assembly's time was devoted to enacting sumptuary legislation, designed to regulate habits and morals, as required by provisions of Penn's Charter detailed below. Robert Proud listed sixty-one such statutes in his famous history.[34]

Upon Penn's arrival there were countless official and personal duties demanding attention, including discontented Delawarans. A major irritation was their subordination to the more numerous Pennsylvanians in the General Assembly. Fueling those sentiments were Quakers' novel beliefs and peculiarities thought to be "queer," "radical" and lacking in experience. The latter was undoubtedly true because of their apolitical approach to secular government, over which Jesus said Caesar had jurisdiction. The subordination issue changed radically in 1701 when Delaware's legislature was granted full responsibility for its actions.[35]

More serious were intractable disputes over boundaries and related issues which the Duke of York and Penn hoped to avoid. Lord Baltimore, the Proprietor of Maryland, was also concerned and became the spokesman for Delaware's colonists as well as his own. Negotiations were complicated for several reasons, including early Dutch and Swedish claims; erroneous topographic surveys and the meandering character of the Delaware River, which restricted heavy vessels to deep channels. Moreover, interruptions along the Atlantic coast by pirates and other enemy ships were constant hazards. All three of those colonies and also New Jersey considered these issues vital to their survival and welfare. Delaware's legal status remained flawed until 1776 when, upon recommendation of the Continental Congress, a modified constitution was adopted in 1792, but neither it nor the preceding one was submitted to the voters for approval.[36]

Throughout the colonial period, Pennsylvania's government consisted of a proprietor, a governor, who was either the proprietor himself or his deputy; an executive council; a one-house general assembly; courts of law and local governments established by statutory enactments. The first seventy-two councilmen were chosen by voters. As the number of people and counties grew, the council proposed and the assembly determined apportionment ratios and district boundaries. The general assembly was limited to not more than 500. As mentioned above, the first one met at Chester; the date was December 4–7, 1682.

Altogether, there were five frames of government: the first in 1682; the second in 1683; the third in 1692; the fourth in 1696 (also known as the "Markham Frame"); and the fifth, known as the Charter of Privileges, in 1701, which served the colony until the American Revolution in 1776. All of those were similar in many respects, despite inevitable bickering and factional rivalries.[37] Penn was present on two occasions: in 1683 and 1701. A religious test was required of candidates for public offices, all of whom had to profess belief in Jesus Christ. Moreover, only freemen were eligible to vote.

Despite Penn's eagerness to resolve the southeastern boundary controversy, progress was slow, due largely to legal ambiguities within the respective charters and Lord Baltimore's strong support for a planning device known as a "Twelve Mile Circle." Speaking of that device, Harry Emerson Wildes had this to say:

> The circle boundary, unique in America except for three or four Tennessee counties, was the subject of litigation between Delaware and New Jersey for more than two centuries. Delaware contended that the deeds to Berkeley and Carteret extended only "to the river," which to Delaware meant the eastern bank. By this interpretation, all fishing and navigation rights within that portion of the river included within the Twelve Mile Circle belonged to Delaware. Eventually the United States Supreme Court upheld the Delaware contention.[38]

When Penn (whose wife remained in England) and other Quakers sailed up Delaware Bay aboard the *Welcome,* it docked at New Castle, Delaware, a short distance south of where Philadelphia would soon be situated. Penn was then in his late thirties and well acquainted with proprietary government as it had developed in New Jersey, Maryland and Delaware, but never before had he held such an exalted office as the one detailed in his Charter. Speaking generally of the American colonial charters, they were not only respectful of "Almighty God" but also conformed to political expectations inherited from the medieval past. How prestigious Penn's status was is suggested by these quaint and florid words and phrases:

> Charles the Second by the Grace of God, King of *England,* Scotland, France and Ireland, Defender of the

163

Faith, Etc. Our Trustie and well-beloved Subject William Penn, Esquire, Sonne and heir of Sir William Penn deceased, out of a commendable Desire to enlarge our *British* Empire, and promote such useful commodities as may be of Benefit to us and our Dominions, as also to reduce the savage Natives by gentle and just manners to the Love of Civil Societie and Christian Religion hath humbly besought leave of Us to transport an ample Colonie unto a certaine Countrie hereafter described, in the Parties of *America* not yet cultivated and planted. . . [39]

Proceeding on the premises set forth by St. Paul, Penn prefaced his first frame of government with these extracts:

I do not find a model in the world, that time, place and some singular emergencies have not necessarily altered; nor is it easy to frame a civil government, that shall serve all places alike. I know what is said by the several admirers of *monarchy,* which are the rule of one, a few, and many, and are the three common ideas of government, when men discourse on the subject. But I chose to solve the controversy with this small distinction, and it belongs to all three: *Any government is free to the people under it* (whatever the frame) *where the laws rule, and the people are a party to those laws,* and more than this is tyranny, oligarchy, or confusion . . .

Governments, like clocks, go from the motion men give them; and as governments are made and moved by men, so by them are ruined too. Wherefore more governments rather depend upon men, than men upon governments. Let men be good, and the government cannot be bad; if it be ill, they will cure it. But, if men be bad, let the government be never so good, they will endeavor to warp and spoil it to their turn. [40]

Hinged upon goodness and badness, Penn's famous *Preface* was much too simplistic and subjective for easy institutionalization. Equally important were knowledge, judgment, experience and wisdom. Indeed, anarchy and tyranny, like death, have been ever-present threats to civil governance, even among well-intentioned subjects or citizens, as witnessed by the Nazi Holocaust of recent times.

Penn's Charter mentioned the "Grace of God" and passing references to a Divine Being, but the term "Quaker" is unmentioned. Relying upon God, the Charter stipulated that a long list of statutory offenses mentioned above be enacted by the colonial legislature. That list included the following:

> All such offenses against God, as swearing, cursing, lying, prophane talking, drunkenness, drinking of healths, obscene words, incest, sodomy, rapes, whoredom, fornication, and other uncleanness (not to be repeated) all treasons, misprisons, murders, duels, felony, seditions, maimes, forcible entries, and other violences, to the persons and estates of the inhabitants within this province; all prizes, stage-plays, cards, dice, May-games, gamesters, masques, revels, bull-baitings, cock-fightings, bear-baitings, and the like, which excite the people to rudeness, cruelty, looseness, and irreligion, shall be respectfully discouraged, and severely punished, according to the appointment of the Governor and freemen in provincial Council and General Assembly; as also all proceedings contrary to these laws, that are not here made expressly penal.[41]

While in Pennsylvania, Penn quickly discovered that factionalism was rampant over such fundamental issues as individual rights versus the proprietary principle which was essentially autocratic. Speaking of that difference, Frederick Tolles reported:

> As two major parties assumed definite form, their social basis became clearly apparent. Both were Quaker parties and both sincerely professed allegiance to the principles of Whiggism, but the familiar political process of fission was taking place. Friends were dividing into a radical "country party," led by the brilliant and somewhat unscrupulous lawyer David Lloyd, and a conservative party dominated by city merchants under the leadership of the Proprietor's secretary, James Logan (1674-1751). A third party, composed chiefly of Anglicans, was begin-

ning to emerge, but it was overshadowed by the two Quaker factions and was not to figure importantly in Pennsylvania politics for several decades to come.[42]

There were, however, positive achievements for Penn to dwell upon as he left for London during the summer of 1684. Heading that list was an imaginative comprehensive plan for Philadelphia developed by Thomas Holme which at that time was a novelty. Also notable was the "Great Treaty" agreed upon with the Lanape Indians signed at Shackamaxon, which is now part of Philadelphia. Although mystery still surrounds that document, it has since symbolized early Quakerism at its best.

Another memorable event was Penn's prayer for his colony abbreviated here:

> My love and life is to you, and with you; and no water can quench it, nor distance wear it out, or bring it to an end: I have been with you, cared over you, and served you with unfeigned love; and you are beloved of me, beyond utterance. I bless you, in the name and power of the Lord. . . . Oh, now you are come to a quiet land, provoke not the Lord to trouble it: And now liberty and authority are with you, and in your hands; let the government be upon his shoulders, in all your spirits; that you may rule for him, under whom the princes of this world will one day esteem it their honor to govern and serve, in their place. . . . And, thou, *Philadelphia,* the virgin settlement of this province, named before thou wert born, what love, what care, what service, and what travail has there been, to bring thee forth. And preserve thee from such as would abuse and defile thee! . . . My soul prays to God for thee.[43]

Penn's departure, after a stay of about twenty-two months, was a disillusioning blow for not only himself and family but also the fledgling colony. At that time, the number of Friends in Philadelphia was about 1,100, by 1690 there were an estimated 2,200 Friends in the province and by 1760 the last mentioned figure had grown to about 12,922.[44] Meanwhile Quakers had become a minority of total population.

166

While in Pennsylvania and immediately afterward, Penn recognized that additional sources of revenue were desperately needed, not only for the colony but also himself. The expectation had been that quitrents would meet essential needs, but experience showed they were widely disliked and difficult to collect. With that in mind, Penn appointed a Deputy Governor, the former John Blackwell. Although a non-Friend, he was well known by Penn; he had been a cavalry officer formerly associated with Oliver Cromwell and presently a businessman temporarily situated in Boston. Impressed by those credentials and his accessibility, Blackwell was appointed on July 12, 1688, a circumstance which produced a fiasco, not only because of his military background but also because of the bungling way the appointment was made. Spurned by his colleagues, including the Colonial Assembly, Blackwell exchanged his Deputyship for Receiver General (a Quitrent Treasurer), a post which he held briefly and surrendered in disgust. His lack of tact was a contributing factor.

That imbroglio was not only embarrassing but it also intensified rivalries which Penn deplored. Speaking of those, Harry Emerson Wildes made these provocative observations:

> Royalists opposed Penn's partisans; Anglicans attacked Quakers; farmers disliked city folk; national minorities— Germans, Welsh, Irish, Swedes, and Dutch—quarreled with one another, though all ganged up against the English. Everyone, of course, made matters difficult for tax collectors. Vice and corruption were rampant; criminals terrorized the towns; pirates ruled the waterfronts. Brotherly love had vanished. Unless Penn acted quickly and decisively, the Holy Experiment was a failure. Or so, at least, ran the hysterical reports.[45]

Although widely perceived as a wealthy person, Penn was often indiscreet where money matters were involved. A contributing factor was his underestimation of quitrent-income which steadily dwindled after 1682.[46] Having made that mistake, he dealt more firmly with persons charged with responsibility for such matters.

Moreover, both he and his lovely wife, Gulielma, who was personally well-to-do, had a penchant for elegant living. Their principal home in England, known as *Worminghurst,* was located about fifty miles south of London and exemplified their life-style. It was of ancient vintage and spacious enough to accommodate their growing family, distinguished guests, relatives and servants. Their *Pennsbury Manor,* located twenty-four miles north of Philadelphia also displayed splendor. The estate consisted of several thousand acres of forested land accessible chiefly by boat up and down the Delaware River, although much of the time Penn and other members of the family lived in commodious housing within Philadelphia. Aides were plentiful, among whom were both indentured white servants and black slaves, all of whom were later set free. The *Manor* disintegrated gradually after the Penns ceased living there; it was, however, beautifully restored by the Pennsylvania Historical and Museum Commission during the mid-1900s. Following Gulielma's death, Penn and his second wife, Hanna, lived spaciously at several locations; the final one, named *Ruscome,* at Reading in the Berkshires. Generally speaking, the homes mentioned were quite large and tastefully appointed, but not necessarily extravagant.

Penn's Relationship with Royal Monarchs

Sir William Penn's relationships with both restored Stuarts, Charles II and James, then Duke of York, were friendly despite his former allegiance to, and collaboration with, Oliver Cromwell. Son William was at that time 16, Charles was 30 and the Duke 27.

Much later, in 1688-89, after William and Mary had ascended the throne, Penn was accused of Jacobitism and treason inasmuch as he had previously been a close friend of the deposed King James. Little is known about the details of that trial, but Penn's imprisonment lasted less than two weeks. At stake was his estate and imprisonment for life. Frightened by those prospects, Penn turned to his trusted agent, Philip Ford, for fail-safe insurance provided at considerable expense.[47]

Embarrassed though Penn was by those accusations, he sought advice from London Yearly Meeting in May, 1689, and received this response:

> Walk wisely and circumspectly toward all men, in the peaceable Spirit of Christ Jesus, giving no offense nor occasions to those in outward government, nor way to any controversies, heats or distractions of this world, about the kingdoms thereof. But pray for the good of all;

and submit all to that Divine power and wisdom which rules over the kingdoms of men. That, as the Lord's hidden ones and wise in heart, who know when and where to keep silent, you may all approve your hearts to God; keeping out of all airy discourses and words, that may always become snares, or hurtful to Friends, as being sensible that any personal occasion of reproach causes a reflection upon the body.[48]

Following Penn's release, his charter was revoked for a period of six years (1688-1694) and not fully restored until five years later. During that period Pennsylvania was annexed to the Crown Colony of New York, the Governor of which was Benjamin Fletcher. That action probably had little to do with the criminal charges leveled against Penn, but more likely it was due to rivalries between England, France and associated European coalitions, variously known as King William's War and the French and Indian War. At stake was domination of North America. That contest lasted for seventy-two years.

Although Penn was in royal disfavor, he nevertheless kept in touch with confidants, one of whom was George Fox, who was then quite ill and died shortly thereafter in January, 1691, when about sixty-six years of age. Penn's eulogy, published four years later in the original edition of Fox's *Journal*, included these comments:

Thus he lived and sojourned among us; and as he lived, so he died; feeling the same eternal power, that had raised and preserved him, in his last moments. So full of assurance was he that he triumphed over death; and so even to the last, as if death were hardly worth notice or a mention; recommending to some with him the dispatch and dispersion of an epistle just before written to the Churches of Christ throughout the world, and his own books; but, above all, Friends, and of all Friends, those in Ireland and America, twice over saying "Mind poor Friends in Ireland and America." And to some that came in and inquired how he found himself, he answered, "Never heed, the Lord's power is over all weakness and death; the Seed reigns, blessed by the Lord!" which was about four or five hours before his departure out of this world.[49]

During the period just reviewed, Penn had not only serious political problems but also domestic. His beloved Gulielma died in 1694, whereupon he married Hanna Callowhill, who was then about thirty years of age. Both spouses had heirs who might have become Pennsylvania proprietors, although that possibility ended when the American Declaration of Independence was signed in 1776.

At long last, Penn made his second visit to Pennsylvania in 1699, accompanied by Hanna, who had already demonstrated her managerial talents and would later serve as Acting Governor during his declining years. His mental and physical health were still up to par, despite the vexatious trials and tribulations of recent years. That visit was his "last hurrah" as Proprietor and Governor.

Upon arrival, Penn was again impressed with the area's beauty and *Pennsbury Manor,* then nearing completion. He was also pleased with the generous welcome received and the region's development, but fundamentally serious problems remained, such as disputes over demands emanating from London, bickering over land sales, intense partisanship, money shortages, the continuing Delaware Boundary controversy and the unresolved conflict between himself and the Fords, Philip and Bridget. Returning to London after nearly two years, Penn was again confronted with debts owed by the Fords, both of whom were Quakers. Penn had known Philip before his marriage to Gulielma and later engaged him to handle financial details. Penn was often careless about such matters and, in retrospect, relied too heavily upon his assistant.

The Fords had earlier submitted an invoice totaling £75,000 for services rendered but later reduced it to £7,600, a sum which was lent to Penn by friends and secured by the Province of Pennsylvania. During those lengthy proceedings, Philip died and Quakers proffered arbitration but to no avail, whereupon Penn was forced to seek court protection and report occasionally at Fleet Prison for about a year. That affair terminated in 1708, after two decades of sordid bickering, which may have contributed to his stroke four years later.

Penn died on July 30, 1718. Burial was at Jordans near other members of the family. He was the first of only two Quaker statesmen, although there were and have since been numerous distinguished men and women of that persuasion. The second was another Englishman, John Bright (1811-1889), champion of free trade, famous orator and statesman, opponent of the Crimean War and slavery during the American Civil War.

Before Penn had his stroke he and the Queen attempted to nego-
tiate selling the proprietorship, but that became impossible when
Penn's condition worsened, despite strenuous efforts on Hanna's part.
Upon his death the proprietorship was deeded to three sons, born of
Hanna: John, Richard and Thomas, none of whom became Quakers.
The first son listed became known as "John (the American)" because
he was the only one sired by Penn in that distant land. The other two
sons left grandsons, John and Thomas as sole proprietors and heirs.
Three other Penns served later as Lieutenant Governors, but John was
the only one who lived to celebrate the Fourth of July, 1776. Technically, however, it was not until the Treaty of Peace of 1783 that England's claims were legally terminated. The title for the original William Penn was simply "Proprietor" but when in Pennsylvania it became "Proprietor and Governor."

Altogether, members of the Penn families held prestigious offices
for 95 years. Meanwhile, officials charged with operating the provi-
sional government included Lieutenant Governors, Deputies, Presi-
dents of Council and Presiding Judges. Quakers held some of those
offices but by no means all of them, partly because of their religious
scruples. Terms of office were variable except for Proprietors; the
longest were ten and eight years. Terms of one, two and three were
quite common. William Keith had the distinction of serving as Lieutenant Governor on two non-consecutive occasions, one briefly, the
other for eight years.[50] Many of those officers were non-Quakers, a
circumstance which accounted for not only much contentiousness but
also the steady decline of Penn's "Holy Experiment."

Bickering among Pennsylvanians became increasingly intense
after William Penn's demise. Customarily, Quakers outnumbered
assemblymen of other faiths, but when the friendly Delaware Indians
allied themselves with French forces on the Western Frontier, most
Quaker members withdrew from the Assembly. Henceforth, Quakers
and other genuine pacifists were either punished severely or allowed
to perform humanitarian services, as explained by Rufus M. Jones:

> In the American War for Independence patriotic feelings
> were profoundly stirred. Many young Friends broke an-
> chor and were swept into war by the spirit of the times.
> The largest group of this type was in Philadelphia. A
> small group of Quaker patriots organized an independent
> Society, called the "Free Quakers." They renounced the

171

ancient testimony against war and claimed individual freedom in their relation to the State and to public life. The defection was, however, too small to affect very seriously the main body of Friends, and the little band itself found it impossible to maintain a separate existence on its somewhat anomalous basis. . . . By actual count of cases in the minutes of Monthly Meetings it appears that no less than four hundred members of Philadelphia Yearly Meeting were expelled for their participation in some form of military service during the Revolutionary period (1776-1783).[51]

As this chapter ends, Penn's message spoken more than three centuries ago is still honored by the following abstracts set forth in Pennsylvania's Declaration of Rights:[52]

Political Powers

All power is inherent in the people, and all free governments are founded on their authority and instituted for their peace, safety and happiness. For the advancement of these ends they have at all times, an inalienable and indefeasible right to alter, reform or abolish their government in such manner as they may think proper.

Religious Freedom

All men have a natural and indefeasible right to worship Almighty God according to the dictates of their own consciences; no man can of right be compelled to attend, erect or support any place of worship, or to maintain any ministry against his consent; no human authority can, in any case whatever, control or interfere with the rights of conscience, and no preference shall ever be given by law to any religious establishments or modes of worship.

NOTES

Foreword

[1]*The Development of Religious Toleration in England* (Cambridge: Harvard University Press, 4 vols., 1932-1938) III, pp. 176-177.

Chapter 1

[1]The Gospel of St. John: 17, 14-18.

[2]*The Inner Life of the Religious Societies of the Commonwealth* (London: Hodder and Stoughton, 1876), pp. 193-194.

[3]For those two books and others see: *Complete Works of John Bunyan,* edited by Henry Stebbing (George Olms Verlag, Hildeseim, New York; Johnson Reprint Corporation, New York, 4 vols, 1970).

[4]That tragic but heroic story is detailed in a small book written by the Reverend B. Richings and entitled: *Narrative of the Persecutions and Sufferings of the Two Martyrs, Robert Glover and Mrs. Lewis* (London: L. & G. Seeley, 3d ed., 1842). Brief accounts of several other martyrs from the Mancetter area are included.

[5]*George Fox and the Valiant Sixty* (London: Hamish Hamilton Ltd., 1975), p. 3.

[6]*Journal,* pp. 1-2, 71, 192.

[7]William Penn's Preface to the *Journal of George Fox* (1831 Ed., 2 Vols.), I, p. xxiv.

[8]*Ibid.,* pp. 48, 71.

[9]*Ibid,* p. 1.

[10]*Ibid.,* pp. 6, 673.

[11]T. Joseph Pickvance: *George Fox and the Purefeys* (London: Friends Historical Society, 1970), pp. 5, 26-27.

[12]*Ibid.,* p. 2.

[13]*Ibid.,* pp. 4-5.

[14]William C. Braithwaite: *The Beginnings of Quakerism* (London: Macmillan and Co., Limited, 1912), p. 30.

[15]*The General History of the Quakers* (English ed., 1696), p. 14. Croesce was a Dutch pastor but never a Quaker.

[16]William Sewel, *The History of the Rise, Increase and Progress of the Christian People Called Quakers* (New York: Baker and Crane, 2 vols, 1844) I, p. 20.

[17]Vol. VII, p. 561.

[18]*George Fox and the Valiant Sixty* (London: Hamish Hamilton, 1975), p. 5.

[19]*Journal*, p. 2.

[20]*Journal*, p. 3.

[21]*Op. Cit.*

[22]*Ibid.*, p. 7. See also the *Dictionary of National Biography*, Vol. XX, p. 118 (London: Macmillan & Co., 1889). This sketch of Fox was written by The Reverend Alexander Gordon.

[23]Eduard Bernstein: *Cromwell and Communism; Socialism and Democracy in the Great English Revolution* (New York: Schocken Books, 1963), p. 227.

[24]*Journal*, pp. 4-5.

[25]*Ibid.*, pp. 11-12. The exact date is unknown, but mid-1674 is a likely one.

[26]*Ibid.*, p. 21.

[27]Sewel, *op. cit.*, I, p. 28. The use of "professor" probably referred to persons professing their beliefs, not academics.

[28]Gerard Croesce: *The General History of the Quakers* (1696, part I, p. 37). This and other details mentioned were published by Emily Manners, with notes, etc., by Norma Penny under the title: *Elizabeth Hooton First Quaker Woman Preacher* (London: Headley Brothers, 1914), *passim*.

[29]*Journal*, p. 11.

[30]*Ibid.*

[31]*Op. cit.*, I, p. 26.

[32]*The Social Development of English Quakerism 1655-1755* (Cambridge, Mass.: Harvard University Press, 1969), p. 7.

[33]Further references to the group mentioned are scattered throughout this study. See the Index and the indispensable account of Rufus M. Jones: *Studies in Mystical Religion* (London: Macmillan and Co., 1923, *passim*.

[34]Chapters 2, 3.

174

[35]T. Canby Jones: *George Fox's Attitude Toward War* (Richmond, Indiana: Friends United Press, 1972), pp. 59-70.

[36]*Journal*, pp. 39-43.

[37]Act of Mary, st. 2, cap. 3; Braithwaite: *Beginnings, op. cit.,* pp. 133, 450; Barclay (Tottenham), *op. cit.,* pp. 269-270.

[38]For both accounts, see, *Journal*, pp. 40-45.

[39]The term "capital punishment" was well known at that time, but "pacifism" was not until 1905. The latter was a derivative of "pacific" which referred to a doctrine or belief that it is desirable and possible to settle international disputes by peaceful means. Presently, it suggests various forms of peaceable behavior including those stated in the Sermon on the Mount.

[40]*Journal*, p. 66; Sewel, I, p. 50.

[41]*Journal*, pp. 66-67.

[42]Which stated: "From whence came wars and fightings among you? Come they not hence, even of your lusts that war in your members?"

[43]*Ibid.*, p. 65.

[44]It is worth noting at this point that Gerard Croesce, a learned German Protestant well versed in Quakerism wrote an account of Fox's imprisonment at Derby which differs considerably from that quoted above, but there is no reference to it in the *Journal*. Croesce's book was first published in English in 1696, a year after Thomas Elwood's version of the *Journal* appeared. The latter benefitted from numerous revisions. An abbreviated citation of Croesce's book is: *The General History of the Quakers*. . . (London: printed by John Dunton, 1696). Some of the data used were supplied by William Sewel.

[45]*Ibid.*, p. 67.

Chapter 2

[1]F. W. Maitland: *The Constitutional History of England* (Cambridge: at the University Press, 1950), p. 341.

[2]James Brown Scott (Ed.): *The Classics of International Law* (New York: Oceana Publications, Inc., 3 vols., 1964).

[3]James Brown Scott (Ed.): *The Classics of International Law* (New York: Oceana Publications, Inc., 3 vols., 1964).

[4]Frederick B. Tolles and E. Gordon Alderfer: *The Witness of William Penn* (New York: The Macmillan Company, 1957), p. 138.

[5]*The Divine Right of Kings* (New York: Harper and Row, Torchbook edition, 1966), pp. 6-8. Perspective is provided by mentioning here that Archbishop Charles Ussher's calculations showed that creation, as detailed in the Book of Genesis, occurred in 4004 B.C. John Calvin's estimate was about 3500 B.C. Ussher's dates of other happenings are shown marginally throughout some Bibles. For his chronology see *Anales Veteris et Novi Testment* (2 vol., 1650-1654); C. R. Elrington and J. H. Todd (eds.): *Works* (17 vols., 1847-64); W. R. Wright: The *Ussher Memoirs* (1888). For the date mentioned by John Calvin see his *Institutes,* vol. II, p. 205. Recent scientific studies indicate that the earth is 4.5 billion years old (*The World Book Year Book,* Chicago, London, Sydney, Toronto, 1984), p. 322.

[6]Figgis: *op. cit.,* pp. 5-8.

[7]George H. Sabine: *Encyclopedia of the Social Sciences* (New York: The Macmillan Company, 1937, 8 vols.), VII, p. 328.

[8]John H. Ferguson and Dean E. McHenry: *The American System of Government* (New York: McGraw-Hill Book Company, 14th ed., 1981), pp. 484-485.

[9]Elliott Rose: *Cases of Conscience Alternatives Open to Recusants and Puritans under Elizabeth I and James I* (London: Cambridge University Press, 1975), pp. 11-22.

[10]Rose, *op. cit.,* pp. 13-14.

[11]*The Digger Movement in the Days of the Commonwealth* (London: Holland Press & Merlin Press, 1961), p. 14.

[12]Antonia Fraser: *Cromwell The Lord Protector* (New York: Knopf, 173), pp. 566-577.

[13]*The Origins of Sectarian Protestantism* (New York: Macmillan Company, paperback ed., 1964), p. 14.

[14]*Ibid.,* pp. xv-xvi.

[15]*Ibid.,* p. 45.

[16]*Ibid.,* p. xvii.

[17]William R. Estep Jr.: *Anabaptist Beginnings (1523-1533):* (Nieuwkoop: B. De Graaf), p. 1.

[18]John Horst: *Mennonites in Europe* (Scottsdale, Pa.: Mennonite Publishing House, 1942), pp. 129-210.

[19]*The Inner Life of the Religious Societies of the Commonwealth* (London: Hodder and Stoughton, 3d. ed., 1879), pp. 11-12.

[20]*Studies in Mystical Religion* (New York: Macmillan, 1923), p. 1.

[21] Robert Friedman: *The Theology of Anabaptism* (Scottdale, Pa. and Kitchener, Ontario, 1973), p. 28. See also, p. 30.

[22] John A. Garraty and Peter Gay (eds.): *The Columbia History of the World* (New York: Harper and Row, 1972), p. 231.

[23] *Adam, Eve, and the Serpent* (New York: Vintage Books, 1988), p. 152.

[24] *The Eclipse of the Historical Jesus,* Haverford Library Lectures at Haverford College, Haverford, Pennsylvania, April, 1964), pp. 33-34.

[25] *Institutes of the Christian Religion,* a New Translation by Henry Beveridge (Grand Rapids, Michigan: Wm. B. Eerdmans Publishing Company, 1953, II vols.), I, p. 519.

[26] Robert Barclay (Tottenham): *The Inner Life of the Religious Societies of the Commonwealth* (London: Hodder and Stoughton, 3rd ed., 1879), p. 242.

[27] John Horst: *Mennonites in Europe* (Stockdale, Pennsylvania, 2 vols., 1942), Vol. I, p. 139.

[28] *Ibid.,* pp. 226-227.

[29] *Ibid.,* pp. 231-232.

[30] Translation and Introduction by Peter Erb, Preface by Winfried Zeller (New York: Paulist Press, 1978). The words quoted are at p. xvii.

[31] *Milton and Jacob Boehm, A Study in German Mysticism in Seventeenth Century England* (New York: Oxford University Press, 1914), p. 57.

[32] *Mennonite History,* vol. I, "Mennonites in Europe?" (Mennonite Publishing House, Scottsdale, Pennsylvania, 2nd ed., 1950), p. 389. For a more recent and detailed account of these developments see Champlin Burrage: *The Early English Dissenters in the Light of Recent Research* (New York: Russell and Russell, 2 vols., published in 1912 but revised in 1967), pp. 221-269.

[33] The Eastern Orthodox Church, centered in Constantinople, and the Roman Catholic Church had formally separated in 1054, after centuries of disputation over the claim to headship made by the Bishop of Rome (the Pope). The Eastern Church was not greatly affected by the Protestant Reformation.

[34] *Political Thought from Gerson to Grotius 1414-1625* (New York: Harper and Row, Torchbook ed., 1960), p. 5.

[35]A Catholic dogma insisting that the Eucharist, or Lord's Supper, literally transformed bread and wine into the body and blood of Christ.

[36]Philip Schaff: *op. cit.,* vol. I, p. 363.

[37]John A. Garraty and Peter Gay (eds.), *op. cit.,* pp. 524-525.

[38]*Op. cit.,* pp. 361-362.

[39]*Ibid.,* pp. 373-374.

[40]Ross William Collins (F. D. Blackley, ed.): *Calvin and the Libertines of Geneva* (Toronto: Clarke, Irwin and Company, 1968), p. 43. See also James Mackinnon: *Calvin and the Reformation* (New York: Russell and Russell, Inc., 1962), pp. 39-51.

[41]*Institutes of the Christian Religion* (Grand Rapids, Michigan: William H. Erdmans Publishing Co., 2 vols., 1953), vol. II, p. 206.

[42]*Ibid.,* pp. 210-211.

[43]*Ibid.,* p. 206.

[44]Cf. Joseph Frank: *The Levellers* (Cambridge, Mass.: Harvard University Press, 1955), p. 3.

[45]*Ibid.*

[46]John H. Leith, *op. cit.,* p. 192.

Chapter 3

[1]Braithwaite: *Beginnings,* p. 307.

[2]See, for example, the detailed and sensitive account of her life by Isabel Ross: *Margaret Fell: Mother of Quakerism* (New York: Longmans, Green and Co., 1949).

[3]*Journal,* p. 119.

[4]*The Quakers in Peace and War* (London: Swarthmore Press, 1923), p. 45. Her list is at Appendix A, pp. 527-529.

[5]Barry Reay: *The Quakers and the English Revolution* (New York: St. Martin's Press, 1985), pp. 18-19.

[6]Braithwaite: *op. cit.,* p. 120.

[7]Hugh Barbour and Arthur O. Roberts (eds.): *Early Quaker Writings 1650-1700* (Grand Rapids, Michigan: Williams B. Eerdmans Publishing Company, 1973), *passim;* Hugh Barbour: *The Quakers in Puritan England* (New Haven and London: Yale University Press, 1964), Chapter 2.

[8]John H. Leith (ed.): *Creeds of the Churches* (Richmond, Virginia: John Knox Press, Rev. ed., 1973), pp. 302-308.

[9]Use of the word "equality" has been avoided here because of its imprecise and changing meaning.

[10]Mark 16:15.

[11]*Journal,* Preface xliii.

[12]Barclay (Tottenham): *op. cit.,* p. 361.

[13]*Ibid.*

[14]*Op. cit.,* pp. 32-33.

[15]Barclay (Tottenham), *op. cit.,* p. 349. For other details see Braithwaite, *op. cit.,* pp. 181-185.

[16]The *Journal* account of what happened is brief and sketchy. For details see: Sewel, *op. cit.,* Vol. I, pp. 179-209; Braithwaite, *op. cit.,* pp. 238-275.

[17]*The Autobiography of Richard Baxter,* edited with introduction & notes by J. M. Lloyd Thomas (London: J. M. Dent & Sons; New York: E. P. Dutton & Co., Inc.), Notes, p. 285.

[18]Barclay (Tottenham), *op. cit.,* p. 340.

[19]Barclay (Tottenham), *op. cit.,* p. 430.

[20]*Op. cit.,* pp. 430-432.

[21]*The Anarchy of the Ranters, and other Libertines, the Hierarchy of the Romanists and the Pretended Charles, Equally Refused and Refuted in a two-fold Apology of the Church and People of God, called in Derision Quakers.* First published in 1674.

[22]*George Keith (1653-1716),* D. Appleton-Century Company (New York and London, 1942), p. 83.

[23]*Quakers and Politics Pennsylvania 1681-1726* (Princeton, New Jersey: Princeton University Press, 1968), pp. 144, 161.

[24]For the text, see Sewel, *op. cit.,* Vol. II, p. 377. Both Sewel and Braithwaite deal extensively with the controversy.

[25]*Op. cit.,* p. 111.

[26]Sewel, *op. cit.,* p. 180; Barclay (Tottenham), *op. cit.,* pp. 394-395; Davis, *op. cit.,* pp. 376-382.

[27]*Op. cit.,* pp. 395-398. Barclay lists nineteen Canons but for reasons unexplained the sixteenth is omitted. See also, Davis, *op. cit.,* pp. 378-381.

[28]An American term which was not used in England until much later.

Chapter 4

[1]For a copy of the Petition see George Burton Adams and H. Morse Stephens (eds.): *Select Documents of English Constitutional History*

(New York: Macmillan, 1914), p. 339. For the "Remonstrance" and the King's rebuttal, see *ibid.*, pp. 376-382.

[2] Ivan Roots: *The Great Rebellion 1642-1660* (London: B. T. Batesford, 1966), pp. 12-13.

[3] F. W. Maitland: *op. cit.*, p. 298. See also Corrine Weston and Janelle Renfrow Greenberg: *Subjects and Sovereignty in Stuart England* (Cambridge: at the University Press, 1981), *passim*.

[4] Quoted in Sir John A. R. Marriott: *The Crisis of English Liberty: A History of the Stuart Monarch and the Puritan Revolution* (Westport, Connecticut: Greenwood Press Publishers, reprinting 1970), p. 9.

[5] *The Levellers and the English Revolution,* edited and prepared for publication by Christopher Hill (Stanford University Press, 1961), p. 19.

[6] H. N. Brailsford, *op. cit.*, pp. 31, 638-640.

[7] *The Oxford Universal Dictionary,* Third Ed. Revised with Addenda (Oxford at the Clarendon Press, 1955).

[8] *Pacifism in the United States From the Colonial Era to the First World War* (Princeton, New Jersey: Princeton University Press, 1968), p. 8.

[9] *Ibid.*

[10] *Ibid.*

[11] For a copy see Adams and Burton, *op. cit.*, pp. 383-386.

[12] Sir James Fitzjames Stephens: *A History of the Criminal Law of England* (New York: Burt Franklin, 3 vols., originally published in London: 1883), II, p. 404.

[13] *The Writings and Speeches of Oliver Cromwell* (Cambridge: Harvard University Press, 4 vols., 1945), Vol. III, p. xv.

[14] For the speech, see *ibid.*, pp. 434-443.

[15] *Ibid.*, p. 828.

[16] *Ibid.*, p. 837.

[17] *Ibid.*, p. 845.

[18] *Ibid.*, p. 848.

[19] *Op. cit.*, p. 57.

[20] William Haller and Godfry Davis (eds.): *The Leveller Tracts 1647-1653* (Columbia University Press in cooperation with Henry E. Huntington Library and Art Gallery, 1944), p. 7.

[21] Theodore Calvin Pease: *The Leveller Movement, A Study in the History and Political Theory of the English Great Civil War* Washington: (American Historical Association, London: Humphrey Mil-

ford, Oxford University Press, 1916), pp. 88-92; Frank, *op. cit.*, pp. 16-25.

[22]*Free-born John A Biography of John Wilburne* (London Toronto Wellington Sydney, 1961), p. 41.

[23]*Op. cit.*

[24]Quoted by Pauline Gregg: *op. cit.*, p. 221.

[25]*The Oxford Universal Dictionary* (Third Edition Revised with Addenda (1955) says the word "common" and "levelling" were generally known by 1580. The words "communalism," "communism" and "socialism" gained acceptance during the mid-1800's. Robert Barclay (Urie) used both "common" and "levelling." For the early Quaker period, we prefer the word "communalism" to distinguish it from what today is meant by "communism" and "socialism."

[26]*Op. cit.*, pp. 382-383.

[27]*Ibid.*, pp. 318-328.

[28]William Cortez Abbott et al: *The Writings and Speeches of Oliver Cromwell* (Cambridge: Harvard University Press, 4 vols., 1945), III, pp. 435-436.

[29]*Ibid.*, p. 433.

[30]Note also Bushell's Case and Zenger's Trial, *infra*.

[31]M. A. Gibbs: *op. cit.*, pp. 344-345; Joseph Frank: *The Levellers* (Cambridge, Mass.: Harvard University Press, 1955), p. 242.

[32]H. N. Brailsford: *op. cit.*, xi.

[33]*Op. cit.*, p. 161.

[34]*Op. cit.*, p. 245.

[35]The dates shown had previously been uncertain. A recent scholar, T. Wilson Hayes, provided the years mentioned in his *Winstanley the Digger* (Cambridge, Massachusetts and London, England: Harvard University Press, 1979), p. 3.

[36]*Ibid.*

[37]The uncertainty is due to differences between the accounts of Lewis H. Berens in his book entitled *The Digger Movement in the Days of the Commonwealth* (London: Holland Press and Martin Press, 1961), p. 15, and Rufus M. Jones' volume *Studies of Mystical Religion* (London: Macmillan, 1923), p. 428. Berens preferred David George while Jones preferred Nicholas; the former cites for his authority three unpublished manuscripts preserved in the Matschappy Library in Leydon. See also T. Wilson Hayes: *op. cit.*, p. 88.

[38]Eduard Bernstein: *Cromwell and Communism* (New York: Schocken Books, 1930), pp. 105-106.

[39]*Op. cit.*, p. 47.

[40]*Op. cit.*, p. 131.

[41]*Op. cit.*, p. 494.

[42]Berens, *op. cit.*, p. 183.

[43]*Ibid.*, p. 230.

[44]*George Fox and the Light Within 1650-1660* (Philadelphia: Friends Book Store, 1940), pp. 24-26.

[45]*Studies in Mystical Religion, op. cit.*, p. 499.

[46]Pp. 488-489.

[47]A. Ruth Fry: *John Bellers 1654-1725, Quaker, Economist and Social Reformer, His Writings Reprinted with a Memoir* (London, Toronto, Melbourne and Sydney: Cassel and Company, Ltd., (First published 1935), p. 22.

[48]*Ibid.*

[49]*Ibid.*, p. 104.

[50]*Ibid.*, p. 105.

[51]Those encounters are recorded in the *Journal* at pages 197-200; 289; and 350.

[52]*Journal*, pp. 319-331; Charles Evans: *Friends in the Seventeenth Century* (Philadelphia: Friends Book Store, New and Revised Ed., 1885), pp. 147-150.

[53]C. H. Firth: *Oliver Cromwell and the Rule of the Puritans in England* (Covent Garden, London, 1935), p. 443; Wilbur Cortez Abbott, *et. al: The Writings and Speeches of Oliver Cromwell* (Cambridge: Harvard University Press, 4 vol., 1947), IV, p. 872.

[54]George Macaulay Trevelyan: *England Under the Stuarts* (New York: G. P. Putnam's Sons; London: Methuen & Co., seventeenth edition, 1938), p. 333. See also C. H. Firth, *op. cit.*, p. 451; Antonia Fraser: *Cromwell: the Lord Protector* (New York: Knopf, 1974), pp. 678-706; Wilbur Cortez Abbott, *et al, op. cit.*, pp. 873-876.

[55]Godfrey Davies: *The Restoration of Charles II 1658-1660* (The Huntington Library San Marino: California 1955), p. 43.

[55]P. 356.

[56]*Oliver Cromwell and the Rule of Puritans in England* (London: Putnam, 1935), pp. 367-368.

[57]*Cromwell: The Lord Protector* (New York: Knopf, 1974), pp. 404-05.

[58]Probably of Particularist persuasion.

[59]George Macaulay Trevelyan, *op. cit.,* p. 310.

[60]Wilbur Cortez Abbott, *et. al.: op. cit.,* pp. 875-876.

[61]It should be noted, however, that from the Royalists' point of view, all official actions taken after the King's execution (for "murder" as they insisted) were null and void. Following that logic, the Restoration began on January 30, 1649, the day Charles I was beheaded. Maitland, *op. cit.,* p. 282.

[62]Isabel Ross: *op. cit.,* pp. 84-85.

[63]David Ogg: *England in the Reigns of James II and William III* (Oxford at the Clarendon Press, 1955), p. 487.

[64]Arthur Lyon Cross: *op. cit.,* p. 360.

[65]John A. Garraty and Peter Gay (Eds.): *The Columbia History of the World* (New York: Harper and Row, 1972), p. 581.

[66]Michael Oakeshotte (Ed.): *Leviathan or the Matter, Forme and Power of a Commonwealth Ecclesiastical and Civil* (Oxford: Basil Blackwell, 1960), p. viii.

[67]P. 242.

[68]*Ibid.;* italics supplied.

[69]*Ibid.,* p. 243.

[70]Evans: *op. cit.,* p. 198.

[71]*Ibid.,* p. 199.

[72]Sewel: *op. cit.,* I, pp. 328-382; Evans: *op. cit.,* pp. 202-207.

[73]Dan.,: 2, 3; Rev.: 20,22; Mt.: 24: 3-25; Luke.: 21; 5-23; I Cor.: 15: 1-28; I Thes.: 3: 13; II Thes.: 8-12; II Pet.: 6-12. See also L. F. Brown: *The Political Activities of the Baptists and Fifth Monarchy Men* (Washington, DC: American Historical Association; London: Henry Frowde, Oxford University Press, 1912), *passim.*

[74]*Op. cit.,* p. 336.

[75]*Margaret Fell Mother of Quakerism* (London, New York: Longmans, Green and Co., 1949), p. 139.

[76]Sewel, *op. cit.,* I, pp. 335-337; *Journal,* pp. 394-405.

[77]P. 335.

[78]*Ibid.,* p. 336. See also Charles Evans, *op. cit.,* p. 211.

[79]For the text see *Journal,* pp. 398-403.

[80]Braithwaite: *Second Period, op. cit.,* 12, 615; *Journal,* p. 359.

[81]Translated from Latin the word "millennium" means a thousand years; belief in it was called "chiliasm" by ancient theologians.

[82]Roberts: *op. cit.,* p. 378.

[83]Marriott: *op. cit.,* pp. 376-378.

[84]That horrible episode has been recounted endlessly. See for example: Trevelyan, *op. cit.*, pp. 429-433; William Bridgewater and Elizabeth J. Sherwood (eds.): *The Columbia Encyclopedia* (New York: Columbia Press, 2nd ed., 1950), pp. 1303, 1308; Braithwaite: *Second Period, op. cit.*, pp. 119-125.

[85]For the text of those indulgences, see Adams and Burton, *op. cit.*, pp. 451-454.

[86]*Ibid.*, pp. 465-465. The Triennial Act of 1694 amended the last mentioned right by saying that "henceforth a Parliament shall be holden once in three years at least." It should also be noted that the provisions mentioned were inapplicable to Catholics.

Chapter 5

[1]Howard H. Brinton: *The Religious Philosophy of Quakerism* (Pendle Hill Publications: Wallingford, Pennsylvania, 1973), pp. 24-43.

[2]Epistole 402.

[3]*Apology*, p. 109. For Fox's views, see his *Works*, VII, passim.

[4]*Journal*, p. 70.

[5]*Journal*, p. 182.

[6]Craig W. Horle: *The Quakers and the English Legal System 1660-1688)* (Philadelphia: University of Pennsylvania Press, 1988), pp. 63, 87, 172.

[7]*Ibid.*, pp. 172-173.

[8]*Journal*, pp. 398-404. For this and other Quaker pacifist declarations see also T. Canby Jones, *op. cit.*

[9]*Apology*, p. 72.

[10]Published in French in 1748 and in English two years later.

[11]*Apology*, pp. 462-463.

[12]*Beginnings*, p. 519.

[13]*Ibid.*, p. 601.

[14]*Ibid.*

[15]Isaac Sharpless: *A History of Quaker Government in Pennsylvania* (Philadelphia: T.S. Leach and Co., 2 vols., 1900) II. pp. 172-206.

[16]*London Yearly Meeting*, 2 vols., 1753. These data show local persecutions for the years 1651-1689. They were gathered in all but a few counties in England and Wales through Quaker Meetings and assembled by the "Meeting for Sufferings" at London Yearly Meeting for presentation to governmental authorities.

[17]*Beginnings*, pp. 464-465.

[18]Isaac Sharpless: *A History of Quaker Government in Pennsylvania* (Philadelphia: T. S. Leach and Co., 2 vols., 1900, I, p. 19.

[19]*Op. cit.*, pp. 475-476.

[20]Arthur Lyon Cross: *A Shorter History of England and Greater Britain* (New York: The Macmillan Company, 126), pp. 142-143.

[21]Norman Penny (ed.): *Extracts of State papers Related to Friends 1654-1672* (London, E.C.: Friends Reference Library, Devonshire House), p. 37.

[22]That controversy has been reported repeatedly. We have relied primarily upon Besse, *op. cit.*, pp. 416-426; Catherine Owens Peare: *William Penn a Biography* (Philadelphia and New York: J. B. Lippencott, 1957), pp. 111-124; F. W. Maitland: *The Constitutional History of England* (Cambridge: University Press, 1950), pp. 311-320; Julius J. Marke: *Vignettes of Legal History* (South Hackensack, N.J.: Fred B. Rothman & Co., 1965); and Penn's version of the trial entitled *The Peoples' Ancient and Just Liberties Asserted in the Trial of William Penn and William Meade . . . Against the Most Arbitrary Procedure of that Court,* republished in 1919.

[23]The literature on speech and press is extensive. For a brief account see Julius J. Marke, *op. cit.*, pp. 225-240.

[24]*Ibid.*, p. 54.

[25]Besse, op. cit., Vol. I, p. 77. Incidentally, Edward Bourne was a Quaker physician who lived in the Midlands and often jailed.

[26]*Ibid.*

[27]*Ibid.*, p. 9.

[28]See, for example, their *Capital A Critique of Political Economy* (New York: The Modern Library, 1906), pp. 147, 358, 467.

[29](London: The Bannisdale Press, 1951).

[30]*The Social Development of English Quakerism 1655-1755* (Cambridge, Mass., 1969), p. 55. Vann counts Gervase Benson a gentleman, since as a colonel and a judge he clearly would have been regarded as such.

[31]*The Social Development of English Quakerism 1655-1755* (Cambridge, Mass., 1969).

[32]"The Social Origins of the Early Friends," *Journal of the Friends Historical Society,* 48 (London, 1956-58).

[33]For the above comments, see Vann, p. 49.

[34]*Ibid.*, p. 73.

Chapter 6

[1]J. F. Jones: *County and Court, England, 1658-1714)* (Cambridge, Mass.: Harvard University Press, 1976), p. 135.

[2]*Ibid.*, pp. 95-96; Harry Emerson Wildes: *William Penn* (New York: Macmillan Publishing Co., Inc., 1976), pp. 19-20.

[3]George Macaulay Trevelyn; *op. cit.*, p. 315.

[4]Melvin B. Endy, Jr.: *William Penn and Early Quakerism* (Princeton, N.J.: Princeton University Press, 1973), p. 97.

[5]William I. Hull: *Eight First Biographies of William Penn in Seven Languages and Seven Lands* (Swarthmore College Monographs on Quaker History, Number Three, 1936), p. 31.

[6]Peare: *op. cit.*, p. 40.

[7]Charles M. Andrews: *The Colonial Period of American History* (New Haven: Yale University Press, 1937, 3 vols.) III, p. 268.

[8]Braithwaite: *Second Period, op. cit.*, pp. 61-62.

[9]Peare, *op. cit.*, pp. 438-444; Richard H. Dunn (ed.): *The Papers of William Penn* (Philadelphia: University of Pennsylvania Press, 1982).

[10]William I. Hull: *William Penn, A Topical Biography* (Oxford University Press, London, New York, Toronto, 1937), pp. 181-197.

[11]Braithwaite: *Beginnings, op. cit.*, pp. 402-405.

[12]Rufus M. Jones: *Quakers in the American Colonies* (London: Macmillan and Co., 1911), pp. 3-4.

[13]James Bowden: *The History of the Society of Friends of America* (London: Charles Gilpin, 5, Bishopsgate Street Without, 1850, 2 vols.), I, pp. 46-47.

[14]*The Quakers in the American Colonies* (London: Macmillan and Co., 1911, p. xv.

[15]Rufus M. Jones: *op. cit.*, p. 117.

[16]Leon R. Camp, "Roger Williams vs. 'The Upstarts': The Rhode Island Debates of 1672": *Quaker History* 52, p. 69.

[17]*Op. cit.*, p. 122.

[18]Commonwealth of Pennsylvania: *The Pennsylvania Manual*, Vol. 106, 1982-1983, p. 11.

[19]*History of the Mennonites* (Philadelphia: Daniel K. Cassel, 1888), pp. 74-80.

[20]*Op. cit.*, pp. 99-100.

[21]John W. Barber and Henry Howe: *Historical Collections of the State of New Jersey* (New York: S. Tuttle, 1844), p. 15.

[22]John Howard Hinton, *et. al,: The History and Topography of the United States of North America* (Boston: Printed and published by Samuel Walker, 1881), p. 118.

[23]William I. Hull: *The Rise of Quakerism in Amsterdam 1655-1665, op. cit.,* pp. 1-18.

[24]John W. Barber and Henry Howe: *op. cit.,* p. 15.

[25]For an official summary, see *The Minutes of the Board of Proprietors of the Eastern Division of New Jersey from 1685 to 1705,* published in Perth Amboy by The Board of Proprietors, February, 1949, pp. 14-15, cited hereafter as *BPEDNJ.*

[26]*BPEDNJ,* p. 2; John E. Pomfred: *The Province of East Jersey* (Princeton, N.J.: Princeton University Press, 1962), p. 173; D. Elton Trueblood: *Robert Barclay* (New York, Evanston and London, 1968), Ch. VI.

[27]*Ibid.,* p. 8.

[28]*BPEDNJ,* pp. 13-14, 232. See also D. Elton Trueblood: *op. cit.,* pp. 104-105.

[29]Charles M. Andrews: *The Colonial Period of American History* (New Haven: Yale University Press, 3 vols., 1937), III, pp. 167-168.

[30]John W. Barger and Henry Howe: *op. cit.,* p. 20.

[31]Edwin B. Bonner: *William Penn's "Holy Experiment" The Founding of Pennsylvania 1681-1701* (New York and London; Temple University Publications, Distributed by Columbia University Press, 1962), p. 27.

[32]Peare: *op. cit.,* p. 230.

[33]Tolles and Alderfer: *op. cit.,* p. 108.

[34]*The History of Pennsylvania* . . . (Philadelphia: Zacharia Poulson, Jr., 2 vols., 1707-1799), I, pp. 207-208.

[35]Francis Newton Thorpe: *Federal and State Constitutions, Colonial Charters, and Other Organic Laws* . . . (Washington, D.C.: Government Printing Office, 7 vols.), I, p. 559, hereafter cited as Thorpe.

[36]*Ibid.,* I, pp. 562, 568.

[37]Klein and Hoogenboom: *op. cit.,* pp. 29-30.

[38]*William Penn* (New York: Macmillan Publishing Co., Inc./London: Collier Macmillan Publishers), p. 161. See also: 206 *United States Reports* (April 1907), p. 550; 291 *United States Reports* (February 1934), pp. 251-285.

[39]Thorpe: *op. cit.,* V, p. 3036.

[40]*Ibid.*, p. 3054.

[41]*Ibid.*, p. 3063.

[42]*Op. cit.*, p. 15.

[43]Robert Proud: *op. cit.*, I, 288-289.

[44]Jack D. Marietta: *The Reformation of American Quakerism. 1748-1783* (Philadelphia: University of Pennsylvania Press 1984), pp. 47, 54.

[45]Harry Emerson Wildes: *op. cit.*, p. 248.

[46]Bronner: *op. cit.*, pp. 72-75.

[47]Published accounts of those events are numerous. Three of them are: Braithwaite, *Second Period, op. cit.*, pp. 14, 151-168; Brenner: *op. cit.*, pp. 70-86; Peare: *op. cit.*, pp. 314-332.

[48]Braithwaite, *Second Period, op. cit.*, pp. 160-161.

[49]Pp. xviii.

[50]The Commonwealth of Pennsylvania: *The 1955-1956 Pennsylvania Manual*, pp. 74-75, 731-732.

[51]*The Latter Periods of Quakerism* (Macmillan and Co., Limited St. Martin's Street, London 1921), p. 715. *See also:* Isaac Sharpless, *op. cit.*, Ch. IX.

[52]Commonwealth of Pennsylvania: *The 1955-1956 Pennsylvania Manual*, p. 33.

BIBLIOGRAPHY

Abbott, Wilburt Cortez: *The Writings and Speeches of Oliver Cromwell* (Cambridge: Harvard University Press, 4 vol., 1945).

Adams, George Burton and H. Morse Stephens (eds.): *Select Documents of English Constitutional History* (New York: Macmillan, 1914).

Ashley, Maurice: *Charles II: The Man and the Statesman* (New York and Washington: Praeger Publishers, 1971).

Andrews, Charles M. L.: *The Colonial Period of American History, The Settlements, III* (New Haven: Yale University Press, 1937).

Baltzell, Edward Digby: *Puritan Boston and Quaker Philadelphia* (New York: Free Press, 1979).

Bailey, Margaret Lewis: *Milton and Jacob Boehm: A Study in German Mysticism in Seventeenth-Century England* (New York: Oxford University Press, 1914).

Barber, John W. and Henry Rowe: *Historical Collections of the State of New Jersey.* (New York: S. Tuttle, 1833).

Barbour, Hugh and Arthur O. Roberts (eds.): *Early Quaker Writings* (Grand Rapids, Michigan: William B. Eerdmans Publishing Company, 1973).

Barclay (Urie), Robert: *The Anarchy of the Ranters.* First Published in 1674.

Barclay (Tottenham), Robert: *The Inner Life of the Religious Society of the Commonwealth* (London: Hodder and Stoughton, 1876).

Barker, Ernest: *The Politics of Aristotle* (London: Oxford; at the Clarendon Press. Reprinted with corrections, 1961).

Berens, Lewis: *The Digger Movement in the days of the Commonwealth* (London: Holland Press & Merlin Press, 1961).

Bernstein, Eduard: *Cromwell and Communism, Socialism and Democracy in the Great Revolution* (New York: Schocken Books, 1930).

Besse, George: *A Collection of the Sufferings of the People Called Quakers* (London Yearly Meeting, 2 vols., 1753).

Board of Proprietors: *Minutes of the Board of the Eastern Division of New Jersey from 1685 to 1705* (Published in Perth Amboy, 1949).

Bouquet, A. C.: *Everyday Life in New Testament Times* (New York: Charles Scribner's Son, 1953).

Bowden, James: *The History of the Society of Friends of America* (London: Charles Gilpin, 5, Bishopsgate Street Without, 1850, 2 vols.).

Brailsford, H. N.: *The Levellers and the English Revolution*, edited and prepared for publication by Christopher Hill (Stanford University Press, 1961).

Braithwaite, William C.: *The Beginnings of Quakerism* (London: Macmillan and Co., Limited, 1912).

Braithwaite, William C.: *The Second Period of Quakerism* (Macmillan and Co., Limited, 1919).

Brayshaw, A. Neave: *The Personality of George Fox,* 1918. Revised and extended edition (London: Allenson & Co., Ltd., 1933).

Brinton, Howard H. (ed.): *Children of Light: In Honor of Rufus M. Jones* (New York: The Macmillan Company, 1938).

Brinton, Howard H.: *The Religious Philosophy of Quakerism* (Wallingford, Pa.: Pendle Hill Publications, 1973).

Brock, Peter: *Pacifism in the United States from the Colonial Era to the First World War* (Princeton, New Jersey: Princeton University Press, 1968).

Bronner, Edwin B.: *William Penn's "Holy Experiment": The Founding of Pennsylvania: 1681-1701* (New York and London: Temple University Publications. Distributed by Columbia University Press, 1962).

Brown, L. F.: *The Political Activities of the Baptist and Fifth Monarchy Men* (Washington, D.C.: American Historical Association; London: Henry Frowde, Oxford University Press, 1912).

Bunyan, John: *Complete Works of John Bunyan,* edited by Henry Stebbing (George Olms Verlag, Hildeseim, New York; John-Repring Corporation, New York, 4 vols., 1970).

Burnet, George B.: *The Story of Quakerism in Scotland 1650-1850* (London: James Clarke & Co., Ltd).

Burrage, Chaplin: *The Early English Dissenters in the Light of Recent Research* (New York: Russell and Russell, 2 vols., published in 1912 but revised in 1967).

Cadbury, Henry J.: *The Eclipse of the Historical Jesus* (Haverford Library Lectures at Haverford College, Haverford, Pennsylvania, April, 1963).

Calvin, John: *Institutes of the Christian Religion,* A Translation by Henry Beveridge (Grand Rapids, Michigan: Wm. B. Eerdmans Publishing Company, 1953, 2 vols.).

Camp, Leon R.: "Roger Williams" vs. "The Upstarts"; "The Rhode Island Debates of 1672." *Quaker History* 52, p. 69.

Clarendon, Edward Hyde: *History of the Rebellion* (3 vols., 1702-1704).

Clarke, George (ed.): *John Bellers, His Life, Times and Writings* (London and New York: Routledge & Kegan Paul, 1987).

Cochrane, A. C. (ed.): *Reformed Confessions in the 16th Century* (Westminster Press, 1966).

Cole, Alan: "The Social Origins of the Early Friends,": *Journal of Friends Historical Society,* 48 (London, 1956-58).

Collins, Ross William (F. D. Blackley, ed.): *Calvin and the Libertines of Geneva* (Toronto: Clarke, Irwin and Company, 1968).

Croesce, Gerard: *The General History of Quakers* (English ed., 1696).

Cross, Arthur Lyon: *A Shorter History of England and Great Britain* (New York: The Macmillan Company, 1926).

Davies, Godfrey: *The Restoration of Charles II* (The Huntington Library, San Marino: California 1955).

Dictionary of National Biography, Vol. XX (London: Macmillan Co., 1889), p. 118.

Donehoo, George P.: *Pennsylvania: A History* (Lewis Historical Publishing Co., N.Y. and Chicago, 1926).

Dunn, Richard H. (ed.): *The Papers of William Penn* (Philadelphia: University of Pennsylvania Press, 1982).

Dunn, Mary Maples: *Wm. Penn: Politics and Conscience* (Princeton, N. J.: Princeton University Press, 1967).

Endy, Melvin B., Jr.: *William Penn and Early Quakerism* (Princeton, N. J.: Princeton University Press, 1973).

Estep, William R., Jr.: *Anabaptist Beginnings 1523-1533* (Nieuwkoop: B. De Graaf).

Evans, Charles: *Friends of the Seventeenth Century* (Philadelphia Friends Book Store, Revised Ed., 1885).

Farmer, D. L.: *Britain and the Stuarts* (London: G. Bell and Sons Ltd., 1965).

Ferguson, John H. and Dean E. McHenry: *The American System of Government* (New York: McGraw Hill Book Company, 14th edition, 1981).

Figgis, John Neville: *The Divine Right of Kings* (New York: Harper and Row, Torchbook edition, 1966).

Figgis, John Neville: *Political Thought from Gerson to Grotius 1414-1625* (New York: Harper and Row, Torchbook ed., 1960).

Firth, Charles Harding: *The Last Years of the Protectorate 1656-1658*, 2 vols. (New York: Russell & Russell, Inc., 1964).

Firth, C. H.: *Oliver Cromwell and the Rule of the Puritans in England* (Covent Garden, London, 1935).

Fiske, John: *The Dutch and Quaker Colonies* (New York: Houghton and Mifflin Publishing Co., 1980).

Fox, George: *Journal,* revised edition by John L Nickalls, with an epilogue by Henry J. Cadbury and introduction by Geoffrey F. Nuttall (London: Religious Society of Friends, 1975).

Frank, Joseph: *The Levellers* (Cambridge, Mass.: Harvard University Press, 1955).

Frank, Joseph: *The Levellers: A History of the Writings of Three Sixteenth Century Democrats, John Wilburne, Richard Overton and William Walwin* (Cambridge: Harvard University Press, 1965).

Fraser, Antonia: *Cromwell and Lord Protector* (New York: Knopf, 1973).

Fraser, Antonia: *Charles II and the Restoration* (New York: Alfred A. Knopf, 1979).

Friedman, Robert: *The Theology of Anabaptism* (Scottsdale, Pa. and Kitchener, Ontario, 1973).

Fry, A. Ruth: *John Bellers 1654-1725, Quaker, Economist and Social Reformer* London, Toronto, Melburne and Sydney: Cassel and Company, Ltd., 1935).

Garraty, John A. and Peter Gay (eds.): *The Columbia History of the World* (New York: Harper and Row, 1972).

Gibb, M.A.: *John Wilburne The Leveller* (Lindsay Drummond Ltd., London, 1947).

Gregg, Pauline: *Free-born John: A. Biography of John Wilburne* (George G. Harrap & Co.: London, Toronto, Wellington, Sydney, 1961).

Gwyn, Douglas: *Apocalypse of the Word The Life and Message of George Fox* (1624-1691): (Richmond, Indiana: Friends United Press, 1984).

Haller, William and Godfrey Davies: *The Leveller Tracts* 1647-1653 (Columbia Uniersity Press, in cooperation with Henry E. Huntington Library and Art Gallery, 1944).

Hayes, T. Wilson: *Winstanley the Digger* (Cambridge, Massachusetts and London, England: Harvard University Press, 1979).

Hill, Christopher, Barry Reay and William Lamont: Reprinted in 1983 as "The Muggletonians: An Introductory Survey," pp. 23-63.

Hill, Christopher: *God's Englishman, Oliver Cromwell and the English Revolution* (New York: The Dial Press, 1970).

Hill, Christopher: *Puritanism and Revolution: Studies in Interpretation of the English Revolution of the 17th Century* (London: Secker & Warburg, 1958).

Hill, Christopher: *Society and Puritanism in Pre-Revolutionary England* (Schocken Books, New York, 2nd ed., 1967).

Hill, Christopher: *The Century of Revolution: 1603-1714* (Edinburgh: Thomas Nelson & Sons Ltd., 1961).

Hinton, John Howard, et. al.: *The History of Topography of the United States of North America* (Boston: Samuel Walker, 1881).

Hirst, Margaret: *The Quakers in Peace and War* (London: Swarthmore Press, 1923).

Holder, Charles Frederick: *The Quakers in Great Britain and America* (New York, Los Angeles, London: Neuner, 1913).

Horle, Craig W.: *The Quakers and the English Legal System 1660-1688* (Philadelphia: University of Pennsylvania Press, 1988).

Horsch, John: *The Hutterian Brethren: A Story of Martyrdom and Loyalty, 1528-1931* (Goshen, Indiana, 1931).

Horsch, John: *Menno Simons, His Life, Labors, and Teachings* (Published at Scottdale, Pa., 1916).

Horsch, John: *The Principle of Nonresistance as Held by the Mennonite Church* (Scottdale, Pa., revised and enlarged, 1929).

Horst, John: *Mennonites in Europe* (Scottdale, Pa.: Mennonite Publishing House, 1922).

Hostetler, John A.: *Amish Society* (Baltimore and London: The John Hopkins University Press, 3rd. ed., 1980).

Howell, Robert, Jr.: *Cromwell* (Boston: Little Brown, 1977).

Hull, William I.: *Eight First Biographies of William Penn in Seven Languages and Seven Lands* (Swarthmore College Monographs on Quaker History) Number Three, 1936).

Hull, William I.: *The Rise of Quakerism in Amsterdam: 1655-1665* (Swarthmore College Monographs on Quaker History Number Four, 1938).

Jones, J. F.: *County and Court, England, 1658-1714* (Cambridge, Mass.: Harvard University Press, 1978).

Jones, Rufus M.: *Quakers in the American Colonies* (London: Macmillan and Co., 1911).

Jones, Rufus M.: *Spiritual Reformers of the 16th and 17th Centuries* (London: The Macmillan Co., 1914). First published as a paperback in 1959 by permission of The Macmillan Co.

Jones, Rufus M.: *Studies in Mystical Religion* (London and New York: Macmillan, 1923).

King, Hadley: *George Fox and the Light Within: 1650-1660* (Philadelphia: Friends Book Store, 1940).

Kirby, Ethyn Williams: *George Keith (1638-1716)* (New York and London: D. Appleton-Century Company, 1942).

Klein, Philips S. and Ari Hoogenboom: *A History of Pennsylvania* (McGraw-Hill Book Company, 1973).

Kriebel, Howard W.: *The Schwenkfelders in Pennsylvania* (Lancaster: Pennsylvania German Society, 1904).

Leith, John H. (ed.): *Creeds of the Churches* (Richmond, Virginia: John Knox Press, Rev. ed., 1973).

Little, Franklin Hamlin: *The Origins of Sectarian Protestantism* (New York: Macmillan Company, paperback ed., 1964).

Luther, Martin: *Works,* Philadelphia Edition (Philadelphia: Muhlenberh Press, 6 vols., 1932).

Macaulay, Thomas Babington: *The History of England from the Accession of James II,* 5 vols. (New York and Chicago, Hooper Clark and Co., 1858).

Mackinnon, James: *Calvin and the Reformation* (New York: Russell and Russell, Inc., 1962).

Maitland, F. W.: *The Constitutional History of England* (Cambridge: at the University Press, 1950).

Makower, Felix: *The Constitutional History and Constitution of the Church of England* (New York: Burt Franklin, Originally Published in London, 1895).

Manners, Emily: *Elizabeth Hooton: First Quaker Woman Preacher* (London: Headley Brothers, 1914).

Marke, Julius: *Vignettes of Legal History* (South Hackensack, N.J.: Fred B. Rotham & Co., 1965).

Marriott, Sir John A. R.: *The Crisis of English Liberty: A History of the Stuart Monarch and the Puritan Revolution* (Westport, Connecticut: Greenwood Press Publishers, reprinting 1970).

Marx, Karl and Frederick Engles: *Capital: A Critique of Political Economy* (New York: The Modern Library, 1906).

Moore, John M.: *Friends in the Delaware Valley, Philadelphia Yearly Meeting, 1681-1981* (Philadelphia: Friends Historical Association, 1981).

Nash, George B.: *Quakers and Politics Pennsylvania 1681-1726* (Princeton, N.J.: Princeton University Press, 1968).

Nuttall, G.F.: *Studies in Christian Enthusiasm* (Pendel Hill, Wallingford, Pa., 1948).

Oakeshotte, Michael (ed.): *Leviathan on the Matter, Forme and the Power of a Commonwealth Ecclesiastical and Civil* (Oxford: Basil Blackwell, 1960).

Ogg, David: *England in the Reign of James II and William III* (Oxford at the Clarendon Press, 1955).

Pagels, Elaine: *Adam, Eve, and the Serpent* (New York: Vintage Books, A Division of Random House, Inc., 1988).

Peare, Catherine Owens: *William Penn a Biography* (Philadelphia and New York: J. B. Lippincott, 1957).

Pease, Theodore Calvin: *The Leveller Movement, A Study of the History and Political Theory of the English Great Civil War* (Washington: The American Historical Association; London: Humphrey Milford, Oxford University Press, 1916).

Penny, Norman (ed.): *Extracts of State Papers Related to Friends 1654-1672* (London, E. C.: Friends Reference Library, Devonshire House).

Pickvance, T. Joseph: *George Fox and the Purefeys* (London: Friends Historical Society, 1970).

Pomfret, John E.: *Colonial New Jersey: A History* (New York: Charles Scribners, Sons, 1973).

Pomfret, John E.: *The Province of West New Jersey 1609-1702* (Princeton, N.J., 1956).

Proud, Robert: *The History of Pennsylvania* (Philadelphia: Zacharia Poulson, Jr., 2 vols., 1797-1799).

Punshon, John: *Portrait in Grey, A Short History of the Quakers* (London: Quaker Home Service, 1984).

Qualben, Lars P.: *The Lutheran Church in Colonial America* (New York: Thomas Nelson and Sons, 1940).

Reay, Barry: *The Quakers and the English Revolution*, Foreword by Christopher Hill (New York: St. Martin's Press, 1985).

Richings, Reverend B.: *Narrative of Persecutions and Sufferings of the Two Martyrs, Robert B. Glover and Mrs. Lewis* (London: L. & G. Seeley, 3rd ed., 1842).

Robers, Clayton: *The Growth of Responsible Government in Stuart England* (Cambridge: University Press, 1966).

Robertson, D. B.: *The Religious Foundations of Leveller Democracy* (New York: Kings Crown Press, Columbia University, 1951).

Robinson, James M.: *The Nag Hammadi Library in English* (San Francisco: Harper & Row, 1978).

Roots, Ivan: *The Great Rebellion 1642-1660* (London: B.T. Batesford, 1966).

Rose, June: *Elizabeth Fry* (London: Macmillan London Ltd., 1980. Paperback, 1981).

Ross, Elliott: *Cases of Conscience Alternatives Open to Recusants and Puritans Under Elizabeth I and James I* (London: Cambridge University Press, 1975).

Ross, Isabel: *Margaret Fell Mother of Quakerism* (London, New York: Longmans, Green and Co., 1948).

Russell, Jeffrey Burton: *Medieval Civilization* (New York; Wiley, 1968).

Russell, Jeffrey Burton: *Religious Dissent in the Middle Ages* (New York: Wiley, 1968).

Russell, Jeffrey Burton: *Witchcraft in the Middle Ages* (Ithaca and London: Cornell University Press, 1972).

Schaff, Philip: *Creeds of Christendom with a History of Critical Notes*, 3 vols. (New York and London: Harper & Bros., 1931).

Schultz, Selina G. *Caspar Schwenckfeld von Ossig (1489-1561)*, 1977. Published by the Board of Publications, Schwenkfelder Church, Pennsbury, Pa.

Scott, James Brown (ed.): *The Classics of International Law* (New York: Oceana Publications, Inc., 3 vols., 1964).

Sewel, William: *The History of the Rise, Increase and Progress of the Christian People Called Quakers* (New York: Baker and Crane, 2 vols., 1844).

Sharpless, Isaac: *A History of Quaker Government in Pennsylvania* (Philadelphia: T. S. Leach & Co., 2 vols., 1900).

Simons, Menno: *The Complete Writings of Menno Simons, c. 1496-1561* (Scottdale, Pa.: Herald Press, 1956).

Stephens, Sir James: *A General View of the Criminal Law* (London and New York, 2d ed., 1890).

Stephens, Sir James: *History of the Criminal Law of England* (London: Macmillan & Co., 1883, 3 vols.).

Thomas, J. M, Lloyd, Ed. & Notes: *The Autobiography of Richard Baxter* (London: J.M. Dent & Sons, Ltd.; New York: E. P. Dutton & Co., Inc.).

Thorpe, Francis Newton: *Federal and State Constitutions, Colonial Charters, and Other Organic Laws* (Washington: Government Printing Office, 7 vols.).

Tolles, Frederick B.: *Meeting House and Counting House: The Quaker Merchants of Colonial Philadelphia 1682-1763* (Chapel Hill: University of North Carolina Press, 1948).

Tolles, Frederick B., and E. Gordon Alderfer: *The Witness of William Penn* (New York: The Macmillan Company, 1957).

Trevelyan, George Macaulay: *England Under the Stuarts* (New York: G. P. Putnam's Sons; London: Methuen & Co., seventeenth edition, 1938.

Trueblood, D. Elton: *Robert Barclay* (New York, Evanston and London: Harper and Row, 1968).

Vann, Richard T.: *The Social Development of English Quakerism, 1655-1755* (Cambridge, Mass.: Harvard University Press, 1969).

Vipont, Elfrida: *George Fox and the Valiant Sixty* (London: Hamish Hamilton, Ltd., 1975).

Weston, Corrine, and Janell Renfrow Greenberg: *Subjects and Sovereignty in Stuart England* (Cambridge: University Press, 1981).

Whitehead, William: *Contributions to Early History of Perth Amboy and Adjoining Country* (New York: D. Appleton and Co., 1856).

Wildes, Harry Emerson: *William Penn* (New York: Macmillan Publishing Co.; London: Collier Macmillan Publishers, 1976).

Yule, George: *The Independents in the English Civil War* (Cambridge University Press of Melburne, 1958).

INDEX

Abbott, Wilburt Cortez, 78
Act of Supremacy, 28
Act of Uniformity, 105
Anabaptists, 4, 16, 31–39, 42, 47, 52, 55, 56, 81, 102, 107, 115, 116, 124
Anarchism, 26
Andrus, Major Edmund, 158
Angles, 28
Anglicans, 166
Anne, 30
Anne, Queen, 106
Anti-Trinitarians, 32
Aquinas, St. Thomas, 116
Aristotle, 1, 3, 25, 120
Æthelbert, 28
Augsburg Confession, 42
Augustine, St., 116
Austin, Ann, 149, 153
Bailey, Margaret Lewis, 38
Baltimore, Lord, 162, 163
Baptists, 14, 15, 39, 52, 56, 58, 64, 67, 110, 116, 150
Barbour, Hugh, 56
Barclay, John, 160
Barclay, Robert (Tottenham), 2, 3, 33, 37, 63, 70, 128
Barclay, Robert (Urie), 57, 62, 63, 64, 66, 88, 89, 99, 111, 121, 124, 151, 152, 158, 159, 160
Bastwick, John, 81
Baxter, Richard, 62
Beheminists, 38
Bellers, John, 90–91, 141

198

Bennet, Jervase, 19
Berens, Lewis, 87
Berkeley, John, 157
Bernstein, Eduard, 87
Besse, George, 127, 137, 141
Bible, 7, 9, 17, 21, 34, 38, 41, 56, 104, 110, 112, 113, 115, 119,
    122, 123
Bill of Rights, 73, 108
Blackwell, John, 167
Bloody Assize, 107
Boehme, Jacob, 38–39, 42, 116
Book of Common Prayer, 7, 77
Bourne, Edward, 136
Bradford, William, 135
Brailsford, H. N., 75
Braithwaite, William C., 125, 127, 128
Brethren Hutterites, 15, 32
Bright, John, 99, 171
Brock, Peter, 75
Browne, Robert, 16
Bunyan, John, 4, 62, 150
Burnyeat, John, 151
Burrough, Edward, 60
Burroughs, Edward, 95
Bushell's Case, 131–35
Byllinge, Edward, 160, 161
Cadbury, Henry J., 35
Caesar, Julius, 120
Caesarism, 118–27
Calvin, John, 27, 36, 40, 41, 44, 45–49, 52, 57, 111, 122
Calvinism, 15, 16, 28, 43, 46–47, 50, 80, 96
Calvinists, 4
Campbell, Neil, 160
Canons of Institutions, 70
Canterbury, 28
Carteret, Philip, 158
Carteret, Sir George, 157, 158
Cassell, Daniel K., 153
Catholicism, 15, 16, 23, 27, 28, 34, 40, 42, 124
    doctrine, 32

Catholics, 29, 57, 107, 114
    persecution of, 28–30
Charles I, 20, 22, 30, 72, 73, 74, 80, 82, 86, 95, 106, 122
Charles II, 16, 17, 25, 73, 74, 75, 77, 91, 95, 98, 99, 101, 105, 129,
    145, 146, 147, 148, 154, 155, 157, 161, 164, 168
Children of the Light, 52, 68
Christian Quakers, 66
Christianity
    primitive, 3
Christison, Wenlock, 154
Church of England, 16
Civil War, 3, 15, 23, 27, 51, 53, 72, 73, 75, 77, 80, 97, 99, 102,
    110, 125, 127, 131, 135, 146, 147
Clarendon Code, 71, 104
Clarendon, Edward Hyde, 104, 105
Coke, Sir Edward, 74, 80, 99, 150
Cole, Alan, 144
Communalism, 88
Consensus Tigurinus, 44
Constantine, 34
Constitution, 124
Conventical Act, 63, 105, 132
Corporation Act, 105
Croesce, Gerard, 8, 11, 14
Cromwell, Oliver, 17, 20, 30, 31, 53, 54, 60, 62, 72, 73, 74, 77, 78,
    80, 82, 85, 95, 102, 125, 129, 135, 145, 147, 167, 168
    death, 94
    opposing Levellers, 83
    relationship with George Fox, 91–96
    religion, 96
    spy system of, 79
    tolerance, 96
Cromwell, Richard, 30, 72, 94, 98
Crook, John, 69
Cross, Arthur Lyon, 129
Davis, Godfrey, 81
Declaration of 1660, 104
Declaration of Independence, 124, 127
Declaration of Rights, 108
Declaration of Rights (Pennsylvania), 172

Delaware, 162–63
Delaware Indians, 172
Derby, 19, 20, 69, 125, 131
Derby Gaol, 14
Dewell, Elizabeth, 80
Dewsbury, William, 51
Diggers, 86–88, 90
Dissenters, 16
Divine right, 24
Dordrecht Confession, 56
Druids, 28
Dutch Reformed Church, 157
Dyer, Mary, 154
Eckhart, Meister, 116
Edmundson, William, 151
Edward I, 30
Edward VI, 30
Elizabeth, 30
Elizabeth, Princess of the Palatinate, 152
Engels, Friedrich, 90, 141
English Baptists, 16
Episcopalianism, 15, 16
Episcopalians, 53, 60, 62, 63, 67
Erasmus, Desiderius, 43
Familists, 17, 86
Farnsworth, Richard, 51, 55
Fell (Fox), Margaret, 9, 53–55, 95, 103, 114, 131
Fell, Thomas, 53–55
Fenny Drayton, 4, 5, 6, 7, 12, 15, 116, 131
Fenwick, John, 160
Fifth Monarchy Men, 17, 78, 102–4, 117
Fifth Monarchy Uprising, 63, 71
Figgis, John Neville, 49
Firth, C. H., 96
Fisher, Mary, 149, 153
Five Mile Act, 105
Fletcher, Benjamin, 169
Ford, Bridget, 170
Ford, Philip, 169, 170
Fox, Christopher, 5, 6

Fox, George
    and capital punishment, 19–20
    and Cromwell, 91–96
    and Winstanley, 88
    apprenticeship, 7, 8, 10, 12
    as standardizer of Quaker practices, 70
    at Sedgberg, 53
    at Swarthmoor Hall, 53–55
    birth of, 4
    commitment to pacifism, 115
    compared with John Bunyan, 4
    controversial nature, 110
    death, 4, 169
    debates Roger Williams, 151
    difficulties with Naylor, 62
    early ministry, 14
    imprisonment, 18–21
    Journal, 5, 6, 7, 8, 9, 10, 11, 12, 14, 15, 18, 20, 50, 87, 91, 93,
        95, 99, 103, 169
    lack of interest in women, 9
    marriage, 9
    marries, 54
    mystical experience, 12
    on subjection, 22
    pacifism of, 20–21, 125
    parents, 5, 6
    personal characteristics, 13
    pilgrimage, 15, 50
    pilgrimage of, 11, 12, 13
    political attitudes of, 1, 2, 3
    politicization of, 18, 19
    preaching, 13
    preaching of, 57
    puritanical values of, 9
    refusal to swear oaths, 114
    schooling, 7
    youth, 5
Fox, Mary, 5
Francis of Assisi, St., 116
Frank, Joseph, 80, 85

French and Indian War, 150, 169
George I, 30
George III, 127
George, David, 86
George, Henry, 87
Glorious Revolution, 62, 73, 77, 86, 99, 113
Glover, Robert, 5
Goodaire, Thomas, 51
Gregg, Pauline, 81
Grotius, Hugo, 3, 22, 24, 26
Hale, Lord Chief Justice, 114
Haller, William, 81
Harrington, James, 1, 22, 99, 160
Hell, 119
Henrietta Maria, 80
Henry VIII, 16, 28, 30, 72, 107
Hirst, Margaret, 55
Hitler, Adolph, 122
Hobbes, Thomas, 1, 22, 99–100
Holme, Thomas, 166
Holy Roman Empire, 23
Hooton, Elizabeth, 9, 14, 150
Horle, Craig, 114
Howgill, Francis, 60
Hubberthorn, Richard, 98, 100, 101, 102
Huguenots, 45
Hull, William I., 152
Huss, John, 40, 41, 42
Hussite Wars, 41
Independents, 15, 29, 53, 54
Inner Light, 52, 56, 57, 66, 87, 102, 111–13, 124, 127
James I, 22, 30, 49, 72, 80, 152
James II, 25, 73, 74, 91, 106–8, 147, 155, 157, 158, 161, 162, 168, 169
Jasper, John, 145
Jeffries, George, 107
Jesus, 115, 116, 118, 120, 121, 126, 127, 154
Jewish persecution, 30, 129
John, King, 72
Jones, Rufus M., 33, 88, 150, 152, 154, 172

Judicial system, 129–31
Jutes, 28
Katherine of Aragon, 28
Keith, George, 66–68, 158
Keith, William, 171
King's Missive, 154
King, Rachel Hadley, 88
Knox, John, 49
Lanape Indians, 166
Laud, William, 77
Leddra, William, 154
Levellers, 3, 78, 80, 81–86, 90, 106
Lewis, Joyce, 5
Littel, Franklin Hamlin, 32
Lloyd, David, 166
Lloyd, Thomas, 66
Locke, John, 1, 22, 99, 146, 160
Loe, Thomas, 147, 148
Logan, James, 166
Lollards, 27, 81
Louis XIII, 80
Louis XIV, 147
Love, John, 63
Luther, Martin, 36, 37, 38, 40, 41–43, 44, 47, 49, 52, 57, 111, 122
Lutheranism, 15, 16, 42–44, 47, 124
Lutherans, 157
Machiavelli, Niccoli, 25
Magna Carta, 72, 73
Mancetter, 8
Mansfield, 13
Marx, Karl, 90, 141
Mary Tudor, 30, 49
Mary, Queen, 16
Meade, William, 131–35
Melanchthon, Philip Schwartz, 42
Mennonites, 15, 16, 32, 39, 55, 56, 124, 153
Milton, John, 39, 99
Monck, George, 93, 98, 100
Monism, 26, 121
Montesquieu, Charles Lewis, 124

Moses, 119, 121
Muggleton, Ludowicke, 17
Muggletonians, 17
Nash, George B., 67
Naylor, James, 51, 55, 60–61
Naylor, John, 129
New Jersey, 66
    colonization of, 157–61
New Netherlands, 157
Nicholas, Henry, 86
Niclaes, Hendrik, 17
Nottingham, 8, 15, 18, 52, 131
Overton, Richard, 81
Owen, John, 92, 146
Pachyn, Thomas, 103
Pacifism, 75, 20–21, 125
Pagels, Elaine, 34
Parliament, 77, 78, 83, 84, 94, 98, 106, 107
Parliamentarians, 74
Paul, St., 118, 122, 126, 127, 164
Pease, Theodore Calvin, 82, 85
Penn's Charter, 161–65
Penn, Gulielma, 168, 170
Penn, Hanna, 168, 170
Penn, John, 171
Penn, Margaret, 145
Penn, Richard, 171
Penn, Sir William, 145, 147, 148, 168
Penn, Thomas, 171
Penn, William, 6, 57, 62, 63, 66, 91, 99, 107, 121, 128, 129,
    131–35, 158, 160
    college studies, 146
    conversion to quakerism, 148
    death, 171
    eulogizes Fox, 169
    imprisonments, 148–49
    in Pennsylvania, 161–68, 170
    nonconformism of, 146
    on Caesarism, 126
    on peace, 24

Penn, William *(cont.)*
    property of, 168
    relationship with royal monarchs, 168–71
    schooling, 146
    trips to Europe, 151
    writings of, 148
Pennsylvania, 66, 67, 107, 161–68
Penny, Norman, 127, 135, 141
Perrott, John, 63
Petition of Right, 73, 74
Philadelphia, 164, 166, 172
Pico della Mirandola, 43
Pluralism, 26, 121
Pope, 122
Popular sovereignty, 27
Predestination, 47
Presbyterianism, 16, 47, 50, 116
Presbyterians, 50, 53, 60, 75, 77, 114
Pride, Thomas, 77
Primitive Christianity, 33–36, 56, 57, 58, 110, 114
Printz, John, 157
Protestant Reformed Churches, 43
Protestant work ethic, 46
Protestantism, 40, 45, 124
Puritanism, 3, 27, 45
Puritans, 27, 75, 102, 149, 153
Pyott, Edward, 92
Quaker Act, 63, 71, 104
Quakers
    and "higher powers," 122–27
    and Book of Revelation, 104
    and Inner Light, 111–13
    and other sects, 16
    and pacifism, 20–21
    and secular authority, 62
    and slavery issue, 152
    and the Bible, 56
    as "Friends," 52, 68
    biblical approach of, 1
    class status, 141–44

Quakers *(cont.)*
    compared to Mennonites, 56
    difference from Hobbes, 100
    dislike by Puritans, 149
    feelings about Cromwell's death, 95
    institutionalization of, 51–53, 56, 59, 68
    meetings of, 69
    mode of conversion, 59
    origin of name, 19
    "peculiarities" of, 63, 64, 162
    persecution of, 127–41, 127–41, 157
    religious services of, 55
    schisms among, 63
Ranters, 17, 63
Reformation, 15, 23, 28, 41, 57
Restoration, 68, 72, 73, 77, 98, 100, 106, 127, 146, 147, 157
Revelation, Book of, 18, 102, 104, 117
Rhode Island, 150
Robinson, William, 154
Ross, Isabel, 103
Royalists, 74, 75, 77, 94, 127
Salvation, 57
Saxons, 28
Schleitheim Confession, 56
Schwenkfeld, Kaspar von, 36–37, 38, 42
Schwenkfelders, 15
Scott, James, Duke of Monmouth, 106
Sects, 15–18
Sedgberg, 51, 53, 57, 69
Seekers, 16, 53, 55
Separatists, 16, 29, 53
Sermon on the Mount, 115, 116
Sewel, William, 8, 103
Simon, Menno, 16, 32, 40, 52, 111
Smyth, John, 16
Socinians, 17
Socinus, Faustus and Laelius, 17
Sovereignty, defined, 26
Spiritualizers, 32, 36, 38
Starling, Sir Samuel, 132

State, defined, 26
Stephens, Nathaniel, 6, 12
Stevenson, Marmaduke, 154
Story, John, 63
Strafford, Earl of, 77
Stuart, James Francis Edward, 107
Stubbs, John, 151
Swarthmoor Hall, 53–55, 69, 123
Swiss Brethren, 32, 124
Taylor, Ernest E., 55, 141
Thirty Years War, 3, 23, 38, 125
Toleration Act, 108
Tolles, Frederick, 144, 166
Transubstantiation, 45, 47
Trevelyan, George Macaulay, 103
Valiant Sixty, 141
Valiants, 55, 69
Vann, Richard T., 15, 59, 144
Vaughan, Chief Justice, 132
Vincent, Thomas, 148
Vipont, Elfrida, 5, 8
Walwin, William, 81
Wesley, John, 59
Westminster Confession of Faith, 50, 76
Whitehead, George, 63
Whitfield, George, 59
Wilburne, John, 80–86, 88, 129
Wildes, Harry Emerson, 163, 167
Wilkinson, John, 63
William III and Mary, 30, 106, 108, 169
Williams, Ethyn Kirby, 67
Williams, Roger, 150–51
Winstanley, Gerard, 86–88
Wittenberg, 41
Wycliffe, John, 27, 40, 41, 42
Zenger, John Peter, 135
Zwingli, Ulrich, 40, 41, 42, 43–45, 122